Barron's Review Course Series

Let's Review: Spanish

José M. Díaz
María F. Nadel
Hunter College High School
New York, NY

BARRON'S

For Jerry.
J.M.D.

For my husband Mark and my daughter Tamara, with love.
M.F.N.

ACKNOWLEDGMENTS
The authors would like to thank Mr. Dennis James Lavoie of Fairport High School, NY, for his careful review of the manuscript and his insightful comments and suggestions and Dr. John Webb, Chairperson of the Foreign Language Department of Hunter College High School, NYC, whose leadership reflects the latest thinking in the field of foreign language education and whose unwavering support bolsters our efforts to prepare our students to be independent users of Spanish.

We are also grateful to Hunter College High School for granting Mrs. María F. Nadel a Fellowship Award, which allowed her to fully concentrate on the development of this project.

A special note of thanks to Dr. Elie de Comminges and Ms. Sonya Mosco for their friendship and encouragement.

All inquiries should be addressed to:
Barron's Educational Series, Inc.
250 Wireless Boulevard
Hauppauge, NY 11788
http://www.barronseduc.com

International Standard Book Number: 0-7641-0133-1
Library of Congress Catalog Card Number: 98-71304

Printed in the United States of America
9 8 7 6 5 4 3 2 1

Contents

Unit 1 SOCIALIZING

Unit 2 PROVIDING AND OBTAINING INFORMATION

Lesson 4—Providing and Obtaining Information About the Past

Unit 3 **EXPRESSING PERSONAL FEELINGS**

Unit 4 GETTING OTHERS TO ADOPT A COURSE OF ACTION

Unit 5 HYPOTHESIZING

Unit 7 PREPARING FOR THE NEW YORK STATE REGENTS EXAMINATION

APPENDIXES

Regents Examinations

Preface

Let's Review: Spanish is primarily a grammar and usage review book for students who are enrolled in Level III Spanish classes or who have the level of proficiency required for that level. Its aim is to solidify the base that students have acquired in the previous years, and to take them a step further by introducing new material needed for effective communication. It can be used in the classroom as a review book, or independently by students who want to refine their knowledge of Spanish. In or out of the classroom it can be used to prepare for the Spanish Level 3 New York State Regents Comprehensive Examination or any equivalent examination.

Let's Review: Spanish is divided into seven units. The first five units review grammar and usage. The sixth unit offers authentic contexts with which the students can refine their writing skills and actively put to use what they have mastered. Unit seven is designed to help students prepare for the New York State Regents Comprehensive Examination in Spanish. This unit describes the speaking, listening comprehension, reading comprehension, and writing sections of the exam, gives suggestions for improving each skill, and provides practice exercises in each skill.

Two complete New York State Regents Comprehensive Examinations from June 2000 and January 2001 are included in this book after Appendix 10. The listening comprehension sections of these exams do not appear on the CD.

As a bonus, we have included the listening comprehension sections from the June 1997 and January 1998 exams for your practice and review. These listening comprehension sections and the listening comprehension practice exercises appear on the enclosed CD.

Some characteristics of the material are:

- Structures that complement each other are grouped according to the four functions presented in the New York State Syllabus— socializing, providing and obtaining information, expressing personal feelings, and getting others to adopt a course of action.
- Grammar explanations focus on the essentials of grammar at this level, that is, the grammar required to produce accurate and interesting speech.
- Explanations are user friendly and require minimal mediation by the teacher so that students can do most of the grammar review independently.
- Topics are mostly self-contained, allowing both teachers and students to tailor the review of the grammar according to their needs.
- Exercises cover the most common topics students will encounter in dealing with other speakers of the language in their daily lives.

- Mechanical exercises are followed by contextualized, situational exercises designed to help students to further refine and enrich their ability to put the grammar to use.
- Vocabulary used in the examples and exercises is simple enough that it does not stand in the way of the grammatical point being practiced, but rather facilitates its mastery through practice.
- Vocabulary is listed thematically in a series of appendixes. Students are encouraged to refer to the thematic vocabulary while completing some of the open-ended exercises.
- Basics such as numbers, dates, and so on are also listed in appendixes.

We believe that the format of *Let's Review: Spanish* promotes better control of frequent simple structures and, at the same time, facilitates the acquisition of the more complex constructions that students need to produce their own thoughts and feelings with the degree of control required at this level. It is our hope that it will help students to continue to develop their proficiency in Spanish in a painless and interesting way, and at the same time prepare them successfully for the New York State Regents Comprehensive Examination in Spanish or any equivalent exam they may encounter.

José M. Díaz
María F. Nadel

Unit One   **SOCIALIZING**

LESSON 1
Socializing

PART A: Greetings

In Spanish there are several ways to greet a person. One thing you must keep in mind is that there is a formal and an informal way to address a person. If you know the person well, or he or she is the same age as you are, you will use the *tú* form. For someone who you do not know, or who is older than you, you need to use the *usted (Ud.)* form. If you are talking to more than one person, always use *ustedes (Uds.)*.

Note that although the plural of *tú* is *vosotros*, *ustedes (Uds.)* is more commonly used. You will see the *vosotros* form throughout this book in parentheses. You should be able to recognize it, but you will not be asked to produce it because its use is limited to some regions of Spain.

INFORMAL GREETINGS		POSSIBLE RESPONSES *	
Buenos días.	Good morning.	Buenos días.	Good morning.
Buenas tardes.	Good afternoon.	Buenas tardes.	Good afternoon.
Buenas noches.	Good evening.	Buenas noches.	Good evening.
¡Hola!	Hi!	¡Hola!	Hi!
¿Qué tal?	How are you?	Bien, gracias. ¿Y tú?	Well, thanks. And you?
¿Cómo te va?	How is it going?	Muy bien, gracias. ¿Y a ti?	Very well, thanks. And you?
¿Cómo estás?	How are you?	Más o menos. ¿Y tú?	So-so. And you?
¿Cómo están Uds.?	How are you (pl.)?	Regular.	So-so.
		Así, así.	So-so.
¿Qué hay de nuevo?	What's new?	Nada de particular.	Nothing special.

1

FORMAL GREETINGS		POSSIBLE RESPONSES *	
Buenos días.	Good morning.	Buenos días.	Good morning.
Buenas tardes.	Good afternoon.	Buenas tardes.	Good afternoon.
Buenas noches.	Good evening.	Buenas noches.	Good evening.
¿Cómo está Ud.?	How are you?	Muy bien, gracias. ¿Y Ud.?	Very well, thanks. And you?
¿Cómo están Uds.?	How are you (pl.)?	Regular.	So-so.
		Bien, gracias. ¿Y Ud.?	Well, thanks. And you?
¿Cómo le va?	How is it going?	Muy bien, gracias. ¿Y a Ud.?	Very well, thanks. And you?

*Note that these are only possible responses; you can use whichever is appropriate.

EXERCISES

A. While walking down the hall in your school, several people greet you. Respond to their greetings appropriately.

1. ¡Hola! _____

2. ¡Buenos días! _____

3. ¿Cómo te va? _____

4. ¿Qué tal? _____

5. Buenas tardes. _____

B. In the cafeteria you run into some of your teachers. Answer their greetings addressing them by name.

> **MODELO:** ¡Hola! (señor Ramírez)
> *Buenos días, señor Ramírez.*

1. ¿Qué tal? (señorita López) _____

2. ¿Cómo le va? (señor Ayala) _____

3. ¡Hola! (señora García) _____

4. ¿Cómo estás? (señor Moreno) _____

5. Buenos días. (señora Iglesias) _____

2

PART B: Leave-taking

Adiós.	Good-bye.
Chao.	Good-bye.
Hasta luego.	See you later.
Hasta la próxima.	Until next time.
Hasta mañana.	See you tomorrow.
Hasta el (lunes, etc.)	See you . . . (Monday, etc.)
Hasta pronto.	See you soon.
Saludos a . . .	Regards to . . .

EXERCISES

You are saying good-bye to some of your friends and your teacher. Read the situations and then write a logical response. Use a different expression for each situation.

1. You plan to see your friend on Saturday.

_____

2. You say good-bye to your teacher. You will see him/her again tomorrow.

_____

3. Your friend is leaving for a couple of weeks.

_____

4. You send your regards to your cousins.

_____

5. An exchange student is going back to his/her country.

_____

PART C: Introducing

INFORMAL INTRODUCTIONS		POSSIBLE RESPONSES *	
Te presento a . . .	This is . . .	Mucho gusto.	A pleasure.
Les presento a . . .	This is . . .		
Este(a) es . . .	This is . . .	Encantado(a).	Delighted.
Este(a) es mi amigo(a) . . .		This is my friend . . .	
Quisiera presentarte a . . .		I would like to introduce . . . to you.	
Quisiera presentarles a . . .		I would like to introduce . . . to you.	

A possible response to *Mucho gusto* is *El gusto es mío* (The pleasure is mine). If you want to introduce yourself, you may use *Me llamo . . . ¿y tú?*

FORMAL INTRODUCTIONS		POSSIBLE RESPONSES *	
Le(s) presento a . . .	This is . . .	Mucho gusto.	A pleasure.
		Encantado(a).	Delighted.
Quisiera presentarle(les) a . . .	I would like to introduce . . . to you		

A possible response to *Mucho gusto* is *El gusto es mío* (The pleasure is mine). If you want to introduce yourself, you may use *Me llamo . . . ¿y Ud.?*

*Note that these are only possible responses; you can use whichever is appropriate.

EXERCISES

Your school has a welcoming party for teachers and students the first day of classes. Everybody is trying to meet the new faculty and students. Read the following situations and respond logically. Try to use as many different expressions as possible.

1. Your friend Ricardo has not met the two new Spanish teachers. You say:

_____

They respond:

_____

He responds:

_____

2. You introduce a Costa Rican exchange student to the French teachers who also speak Spanish. You say:

_____

They respond:

_____

He/She responds:

_____

3. Your best friend has not met the Costa Rican exchange student. You say:

_____

He/She responds:

_____

He/She responds:

_____

MORE EXERCISES

A. Respond to the following statements in an appropriate manner.

1. —¡Hola!

— _____

2. —Te presento a mi amigo Jorge.

— _____

3. —Hasta luego.

— _____

4. —Quisiera presentarles a mis profesores.

— _____

5. —¿Qué tal?

— _____

6. —Esta es mi amiga Lucía.

—_____

7. —Mucho gusto.

—_____

8. —Le presento al Sr. Sánchez.

—_____

B. There is a new exchange student called Sebastián in your school. In the computer room you find one of your friends and you introduce him to her.

You say: —¡Hola!

Your friend says: —_____

You say: —Te presento a mi amigo Sebastián.

Your friend says: —_____

Sebastián says: —_____

Your friend asks: —¿Cómo te va?

Sebastián answers: —_____

You say: —Tenemos una clase ahora. Hasta luego.

Your friend says: —_____

C. You arrive in your Spanish class for the first time with your friend from Chile. Greet your Spanish teacher. Introduce the new exchange student to him/her, and then say good-bye. Make up the responses he/she may give.

—_____

—_____

—_____

—_____

—_____

—_____

PART D: Thanking

EXPRESSIONS TO THANK SOMEONE		POSSIBLE RESPONSES	
Gracias.	Thank you.	De nada.	Don't mention it.
Muchas gracias.	Thank you very much.	No hay de qué.	Don't mention it.
Muchísimas gracias.	Thank you very much.		

PART E: Apologizing

EXPRESSIONS OF APOLOGY		POSSIBLE RESPONSES	
Lo siento.	I'm sorry.	Está bien.	It's OK.
Lo siento mucho.	I'm very sorry.	No se preocupe.	Don't worry.
Perdón.	Pardon me. (Forgive me.)		
Con permiso.*	With your permission /Excuse me.		

*You will use this expression when you need to interrupt someone, want to pass by a person, etc.

EXERCISES
Read the following situations, then in the blank space respond with a possible response. Try to use as many different expressions as possible.

1. You have just met your friend's boyfriend for the first time.

   He says: —Mucho gusto.

   You respond: —_____

2. You hear that your friend Lupe is very sick. You respond by saying:

   —_____

3. You forgot your friend Lucas' calculator at home.

   You say: —_____

4. Two of your friends see you in the street.

   They say: —¡Hola! ¿Qué tal?

   You respond: —_____

5. After talking to you for a while, one of your friends says:

   —Adiós.

   You respond: —_____

6. You bring one of your friends to your home. You introduce him/her to your parents by saying:

   —_____

7. You are walking down the hall and there are two students talking who are preventing you from passing.

   You say: —_____

8. Your neighbor's cat has died.

   You say: —_____

PART F: Talking on the Telephone

The following are some useful expressions you may need to answer the phone in Spanish.	
Aló.	Hello.
Bueno.	Hello.
Diga.	Hello.
Dígame.	Hello.
¿Está(n) . . . (name[s])?	Is (Are) . . . (name[s]) there?
¿De parte de quién?	Who should I say is calling?
¿Quién habla?	Who is it?
Es . . . (name)	It's . . . (name)
Habla . . . (name)	It's . . . (name)
Un momento, por favor.	Just a moment, please.
Lo siento. . . . (name[s]) no se encuentra(n).	I'm sorry. . . . (name[s]) is (are) not here.
Lo siento. . . . (name[s]) no está(n)	I'm sorry. . . . (name[s]) is (are) not here.
Tiene un número equivocado.	You have a wrong number.

EXERCISES

While babysitting for your neighbor, Mrs. Campos, you get several phone calls. Read the situations and write a logical response.

1. The phone rings. You answer it by saying:

—_____

2. The person on the phone asks you for Mrs. Campos. You respond:

—_____

3. A few minutes later you receive another call. You answer by saying:

—_____

4. Mrs. Campos has returned and you want to find out who is calling. You ask:

—_____

5. You are going to tell Mrs. Campos that she has a call. You tell the person on the phone:

—_____

6. The phone rings and the person asks for the doctor. There isn't a doctor living there. You answer:

—_____

PART G: Salutations and Leave-taking Expressions Used in Writing Notes and Letters

Later in this book you will need to write some formal and informal notes and letters. Study the following greetings and leave-taking expressions so that you become familiar with them.

When writing a letter these are some of the greetings you may use:

FAMILIAR

Querido(a) . . .	Dear . . .
Queridísimo(a) . . .	Dearest . . .
Mi querido(a) . . .	My dear . . .

FORMAL

Muy señor mío (señora mía, etc.):	Dear Sir/Madam:
Muy señor nuestro (señora nuestra, etc.):	Dear Sir/Madam:
Muy estimado(a) Sr./Sra. (last name):	Dear (Esteemed) Sir/Madam (last name):
Estimado(a) amigo(a):	Dear (Esteemed) friend:
Mi distinguido(a) amigo(a):	My dear (distinguished) friend:

When writing a letter these are some of the leave-taking expressions you may use:

FAMILIAR

Besos y abrazos,	Hugs and kisses,
Un abrazo de,	A hug from,
Un abrazo de tu amigo(a),	A hug from your friend,
Tu (amigo, hijo, etc.) que te quiere,	Your (friend, son, etc.) who loves you,
Con todo el cariño de,	With all my affection,
Tuyo(a) afectísimo(a),	Yours truly,
Cariñosos saludos de,	Fondly/Fond greetings from,
Sinceramente,	Sincerely,
Afectuosamente,	Affectionately,
Mis recuerdos a tu familia,	My regards to your family,

FORMAL

Atentamente,	Yours truly,
Suyo(a) afectísimo(a),	Yours fondly,
Queda suyo(a) afectísimo(a),	I remain, fondly yours,
Le saluda cariñosamente,	Warm greetings/Fond regards from,
Se despide afectuosamente,	I remain, affectionately,
Mis recuerdos a su familia,	My regards to your family,

Other expressions you may want to keep in mind when writing a letter:

TO ACKNOWLEDGE RECEIPT OF A LETTER

Le/Les agradezco (agradecemos) su carta del 10 de enero . . .	I (We) acknowledge/thank you for your letter of January 10 . . .
Te agradezco (agradecemos) tu carta del . . .	I (We) acknowledge/thank you for your letter of . . .
He (Hemos) recibido tu/su carta del . . .	I (We) have received your letter of . . .
En respuesta a su/tu carta del . . .	In response to your letter of . . .
Con referencia a su/tu carta del . . .	In reference to your letter of . . .
Acabo (Acabamos) de recibir tu/su carta del . . .	I (We) have just received your letter of . . .

TO REQUEST A RESPONSE

Esperando su/tu respuesta . . .	Awaiting your response . . .
En espera de sus/tus gratas noticias . . .	Awaiting your pleasing news . . .
Ruego (Rogamos) a Uds. una contestación tan pronto como sea posible.	I (We) beg you to respond as soon as possible.

You may also want to go to Appendix 6 to review how to write the date on a letter in Spanish.

EXERCISES

You have to write many letters. For each one you must have the right expressions. Read the descriptions of the letters you have to write and give an appropriate response.

1. A letter to a bookstore to order a book.

Salutation: _____

Conclusion: _____

2. A letter to the mother of the family with whom you stayed on your trip to Ecuador.

Salutation: _____

Conclusion: _____

3. A letter to a computer catalogue address to request information about a particular program.

   Salutation: _____

   Conclusion: _____

4. A note to a family friend who just sent you a gift.

   Salutation: _____

   Conclusion: _____

5. The first few words to acknowledge the receipt of a letter from your aunt.

   _____

6. The first few words to acknowledge the receipt of a letter confirming your reservation in a hotel in Mexico.

   _____

7. The last few words of a letter to your friend in college.

   _____

8. The last few words of a letter to a congresswoman in your community.

   _____

Unit Two PROVIDING and OBTAINING INFORMATION

LESSON 2
Providing and Obtaining Information About Facts

There are several ways to obtain information. One way is to ask a question. We will discuss two types of questions you may use: yes/no questions and questions in which one wants to obtain a specific piece of information.

PART A: Asking for Information

YES/NO QUESTIONS

When Spanish speakers anticipate a yes/no answer, they often turn a statement into a question by simply raising the pitch of their voice at the end of the sentence. In writing such questions, an inverted question mark is placed at the beginning of the sentence and another question mark is placed at the end.

Estudias mucho. (Statement)
You study a lot.

¿Estudias mucho? (Question)
Do you study a lot?

It is also possible to ask a yes/no question by inverting the order of the subject and verb. The pitch of the voice rises at the end of these questions also.

¿Trabajan tus padres los fines de semana?
Do your parents work on weekends?

When asking for confirmation (or rejection) of a statement, the words *¿verdad?* or *¿no?* are added at the end of the statement. The pitch of the voice rises when saying *¿verdad?* or *¿no?* When asking this type of question, a person usually expects confirmation of the statement.

Tu novio es médico, ¿verdad?
Your boyfriend is a doctor, isn't he? (right?)

When answering a yes/no question negatively, it is necessary to place the word *no* before the verb. This *no* is equivalent to the English *not*.

No, no es médico.
No, he is not a doctor.

When answering yes/no questions, it is always possible to give additional information.

¿Es médico tu novio?	Sí, es pediatra.
	No, es abogado.
Is your boyfriend a doctor?	Yes, he is a pediatrician.
	No, he is a lawyer.

EXERCISES

A. Imagine that you and your friend are talking about your plans for the weekend. Read some of the statements your friend makes, then write a follow-up question that would elicit a *yes* or *no* response. Try to use different ways to ask *yes* or *no* questions.

> **MODELO:** Hay un restaurante nuevo en el centro.
> *¿Quieres ir con nosotros?* Or,
> *Vamos a invitar a mi novio, ¿verdad?*

1. Vamos a divertirnos este fin de semana.

   _____

2. No tenemos mucho trabajo.

   _____

3. Yo quiero ir al cine.

   _____

4. Julián y Rosa desean jugar en el parque.

   _____

5. Hay un festival de cine el domingo.

_____

6. Invitas a los amigos de Tomás.

_____

7. Hugo prepara una cena el sábado.

_____

8. Queremos descansar también.

_____

B. One of your friends wants to know more about the place where you live. Answer his questions with complete sentences.

1. ¿Vives en el campo?

_____

2. Tú vives en un apartamento, ¿no?

_____

3. ¿El barrio donde vives es bueno?

_____

4. Hay muchas tiendas en tu barrio, ¿verdad?

_____

5. ¿Sales de compras en el barrio?

_____

6. ¿La escuela está muy lejos?

_____

7. ¿Van tú y tus amigos a la escuela en coche?

_____

8. Tu mejor amigo(a) vive cerca de tu casa, ¿verdad?

_____

QUESTION WORDS

When asking for a specific piece of information, use question words. In this type of question, the word order is generally as follows:

¿Question word + verb?

There are many words and expressions that are used to ask information questions. Which one you use will depend on the piece of information you are requesting:

- To ask about location, use *¿Dónde?*

  ¿Dónde lees? En mi cuarto.
  Where do you read? In my room.

- To ask about place of origin, use *¿De dónde?*

  ¿De dónde son tus padres? De Puerto Rico.
  Where are your parents from? From Puerto Rico.

- To ask about direction, use *¿Adónde?*

  ¿Adónde vas durante el verano? A un campamento.
  Where do you go in the summer? To a camp.

- To ask for an identification or a definition, use *¿Qué?*

  ¿Qué tienes en la mano? Un libro.
  What do you have in your hand? A book.

  ¿Qué libro es? Es un diccionario.
  What book is it? It's a dictionary.

- To ask who does something, use *¿Quién?* (if you expect a plural answer, use *¿Quiénes?*)

  ¿Quién limpia tu cuarto? Yo.
  Who cleans your room? I do.

  ¿Quiénes van al supermercado? Mis padres.
  Who goes to the supermarket? My parents.

- To ask who owns something, use *¿De quién?* (if you think there is more than one owner, use *¿De quiénes?*)

  ¿De quién es la calculadora? De Juana.
  Whose calculator is it? Jane's.

  ¿De quiénes es la casa? De los Aznar.
  Whose house is it? The Aznar's.

- To ask the reason for doing something, use *¿Por qué?*

  ¿Por qué lees ese periódico? Porque tiene artículos interesantes.
  Why do you read that newspaper? Because it has interesting articles.

- To ask the purpose for doing something, use *¿Para qué?*

  ¿Para qué lees ese periódico? Para saber las noticias.
  Why do you read that newspaper? In order to find out the news.

- To ask for whom something is intended, use *¿Para quién?* (if you expect a plural answer, use *¿Para quiénes?*)

  ¿Para quién es el regalo? Para Jorge.
  For whom is the gift? For Jorge.

  ¿Para quiénes son las rosas? Para Elena y Julieta.
  For whom are the roses? For Elena y Julieta.

- To ask about the color of something, use *¿De qué color?*

  ¿De qué color es la cortina? Azul.
  What color is the curtain? Blue.

- To ask when something happens, use *¿Cuándo?*

  ¿Cuándo montas en bicicleta? Todos los días.
  When do you ride a bike? Everyday.

- To ask how many of something, use *¿Cuántos?* (if you are referring to something feminine, use *¿Cuántas?*)

  ¿Cuántos chicos hay? Catorce.
  How many boys are there? Fourteen.

  ¿Cuántas páginas tiene el libro? Trescientas.
  How many pages does the book have? Three hundred.

- To ask how much of something, use *¿Cuánto?* (if you are referring to something feminine, use *¿Cuánta?*)

  ¿Cuánto (dinero) cuesta? Cincuenta centavos.
  How much (money) does is cost? Fifty cents.

  ¿Cuánto dinero necesitas? Cien dólares.
  How much money do you need? A hundred dollars.

  ¿Cuánta tarea tenemos? Muchísima.
  How much homework do we have? A lot.

- To ask how something is done, use *¿Cómo?*

  ¿Cómo vas a la escuela? En autobús.
  How do you go to school? By bus.

- To ask what something or someone is like, use *¿Cómo + ser?*

  ¿Cómo es la casa? Grande y bonita.
  What is the house like? Big and pretty.

¿Cómo es la profesora? Inteligente y simpática.
What is the teacher like? Intelligent and nice.

- To ask how someone or something is at a certain time, use *¿Cómo + estar?*

¿Cómo está Elena? Enferma.
How is Elena? Sick.

¿Cómo están los frijoles hoy? Deliciosos.
What are the beans like today? Delicious.

- To ask which of several possibilities, use *¿Cuál?* (if you expect a plural answer, use *¿Cuáles?*). You may also use *¿Cuál de* + noun? (if you expect a plural answer use *¿Cuáles de* + noun?)

¿Cuál es tu película favorita? *Las guerras de las galaxias.*
What is your favorite film? *Star Wars.*

¿Cuáles son tus zapatos?
Which (ones) are your shoes?

¿Cuál de las blusas te gusta más?
Which of the blouses do you like more?

¿Cuáles de los ejercicios tenemos que hacer?
Which of the exercises do we have to do?

Remember that all interrogative words have a written accent.

EXERCISES

A. What's missing? Read the following questions and answers about meals and eating habits. You will notice that a question word is missing. Using the underlined information write the appropriate question word.

MODELO: *¿Qué* es? Es *una enchilada*.

1. ¿_____ prepara la cena en tu casa? *Mi hermana mayor* prepara la cena.

2. ¿_____ ponen la mesa? *Mi mamá y yo* ponemos la mesa.

3 ¿_____ no prepara la cena tu padre? *Porque él trabaja hasta muy tarde*.

4. ¿_____ es tu plato favorito? Mi plato favorito es *una hamburguesa con papas fritas*.

5. ¿_____ van Uds. a cenar a un restaurante? Vamos a un restaurante _los fines de semana_.

6. ¿_____ van Uds. a cenar los fines de semana? Nosotros vamos _a un restaurante peruano_.

7. ¿_____ cuesta el plato más caro? El plato más caro cuesta _veinte dólares_.

8. ¿_____ es la comida en el restaurante? La comida es _deliciosa_.

B. After reading the paragraphs below, write questions you might ask to obtain the information that is underlined.

María y Marcos van de viaje el mes próximo. Ellos van en coche.
                             ‾‾‾‾‾‾‾‾‾‾‾‾   ‾‾‾‾‾‾‾‾
                                  1   2

Salen el domingo. Quieren ir a las montañas. Su hija Tamara va con
                             ‾‾‾‾‾‾‾‾‾‾‾‾‾ ‾‾‾‾‾‾‾‾‾‾‾‾‾‾
                                  3   4

ellos también. Ella vive en Minnesota porque ella asiste a una
                    ‾‾‾‾‾‾‾‾‾‾‾‾‾‾‾ ‾‾‾‾‾‾‾‾‾‾‾‾‾‾‾‾‾‾
                           5   6

universidad lejos de su casa. Ella viene cuando tiene vacaciones
‾‾‾‾‾‾‾‾‾‾‾‾‾‾‾‾‾‾‾‾‾‾‾‾‾‾‾   ‾‾‾‾‾‾‾‾‾‾‾‾‾‾‾‾‾‾‾‾‾‾‾
                                            7

porque le gusta pasar tiempo con ellos.
‾‾‾‾‾‾‾‾‾‾‾‾‾‾‾‾‾‾‾‾‾‾‾‾‾‾‾‾‾‾‾‾‾
               8

   MODELO: 1. _¿Cuándo van de viaje?_   El mes próximo.

2. ¿_____? En coche.

3. ¿_____? A las montañas.

4. ¿_____? Su hija Tamara.

5. ¿_____? Vive en Minnesota.

6. ¿_____? Porque ella asiste a una universidad lejos de su casa.

7. ¿_____? Cuando tiene vacaciones.

8. ¿_____? Porque le gusta pasar tiempo con ellos.

Graciela va de compras todas las semanas. Los sábados va al
                        ‾‾‾‾‾‾‾‾‾‾‾‾‾‾‾‾   ‾‾
                               9

supermercado porque tiene que comprar alimentos para la familia. Ella
‾‾‾‾‾‾‾‾‾‾‾‾ ‾‾‾
    10   11

19

sale <u>de su casa</u> a las diez. <u>Su esposo</u> limpia la casa y cuando ella re-
₁₂ ₁₃

gresa por la tarde todo está en orden. <u>Por la noche</u> ellos salen a cenar
₁₄

a <u>un restaurante japonés o chino</u>. <u>El restaurante japonés</u> es su restau-
₁₅ ₁₆

rante favorito.

9. ¿_____? Todas las semanas.

10. ¿_____? Al supermercado.

11. ¿_____? Porque tiene que comprar alimentos para la
    familia.

12. ¿_____? De su casa.

13. ¿_____? Su esposo.

14. ¿_____? Por la noche.

15. ¿_____? A un restaurante japonés o chino.

16. ¿_____? El restaurante japonés.

Carlos tiene <u>una bicicleta nueva</u>. Es <u>de Alemania</u>. Es <u>muy buena</u>. Es un
₁₇ ₁₈ ₁₉

regalo de su padre pero Carlos ahorra dinero <u>porque quiere comprar</u>

<u>otra bicicleta</u> <u>para su hermano menor</u>. El tiene <u>un hermano y dos her-</u>
₂₀ ₂₁ ₂₂

<u>manas</u>. Sus hermanas tienen <u>veinte y treinta y un años</u>. Ellas usan el
₂₃

coche de su madre <u>para ir a la oficina</u>.
₂₄

17. ¿_____? Una bicicleta nueva.

18. ¿_____? De Alemania.

19. ¿_____? Muy buena.

20. ¿_____? Porque quiere comprar otra bicicleta.

21. ¿_____? Para su hermano menor.

22. ¿_____? Un hermano y dos hermanas.

23. ¿_____? Veinte y treinta y un años.

24. ¿_____? Para ir a la oficina.

C. Read the following situations. Then, using the cues in parentheses, ask a question in Spanish to find out more information.

> **MODELO:** Juan va de vacaciones. El está muy alegre. Tú le haces varias preguntas.
>
> (where)   *¿A dónde vas de vacaciones?*
>
> (with whom) *¿Con quién vas?*

Elena va de compras. Te llama por teléfono y te habla de su nueva blusa.

1. (how much is it)

_____

2. (what color is it)

_____

Eduardo encuentra una mochila en la escuela. No sabe quién es el dueño *(owner)*.

3. (whose is it)

_____

4. (what does it have inside)

_____

Juan llega a la cafetería. Está buscando a su amiga Adelaida. Ellos tienen una cita *(date)*.

5. (at what time is the date)

_____

6. (where are they going)

_____

7. (when are they coming back)

_____

Tú y unos amigos están en un restaurante. Uds. hablan con el camarero.

8. (how is the food)

_____

9. (how much do the hamburgers cost)

_____

10. (what does your friend want to drink)

_____

PART B: Identifying People, Places, and Things

NOUNS

Nouns are words that name people, places, and things. Nouns can be singular (when they refer to one) or plural (when they refer to more than one).

hermano—brother	hermanos—brothers
ciudad—city	ciudades—cities
computadora—computer	computadoras—computers
árbol—tree	árboles—trees

DEFINITE AND INDEFINITE ARTICLES

The articles *the, a,* or *an* usually precede a noun.

the (a) brother	the cities
the (a) computer	the trees

All Spanish nouns are either feminine or masculine. In order to remember the gender of a Spanish noun, it is better to learn it with its definite article (meaning *the*). The definite article *the* has four forms in Spanish, two masculine *el* (plural *los*) and two feminine *la* (plural *las*).

el hermano	las ciudades
la computadora	los árboles

The indefinite article *a(n)* also has four forms in Spanish, two masculine *un* (plural *unos,* meaning *some*) and two feminine *una* (plural *unas,* meaning *some*).

un hermano	unas ciudades
una computadora	unos árboles

When an article immediately precedes a feminine singular noun beginning with stressed *a* or *ha,* the masculine articles *el* and *un* are used instead of the feminine articles *la* and *una*. Two common nouns of this type are:

el agua—the water   el hambre—the hunger

However, because these nouns are feminine, the adjectives that modify them are feminine.

Por la mañana, siempre tengo mucha hambre.
In the morning, I am always very hungry.

Me gusta tomar agua fría.
I like to drink cold water.

GENDER OF NOUNS

There are few rules regarding the gender of Spanish nouns:

- Nouns that refer to males are masculine (i.e. *el padre*—the father)
- Nouns that refer to females are feminine (i.e. *la mujer*—the woman)
- Nouns ending in *-ista* have the same form for the masculine and the feminine (i.e. el dentista/la dentista)
- Nouns ending in *-dad, -tad, -tud, -sión,* and *-ción* are feminine (i.e. *la ciudad*—city, *la libertad*—freedom, *la virtud*—virtue, *la televisión*—television, *la estación*—season, station)

It is also useful to remember a few general guidelines for determining the gender of Spanish nouns:

- Nouns ending in *-o* are generally masculine (i.e. *el pelo*—the hair)
  La mano (hand) and *la radio* (radio) are important exceptions.
- Nouns ending in *-a* are generally feminine (i.e. *la rosa*—the rose)
  El día (the day) and *el mapa* (the map) are important exceptions.

A number of words that end in *-ma* are also exceptions (i.e. *el idioma*—the language, *el problema*—the problem, *el programa*—the program).

- The names of the letters of the alphabet *(las letras)* are feminine, i.e., *la efe (f), la hache (h), la eñe (ñ),* etc.
- The names of the numbers *(los números)* are masculine, i.e. *el seis, el quince, el veinte,* etc.
- The names of the days of the week *(los días)* are masculine, i.e. *el domingo, el lunes,* etc.
- The names of the languages *(los idiomas)* are masculine, i.e *el español, el inglés, el chino,* etc.

EXERCISES

Your younger friend has just finished reading a book for school. He needs to know a lot of information about it. You help him by asking him questions. Complete the dialogues with the correct definite article *(el, la, los, las)*.

1. —¿Quién es _____ hombre?

   —_____ hombre es _____ padre de Felipe
   Córdoba.

2. —¿Quién es _____ mujer?

   —_____ mujer es _____ madre de Felipe
   Córdoba.

3. —¿Cuál es _____ ciudad?

   —_____ ciudad es Nueva York.

4. —¿Quién es _____ artista?

   —_____ artista es Picasso.

5. —¿Cuál es _____ día?

   —_____ día es miércoles.

6. —¿Cuál es _____ número en _____ puerta?

   —_____ número en _____ puerta es
   _____ cincuenta.

7. —¿Qué idioma hablan?

   —_____ idioma que hablan es _____ español.

8. —¿Qué tiene en _____ mano?

   —En _____ mano tiene _____ mapa.

9. —¿Cuál es _____ canción que cantan?

   —_____ canción es _____ himno nacional.

10. —¿Miran _____ televisión?

    —No, escuchan _____ radio.

USES OF THE DEFINITE ARTICLE

In Spanish, the definite article is:

- Used before titles (but not with *don, doña, san, santo,* and *santa*) when one is not speaking directly to the individual

  La señora López tiene dos hijos.
  Mrs. López has two children.

  But: Santa Teresa escribió muchos poemas.
    Saint Teresa wrote many poems.

  When directly addressing the individual, the article is not used.

  ¿Cómo está Ud., Sr. Gómez?
  How are you, Mr. Gómez?

- Often used instead of the possessive when speaking about the person's own parts of the body and clothing (on the person)

  Mi hermano tiene la pierna rota.
  My brother has a broken leg.

- Used before any noun used in the general sense

  Los jugos de frutas tienen mucha vitamina C.
  Fruit juices have a lot of vitamin C.

  Las palomas representan la paz.
  Doves represent peace.

- Omitted when using the noun *la casa* (the house) to mean *home*

  ¿Vas a casa ahora? No, voy a la casa de mis abuelos.
  Are you going home now? No, I am going to my grandparents' house.

- Used in front of the names of the days of the week and seasons of the year (except after the verb *ser*)

  Hoy es lunes. Nosotros vamos el martes.
  Today is Monday. We are going (on) Tuesday.

- Used with the days of the month (except when dating letters, i.e. Nueva York, 20 de octubre de 1997)

  No me gusta el verano. Regresaré el primero de octubre.
  I don't like summer. I will return (on) October first.

- Used with the names of some countries, cities, and states

la Argentina—Argentina	el Brasil—Brazil
el Canadá—Canada	la China—China
el Ecuador—Ecuador	la Florida—Florida
el Japón—Japan	la India—India

el Perú—Perú   el Paraguay—Paraguay

el Uruguay—Uruguay

NOTE that in a few cases the article is capitalized: La Habana (Havana) and El Salvador.

- Used with the names of languages (except immediately after the verb *hablar* and the prepositions *de* and *en*)

  El chino es importante para los negocios.
  Chinese is important for business.

  No hablamos inglés en la clase de español.
  We do not speak English in the Spanish class.

  Tenemos que escribir una composición en español.
  We have to write a composition in Spanish.

  Remember that when the prepositions *de* and *a* are followed by *el,* they form the contractions *al (a + el)* and *del (de + el).*

  El mercado está cerca del centro.
  The market is near the downtown area.

Also, bear in mind that the feminine form of the definite article is used in front of a cardinal number when expressing the time of the day.

  Es la una.
  It is one o'clock.

  Son las dos (tres, cuatro, etc.).
  It is two (three, four, etc.) o'clock.

  Voy a las cinco.
  I am going at five o'clock.

EXERCISES

Your friend is having difficulty completing some dialogues for homework. You help him by completing them with the correct definite article *(el, la, los, las)* or a contraction *(al, del).* If no article is needed write an X in the space.

1. —Buenas tardes, _____ doña Graciela.

   —Hola, Carlos. ¿Vas _____ estadio hoy?

   —Sí, voy después de _____ clases. No está muy lejos de

   _____ escuela.

—Claro. _____ señor Soler va también. Quiere ver

_____ partido.

—¿_____ partido? No, _____ partido no es hoy.

Hoy es _____ martes. _____ partido es

_____ jueves.

—¿Cómo? Ay. El se equivocó *(made a mistake)*. No habla

_____ inglés muy bien. Su lengua materna es

_____ español.

2. —¿Qué le pasa a Victor?

—Tiene _____ brazo roto *(broken arm)*.

—_____ partidos de fútbol son muy violentos.

—Sí, estoy de acuerdo *(I agree)*.

—Bueno, voy a visitarlo _____ domingo. Hoy no tengo

tiempo.

—¿Dónde está Victor?

—El está en _____ hospital.

—_____ Sra. Ochoa, si Ud. quiere yo voy con Ud.

_____ hospital.

—Buena idea. Ven a mi casa a _____ dos.

—De acuerdo.

USES OF THE INDEFINITE ARTICLE
In Spanish the indefinite article is:
- Generally not used following *ser,* when this verb is used to express a nationality, profession, occupation, religious or political group

Juan y Elena son demócratas.
Juan and Elena are Democrats.

¿Es periodista tu padre?
Is your father a journalist?

Note however that when the nationality, profession, etc. is modified by an adjective, the indefinite article is employed.

Juan y Elena son unos demócratas leales.
Juan and Elena are loyal Democrats.

Mi padre es un gran periodista.
My father is a great journalist.

- Not used with the following words:

otro, otra—another
cierto, cierta—a certain
cien (ciento)—a (one) hundred
mil—a (one) thousand
medio, media—a half

Me encanta este batido. Quisiera otro.
I love this shake. I would like another (one).
Los zapatos cuestan cien dólares.
The shoes cost a hundred dollars.

EXERCISES

A. You have to help your friend with a dialogue about a famous reporter who is celebrating one hundred days in his new position. Complete it with the correct form of the indefinite article *(un, una, unos, unas)*. If no article is needed, write an X in the space.

—¿Es el señor _____ republicano?

—No, él es _____ demócrata. Es _____

reportero muy famoso.

—Ah, él trabaja para _____ otra estación.

—Sí. Hoy celebran _____ aniversario. El está allí

_____ cien días hoy.

—Su padre es _____ médico. El es _____

uruguayo.

—Ahora comprendo. El visita Uruguay regularmente.

—Sí, tiene _____ otro hermano que vive allí.

B. In the following descriptions the articles have been omitted. Complete them with the correct form of the definite or indefinite article. If no article is needed, write an X in the space. In some cases there may be more than one possible response.

1. Yo saludo a Juan con _____ mano. Es _____

   día de su cumpleaños. Hay _____ mapa en la pared y

   _____ estrella cerca del nombre de _____

   ciudad donde él vive. El está lejos de su familia. No está triste

   porque _____ amigos de Ricardo lo celebran con él.

   También él recibe _____ telegramas de sus parientes.

2. _____ actor entra en _____ casa.

   _____ policía está allí. Cuando ve a _____

   pianista se sorprende mucho. _____ acción es muy lenta

   pero es _____ película interesantísima. Hablan

   _____ francés. De pronto, empieza a correr por

   _____ calle, y así termina _____ película.

   _____ público nunca sabe lo que pasa. _____

   director no nos da _____ información que necesitamos

   para entender el final.

PLURAL OF NOUNS

The plural of nouns is formed by adding:

- -s to those ending in a vowel (i.e. *la rosa—las rosas*)
- -es to those ending in a consonant (i.e. *un árbol—unos árboles*)

On words ending in stressed *-án, -és, -ón,* the accent disappears (i.e. *alemán—alemanes, francés—franceses, composición—composiciones*).

The plural of nouns ending in *-z* is formed by changing the *-z* to *-ces* (i.e. *lápiz—lápices*).

SER + NOUN

When requesting information about the identity of people, places, and things, you will use the questions *¿qué es? ¿quién es?* or *¿quiénes son?* The answer to these questions usually follows the structure *ser* + noun.

¿Quién es? Es Aida Cartas.
Who is it? It's Aida Cartas.

¿Qué es? Es una enchilada.
What is it? It's an enchilada.

Remember that when identifying a person's career or profession in Spanish, the indefinite article is omitted when the noun is not described by an adjective.

El señor Gonzalez es profesor. Es un profesor interesante.
Mr. Gonzalez is a teacher. He is an interesting teacher.

HAY

The verb *hay* (meaning, *is there?/are there?/there is/there are*) is often used to identify people, places and things.

¿Qué actividad hay en la escuela hoy?
What activity is there in school today?

Hay dos reuniones, un partido de fútbol y un baile esta noche.
There are two meetings, a soccer game and a dance tonight.

EXERCISES

A. Imagine that a shopkeeper wants to make signs for his fruits and vegetables. He has written all the names in the singular, but that doesn't make much sense. You help him by changing the signs to the plural.

> **MODELO:** la banana   *las bananas*

1. la manzana _____	**7.** el tomate _____
2. la pera _____	**8.** el melocotón _____
3. el melón _____	**9.** la fresa _____
4. el limón _____	**10.** el plátano _____
5. la lechuga _____	**11.** el mango _____
6. la naranja _____	**12.** el espárrago _____

B. Rewrite the following fruits and vegetables using indefinite instead of the definite articles.

> **MODELO:** el limón   *un limón*
> los limones *unos limones*

1. la manzana _____   3. las lechugas _____

2. el tomate _____   4. los espárragos _____

C. Yolanda is having some problems completing a paragraph about her father. Help her finish it by translating the words in parentheses to Spanish.

_____ (A certain) hombre viene a visitarnos. Camina

_____ (a half) milla para llegar porque el autobús no para

cerca de mi casa. El le trae _____ (a thousand) dólares a mi

padre. Mi padre vende zapatos y muchas veces sus clientes no tienen

bastante dinero cuando él los visita. Este señor compra

_____ (a hundred) pares de sandalias cada verano. Este

verano él quiere _____ (another) modelo.

D. What is their profession or occupation? Read the following sentences, then based on the information, identify the profession of the following people. You can refer to the list of professions and occupations in Appendix 4.

> **MODELO:** El Sr. Larra conduce un taxi.
>   *Es taxista.*

1. El Sr. Ramírez trabaja en la corte. _____

2. La Sra. Pérez enseña ciencias. _____

3. Laura Esquivel escribe novelas. _____

4. Diego diseña edificios. _____

5. Gustavo y Georgina escriben para un periódico. _____

6. Susana trabaja en un hospital. _____

7. Julio lleva las cartas y los paquetes a las casas de mi barrio. _____

_____

8. Manuela y Luisa trabajan en el teatro. _____

E. Use the following words to write complete sentences in Spanish. Remember to make the adjectives agree with the nouns they describe.

> **MODELO:** La Sra. Castro/maestra/simpático
> *La Sra. Castro es una maestra simpática.*

1. Ricardo/carnicero/muy bueno _____ _____

2. Angela/cantante/famoso_____

3. El Sr. Rodríguez y la Sra. Ruíz/dentista/excelente_____

   _____

4. José Luis/ingeniero/naval_____

5. Inés/traductor/fenomenal _____

F. What do you have in your room? Use the verb *hay* to tell the things that you have in your room.

> **MODELO:** *En mi cuarto hay una cama . . .*

_____

_____

_____

_____

G. Now write five questions you could ask a friend to find out what he/she has in his/her room.

> **MODELO:** *¿Hay una cama en tu cuarto?*

1. _____

2. _____

3. _____

4. _____

5. _____

PART C: Describing People, Places, and Things

ADJECTIVES

Adjectives describe nouns. Spanish adjectives are generally placed after the noun they modify and agree with the noun in gender and number.

Me gustan las rosas rojas.
I like red roses.

El edificio "Empire State" es un edificio alto.
The Empire State Building is a tall building.

GENDER OF ADJECTIVES

Most adjectives end in *-o* in the masculine singular, and *-a* in the feminine singular.

divertido, divertida—amusing

Adjectives that do not end in *-o* in the masculine singular have the same ending for both genders. An important exception is that adjectives that end in a consonant add an *-a* to the masculine form to express the feminine form.

inglés, inglesa	English
alemán, alemana	German
español, española	Spanish

The plural of adjectives is formed in the same manner as the plural of nouns (see p. 29).

divertido—divertidos
divertida—divertidas
fácil—fáciles
español—españoles
alemana—alemanas

SER + ADJECTIVE

The construction *ser* + adjective is used to describe:

- A person, place, or thing physically

   Mi hermana es pelirroja. Su ropa es bonita.
   My sister is redheaded. Her clothes are pretty.

- A person's personality

   Felipe es trabajador.
   Felipe is hard-working.

- A non-physical characteristic of place or thing

  Las reuniones son aburridas.
  Meetings are boring.

- Nationality

  Los señores Gómez son dominicanos.
  The Gomez's are Dominican.

In order to find out what someone, something, or someplace is like, use the question *¿Cómo + ser?*

¿Cómo es la novela? Es interesante.
What is the novel like? It's interesting.

TENER + PART OF THE BODY + ADJECTIVE

To describe a specific part of the body, use the construction *tener* + part of body (with its definite article) + adjective

Elena tiene las manos bonitas.
Elena has pretty hands.

EXERCISES

A. You are writing a letter to a pen pal and you want to describe some of the people you know. Use at least two adjectives from the list and one of your own to describe the following people and things.

> aburrido/inteligente/rápido/amable/simpático/
> latinoamericano/grande/interesante/divertido/emocionante

MODELO: Mi profesora de arte es *divertida.* Es *amable.*
También es comprensiva.

1. mi mejor amigo(a)

   _____

2. mi escuela

   _____

3. mi profesor(a) de español

   _____

4. mi computadora

   _____

5. mis clases

   _____

B. In your school there are students from all over the world. Tell the nationalities of the following students. You can refer to the list of nationalities in Appendix 4.

> **MODELO:** Sasha (m.) (Rusia)
> *Sasha es ruso.*

1. Luise (el Canadá)

_____

2. José Antonio y Mari Carmen (España)

_____

3. Christophe (Francia)

_____

4. Yoko (f.) y Akira (m.) (el Japón)

_____

5. Sofía (Nicaragua)

_____

6. Isidro (el Uruguay)

_____

C. You want to tell a friend about your favorite actor or actress. Use the verb *tener,* the following nouns, and the adjectives in parentheses to describe him or her.

> **MODELO:** las orejas (grande, pequeño, ancho, estrecho)
> *Mi actor favorito tiene las orejas pequeñas.*

el pelo (largo, corto, rizado, lacio)

_____

los ojos (azul, negro, pardo, gris, verde)

_____

la cara (redondo, largo, ovalado, cuadrado, delgado)

---

la boca (grande, pequeño, ancho, estrecho)

---

la nariz (grande, pequeño, ancho, estrecho)

PART D: Describing Conditions or States

ESTAR + ADJECTIVE

To make a statement about how someone feels, use *estar* + adjective.

> Antonio está contento.
> Antonio is happy.

Estar + adjective is also used to describe conditions or states of being of places and things.

> La ventana está abierta.
> The window is open.

> Ese coche está hecho en Alemania.
> That car is made in Germany.

The question *¿Cómo + estar?* is used to ask for information about how people feel.

> ¿Cómo están tus abuelos? Están contentos.
> How are your grandparents? They are happy.

The same question is used to ask about the condition or state of being of places and things.

> ¿Cómo está la bicicleta? Está rota.
> How is the bicycle? It is broken.

EXERCISES

A. What's the matter? Read the following phrases, then complete the sentences with the condition or state in which the people find themselves.

triste/cansado/mojado/alegre/aburrido/preocupado/
ocupado/nervioso

MODELO: *Después de correr mucho Elisa está cansada.*

1. Antes de un examen, Alicia . . .

2. Cuando salen bien en sus clases Luisa y Alberto . . .

3. Si nosotros no tenemos nada que hacer, nosotros . . .

4. Gerardo tiene mucho trabajo, él siempre . . .

5. Cristóbal y Julia corren diez millas, ellos . . .

6. Llueve mucho y no tienes un paraguas, tú . . .

7. El novio de Inés está en El Salvador desde el año pasado, ella . . .

8. Sonia viene a visitarme pero siempre se pierde, yo . . .

B. Read the following phrases, then use the verb *estar* and one of the adjectives from the list to complete the sentences in a logical way.

sentado/perdonado/cerrado/invitado/dormido/
escondido *(hidden)*

MODELO: *La clase es aburrida. Todos los estudiantes*
están dormidos.

1. No puedo entrar en el cuarto porque la puerta . . .

2. ¿Dónde está Felipe? No lo veo en ninguna parte. Pienso que él . . .

3. Orlando trabaja mucho. No hagas ruido *(noise)*, él . . .

4. Mira, allí están Roberto y Georgina, ellos . . . en una silla.

5. Aquí está la invitación para la fiesta, todos nosotros . . .

6. Aunque *(Although)* dices mentiras, esta vez tú . . .

PART E: Talking About the Location of People, Places, and Things.

In order to find out where something or someone is located use

¿Dónde + estar?
¿Dónde están las cataratas de Iguazú?
Where are the Iguazú Falls?

When stating the location of something or someone use *estar* + location.

Las cataratas de Iguazú están entre la Argentina y el Brasil.
The Iguazú Falls are between Argentina and Brazil.

ADVERBS OF PLACE

Adverbs modify verbs. Adverbs of place tell you where the action takes place. They can answer the question word *¿Dónde?*

Some common adverbs of place are:

aquí—here (definite
  place-near speaker)

allí—over there (definite
  place-far from both)

adentro—inside

afuera—outside

abajo—underneath, downstairs

arriba—above, upstairs

lejos—far

cerca—near

enfrente—in front, across,
  opposite

detrás—behind

delante—in front

encima—on top

debajo—under

La farmacia está cerca.
The pharmacy is nearby.

If you want to be more specific, it is possible to add *de* + noun to some adverbs. For example:

La farmacia está cerca *de mi casa.*
The pharmacy is near *my house.*

Here are some adverb + *de* combinations:

cerca de—near, close to

debajo de—under, beneath

delante de—in front of

dentro de—inside

detrás de—behind

encima de—on, on top of, over

enfrente de—opposite, in front of

fuera de—outside of, beyond

lejos de—far from, distant from

Remember that *de* + *el* = *del.*

    El restaurante está enfrente del hotel
    The restaurant is opposite the hotel.

Also remember that a noun must follow the above combinations.

EXERCISES

A. Julia is very confused. Her friend asks her where certain things are and she answers with the wrong information. You correct her by telling her the opposite of what she says.

      MODELO: ¿La camisa? Está allí.
               No, no está allí, está aquí.

1. ¿Las blusas? Están encima de la mesa.

2. ¿El traje? Está detrás del sillón.

3. ¿La camiseta? Está aquí.

4. ¿Las botas? Están allí afuera.

5. ¿Los zapatos? Están lejos de la caja.

B. Eloisa is describing her neighborhood. You help her by completing her description with the right expression in Spanish.

1. La oficina de correos está _____ (near) la carnicería.

2. El mercado está _____ (far from) mi casa.

3. La casa del perro está _____ (behind) la casa.

4. El banco está _____ (opposite) la peluquería.

5. La farmacia está _____ (inside) mercado.

6. El buzón está _____ (in front of) la zapatería.

PART F: Expressing Ownership

SER + DE

When stating who owns something you may use one of the following constructions:

> possession + *ser* + *de* + owner

> La mochila es de Ester.
> The backpack is Ester's.

> Los patines son de María.
> The skates are María's.

or

> ser + possession + de + owner

> Es la mochila de Ester.
> It is Ester's backpack.

> Son los patines de María.
> They are María's skates.

If you want to ask about ownership, use *¿De quién + ser?* If you expect a plural answer, use *¿De quiénes + ser?*

> ¿De quién son los anteojos?
> Whose glasses are they?

> ¿De quiénes es la computadora?
> Whose computer is it?

EXERCISES

A. Whose objects are these? In one of the classrooms you find different objects and you try to sort them out. Use the following information to identify the owner(s) of the following objects.

1. lápices/Juanita

_____

2. calculadora/Felicia y Pedro

_____

3. mochila/Luis

_____

4. bolígrafos/Julio

_____

5. cuadernos/Antonio

_____

6. libro/Isabel y Guillermo

_____

B. Answer the following questions with the information in parentheses.

1. ¿De quiénes son las tizas? (maestros)

_____

2. ¿De quién es el escritorio? (director)

_____

3. ¿De quién es la bolsa? (Diego)

_____

4. ¿De quiénes es la goma de borrar? (Yolanda y Carlota)

_____

5. ¿De quiénes son las plumas? (Juan y Tito)

_____

POSSESSIVE ADJECTIVES

Another way to express ownership in Spanish is to use possessive adjectives. Possessive adjectives modify nouns by limiting who owns them, for example: It is _my_ book.

There is a long form and a short form of the possessive adjectives.

SHORT FORM OF THE POSSESSIVE ADJECTIVES		
SINGULAR	PLURAL	MEANING
mi	mis	my
tu	tus	your (familiar)
su	sus	his, her, its,
		your (formal)
nuestro, nuestra	nuestros, nuestras	our
vuestro, vuestra	vuestros, vuestras	your (familiar)
su	sus	their, your (formal)

Remember that:

- Like all adjectives, possessive adjectives agree in gender and number with the noun they modify (what is possessed)
- The short form of possessive adjectives is placed before the noun they modify
- *Nuestro* and *vuestro* are the only short forms of the possessive adjectives that have a feminine form

  Es nuestra calculadora.
  It is our calculator.

  Mis primos son guapos.
  My cousins are handsome.

  ¿Tienes su libro?
  Do you have her book?

- The possessive adjective *su* has several different meanings. If its meaning is unclear, it is possible to use *de él, de ella, de Ud., de ellos, de ellas, de Uds.* to clarify the meaning

  Es su libro.
  It is (his/her/your/their) book.

Es el libro de él.	It is his book.
Es el libro de ella.	It is her book.
Es el libro de Ud.	It is your book.
Es el libro de ellos.	It is their book.
Es el libro de ellas.	It is their book.
Es el libro de Uds.	It is your book.

EXERCISES

A. You and a friend are talking about the ways in which you and your friends have fun. Complete the following sentences with the correct possessive adjective according to the subject.

> **MODELO:** Nosotros jugamos con _nuestro_ juego de ajedrez.

1. Yo siempre doy un paseo en _____ bicicleta.

2. Eduardo y Nora escuchan _____ radio portátil.

3. Cristina mira la televisión en _____ cuarto.

4. Nosotros jugamos con _____ pelota.

5. Tú vas a la escuela en _____ patines (*skates*).

6. Ignacio y yo jugamos con _____ juegos electrónicos.

7. Sebastián escucha _____ discos compactos.

8. Carolina va a las montañas en _____ moto.

B. John is very interested in what you have in your school bag. Some things belong to you and others do not. Write six sentences telling him the things you have in the bag.

> **MODELO:** *Son mis libros.* Or, *Tengo los libros de Carlos.*

1. _____

2. _____

3. _____

4. _____

5. _____

6. _____

There is also a long form of the possessive adjectives. These forms are most commonly used after the verb *ser* and have the meaning of *of mine, of yours, of his,* etc.

LONG FORM OF THE POSSESSIVE ADJECTIVES		
SINGULAR	PLURAL	MEANING
mío, mía	míos, mías	(of) mine
tuyo, tuya	tuyos, tuyas	(of) yours
suyo, suya	suyos, suyas	(of) his
suyo, suya	suyos, suyas	(of) hers
suyo, suya	suyos, suyas	(of) yours (formal)
nuestro, nuestra	nuestros, nuestras	(of) ours
vuestro, vuestra	vuestros, vuestras	(of) yours (informal)
suyo, suya	suyos, suyas	(of) theirs
suyo, suya	suyos, suyas	(of) yours (formal)

Juan es amigo mío.
Juan is a friend of mine.

Es problema tuyo.
It is your problem.

Note that the long form of the possessive adjectives:

• Is placed after the noun it modifies

• Has a feminine form for all persons

Remember that, if the ownership is clear, the definite article (not the possessive) is used if you are talking about an article of clothing or parts of the body.

Cristóbal siempre levanta la mano. (obviously it is his own hand.)
Cristóbal always raises his hand.

Mi madre compra los zapatos en el centro comercial.
My mother buys her shoes at the mall.

EXERCISES

A lot of things are happening at the airport. People are talking and you observe certain things. Translate into Spanish the words in parentheses.

MODELO: Tina trae el abrigo _suyo_ (hers).

1. Esas son las maletas _____ (mine).

2. Uds. traen los pasaportes _____ (your).

3. Aquí tienes el billete _____ (mine).

4. Tenemos que darle las tarjetas de embarque _____ (our).

5. Dolores, esa bolsa, ¿es la bolsa _____ (yours)?

6. Hay unas personas en los asientos _____ (our).

7. Pedro pide información sobre el vuelo _____ (his).

8. Diego y Nora leen la guía turística _____ (theirs).

POSSESSIVE PRONOUNS

If a noun has already been stated or is understood, a possessive pronoun may replace it.

POSSESSIVE PRONOUNS		
SINGULAR	PLURAL	MEANING
mío, mía	míos, mías	mine
tuyo, tuya	tuyos, tuyas	yours
suyo, suya	suyos, suyas	his
suyo, suya	suyos, suyas	hers
suyo, suya	suyos, suyas	yours (formal)
nuestro, nuestra	nuestros, nuestras	ours
vuestro, vuestra	vuestros, vuestras	yours (informal)
suyo, suya	suyos, suyas	theirs
suyo, suya	suyos, suyas	yours (formal)

¿De quién es esa bicicleta? Es nuestra.
Whose is that bicycle? It's ours.

Note that in Spanish:

• Possessive pronouns always agree in gender and number with the noun they are replacing (what is possessed)

Las plumas son rojas. Son mías.
The pens are red. They are mine.

• If a pronoun replaces a group of nouns which includes any masculine noun, the masculine plural form is used

La calculadora, la regla y el lápiz son tuyos.
The calculator, the ruler, and the pencil are yours.

EXERCISES

A. In the locker room the coach is trying to find out who owns certain things. Answer his questions with the information in parentheses. Follow the model.

> **MODELO:** ¿Es tu raqueta? (mine)
>
> *Sí, es mía.*

1. ¿Son tus zapatos tenis? (mine)

   _____

2. ¿Es su pelota? (hers)

   _____

3. ¿Son nuestras camisetas? (ours)

_____

4. ¿Son sus gorras? (theirs)

_____

5. ¿Son sus calcetines? (his)

_____

6. ¿Es mi guante? (yours—familiar)

_____

TENER TO EXPRESS OWNERSHIP

The verb _tener_ (meaning, _to have_ or to possess) is often used to express ownership.

¿Qué equipo electrónico tienes en tu cuarto?
What electronic equipment do you have in your room?

Tengo una calculadora, un televisor y un estéreo.
I have a calculator, a television set, and a stereo.

EXERCISES

Students' lockers tell a lot about their owners. Think of your locker and tell everything you have in it.

MODELO: _Tengo unos zapatos tenis, etc._

_____

_____

_____

_____

_____

_____

PART G: Comparing People, Places, Things, and Actions that Are Not Equal

COMPARATIVE OF INEQUALITY

When describing people, places, and things, it is common to make comparisons. To compare the qualities of people, places, and things that are different, use one of the following constructions:

> *más* (more) + adjective + *que* (than)

or

> *menos* (less) + adjective + *que* (than)

Remember that the adjective must change according to the noun it is describing. For example:

> Josefina es más alta que Samuel.
> Josefina is taller than Samuel.

or

> Samuel es más bajo que Josefina.
> Samuel is shorter than Josefina.

When comparing in relation to numbers, use:

> *más de* + number
> (more than + number)

or

> *menos de* + number
> (less than + number)

Necesito más de veinte dólares.
I need more than twenty dollars.

To compare actions that are different, use one of the following constructions:

> *más* + adverb + *que*
> (more + adverb + than)

or

> *menos* + adverb + *que*
> (less + adverb + than)

Hilda trabaja más rápidamente que Graciela.
Hilda works faster than Graciela.

or

> Graciela trabaja más despacio que Hilda.
> Graciela works more slowly than Hilda.

SUPERLATIVE

When people, places, or things are superior (or inferior) to others, use one of the following constructions:

> definite article + [noun] + *más* + adjective + *de*

or

> definite article + [noun] + *menos* + adjective + *de*

> El primer capítulo es el [capítulo] más interesante de la novela.
> The first chapter is the most interesting [chapter] in the novel.

Note that:

- In this type of comparison, the English *in* is translated by *de*
- When it is not needed for clarity, the noun can be omitted

EXERCISES

A. After visiting Luis' class you want to report back to your friends and tell them about the people you met. Use the information below to compare the different people in Luis' class.

> **MODELO:**   Elena (-) José (serio)
> *Elena es menos seria que José.*

1. Guillermo (+) Adela (simpático)

   _____

2. Felicia (+) Beatriz (delgado)

   _____

3. Tomás (-) Georgina (trabajador)

   _____

4. Paula (+) Rosa (inteligente)

   _____

5. Teresa y Domingo (-) Isabel (curioso)

_____

6. Alicia (-) Milagros (romántico)

_____

7. Juan José (+) Leticia y Sandra (alto)

_____

8. Ignacio (-) Jorge (débil)

_____

B. One of your teachers asks you about the different classes in Luis' school. You respond by telling him approximately how many students there are in each class.

> **MODELO:** química (30)
> _En la clase de química hay más (menos) de treinta estudiantes._

1. español (20)

_____

2. historia (40)

_____

3. matemáticas (10)

_____

4. inglés (15)

_____

5. educación física (25)

_____

6. arte (8)

_____

C. Write complete sentences in Spanish comparing the following people and things. Use comparisons of superiority or inferiority.

> **MODELO:** el hermano de Jorge/pequeño/la familia
> *El hermano de Jorge es el más pequeño de la familia.*

1. el profesor de español/exigente/todos los profesores

_____

2. mi mejor amigo/honesto/mis amigos

_____

3. el entrenador (*trainer*) de natación/pesimista/los entrenadores

_____

4. los experimentos de física/interesante/todos los experimentos

_____

5. mi amiga/perezosa/la clase

_____

6. la profesora de gimnasia/fuerte/las profesoras de educación física

_____

D. How do the following people compare to you and your friends? Use the information below to write sentences describing how the following people compare.

> **MODELO:** Mi hermano/entender/+completamente/yo
> *Mi hermano entiende más completamente que yo.*

1. Carl Lewis/correr/+rápido/yo

_____

2. Mick Jagger/cantar/+alto/mi amiga

_____

3. yo/aprender/+fácilmente/tú

_____

4. Carola/leer/-cuidadosamente/su hermana

---

5. Tú/hablar español/-claramente/esos chicos

---

6. Nosotros/llegar/+temprano/el profesor

IRREGULAR ADJECTIVES OF COMPARISON

The following adjectives have irregular forms when used in comparisons. Do not use either *más* or *menos* when using these irregular adjectives of comparison.

> bueno—mejor (good—better)
> malo—peor (bad—worse)
> joven—menor (young—younger)
> viejo—mayor (old—older) (used for people)

> Aida baila mejor que su compañero.
> Aida dances better than her partner.

> Mis notas son peores que las de mi hermano.
> My grades are worse than my brother's.

> Mi hermano y yo somos menores que Uds.
> My brother and I are younger than you.

> Bárbara es mayor que Jorge.
> Bárbara is older than Jorge.

When comparing things in relation to age, use *más nuevo* and *más viejo*.

> Esa película es más vieja que *Lo que el viento se llevó.*
> That film is older than *Gone With The Wind.*

Note the superlative construction when using an irregular adjective:

> Mi abuela es la mejor cocinera de la familia.
> My grandmother is the best cook in the family.

IRREGULAR ADVERBS OF COMPARISON

The only adverbs that have irregular forms are:

bien—well	mejor—better, best
mal—badly	peor—worse, worst
mucho—a lot, much	más—more, most
poco—little	menos—less, least

José habla inglés bien. Habla inglés mejor que sus abuelos.
José speaks English well. He speaks English better than his
grandparents.

Irma trabaja mucho. Trabaja más que su jefe.
Irma works a lot. She works more than her boss.

EXERCISES

A. Contradictions. One of your friends is talking about politics and the
economy of some countries. You express your opinion by saying the
opposite.

> **MODELO:** La agricultura es más importante para Puerto Rico.
> *La agricultura es menos importante para Puerto Rico.*

1. El socialismo es mejor que la democracia.

   _____

2. El gobierno de Chile es más liberal que el de Guatemala.

   _____

3. La situación política de los países en vía de desarrollo es más grave
   que la situación de los países desarrollados.

   _____

4. El presidente de Costa Rica es mayor que el presidente de los
   Estados Unidos.

   _____

5. La economía del Perú está mejor.

   _____

6. Ecuador produce pocas bananas pero Panamá produce menos.

   _____

B. Compare yourself to your friends regarding the following objects, things, and activities.

> **MODELO:** ir al parque
>
> *Yo voy al parque más que mi amigo John.*

1. discos compactos

   _____

2. camisetas

   _____

3. vídeos

   _____

4. tener paciencia (*to be patient*)

   _____

5. tener suerte (*to be lucky*)

   _____

6. jugar al ajedrez (*chess*)

   _____

7. comer en restaurantes caros

   _____

8. sacar buenas notas

   _____

C. While listening to the radio with your friend from Nicaragua you hear students talk about the weather in the United States and the clothing they wear. Express what they say in Spanish so that your friend knows what they are talking about. If you need to review the vocabulary dealing with the weather, check Appendix 4.

1. The weather is bad in Alaska, but it is better in Florida.

   _____

2. It snows more in Maine than in Pennsylvania.

_____

3. My oldest brother wears his oldest coat when he goes skiing.

_____

4. Winter is the worst season in Minnesota.

_____

5. August is the warmest month of the year.

_____

6. It rains more in Seattle than in Los Angeles.

_____

7. Spring is the best season in Washington.

_____

8. In the summer I go swimming with my youngest brother.

_____

PART H: Comparing People, Places, Things, and Actions that Are Equal

COMPARATIVE OF EQUALITY

When you are comparing two or more items that are equal, use the constructions:

> _tan_ + adjective + _como_
> (as + adjective + as)

Or,

> _tan_ + adverb + _como_
> (as + adverb + as)

Los zapatos rojos son tan cómodos como los azules.
The red shoes are as comfortable as the blue ones.

Nosotros llegamos tan temprano como el profesor.
We arrive as early as the teacher.

When comparing in terms of a noun, use the construction

tanto/tanta + noun + *como*
(as much + noun + as)

Or,

tantos/tantas + noun + *como*
(as many + noun + as)

Tenemos tanta tarea como el año pasado.
We have as much homework as last year.

Este libro tiene tantos ensayos como ése.
This book has as many essays as that one.

When you want to say that a person, place, or thing is *very* or *extremely* something, you may:

- Use *muy* before the word (i.e. *unos libros muy raros*)
- If the word ends in a consonant, add *-ísimo, -ísima, -ísimos, -ísimas* (i.e. *un examen facilísimo*)
- If the word ends in a vowel, drop the final vowel before adding *-ísimo, -ísima, -ísimos, -ísimas* (i.e. *una blusa elegantísima*)
- If the letters *c* or *g* appear in the last syllable of a word, change them to *qu* and *gu*, and then add *-ísimo, -ísima, -ísimos, -ísimas* (i.e. *rico-riquísimo, largo-larguísimo*)

EXERCISES

A. You hear some of your friends make comments about certain people. You answer by saying that someone else is on equal terms with them. Follow the model.

> **MODELO:** Michael Jackson canta muy bien.
>
> *Madonna canta tan bien como Michael Jackson.*

1. Bill Gates tiene mucho dinero.

   _____

2. Michael Jordan juega al básquetbol muy bien.

   _____

3. Donald Trump tiene muchos edificios.

   _____

55

4. Los Rolling Stones tienen muchas canciones famosas.

_____

5. Esas tiendas vendieron muchos discos de Janet Jackson.

_____

6. Las canciones de Julio Iglesias son muy románticas.

_____

7. El presidente Carter está muy dedicado a las causas de los pobres.

_____

8. Bruce Willis actúa muy bien.

_____

B. Comparisons. Compare the following topics in relation to last year. You can use any type of comparison (i.e. equal, not equal, superior, or inferior).

      MODELO: el equipo de tenis

         El equipo de tenis juega tan bien como el año pasado. Or,

         Este año el equipo de tenis es mejor que el año pasado.

1. las clases

_____

2. los profesores

_____

3. las diversiones

_____

4. los programas de televisión

_____

5. el tiempo

_____

6. la comida en la cafetería

_____

7. los partidos de fútbol

_____

8. las películas

_____

C. Qualities. Some of your friends are truly exceptional. Compare them to someone who is really admirable. Follow the model.

MODELO: paciencia

Mi amiga Jane tiene tanta paciencia como mi madre. Or,
Mi amiga Jane tiene más paciencia que su abuela.

1. energía

_____

2. optimismo

_____

3. fuerza (*strength*)

_____

4. inteligencia

_____

5. intuición

_____

6. sentido común

_____

D. When you hear a friend make a statement, you correct him by saying that what he is describing is more than he thinks. Follow the model.

> **MODELO:** La calle es corta.
> *No, la calle es cortísima. Or,*
> *No, la calle es muy corta.*

1. El río es largo.

_____

2. El edificio es grande.

_____

3. La avenida es ancha.

_____

4. La película es cómica.

_____

5. El periódico es liberal.

_____

PART I: Talking About Oneself and Others

SUBJECT PRONOUNS

When talking about yourself and others you will often use pronouns. Pronouns are words that replace nouns. Subject pronouns replace the person about which one is saying something.

SUBJECT PRONOUNS	
SINGULAR	PLURAL
yo—I	nosotros, nosotras—we
tú—you, familiar	vosotros, vosotras—you, familiar
él—he	ellos—they, masculine
ella—she	ellas—they, feminine
usted (Ud.)—you, formal	ustedes (Uds.)—you, formal

Note that in Spanish:

- Subject pronouns are usually used only for clarity or emphasis
- *Ud.* and *Uds.* are often included for politeness

- The subject pronoun *ustedes* is often used for the familiar plural *you*

Mi amigo Tomás canta mucho pero yo no canto.
My friend Tomás sings a lot but I don't sing.

¿De dónde son Uds.? De Cuba.
Where are you from? Cuba.

PERSONAL *A*

When the direct object of the verb is a person, the word *a* (called the *personal a*) is placed before the noun or pronoun that represents the person. The *personal a* is not translated into English; it is there to indicate that a person is directly receiving the action of the verb.

¿A quién busca Ud.? Busco a Ricardo.
Whom are you looking for? I'm looking for Ricardo.

Sometimes pets are personalized, and in this case you will also use the *personal a.*

Llevo a mi perro Tigre a la playa.
I take my dog Tiger to the beach.

Remember that *a + el = al.*

Busco al hermano de Sofía.
I am looking for Sofía's brother.

The *personal a* is not used with the verb *tener.*

Tengo muchos amigos puertorriqueños.
I have many Puerto Rican friends.

EXERCISES

What's missing? Imagine that you want to clarify or emphasize the subject of the following sentences. Write the appropriate subject pronoun before the verb and add the *personal a* whenever it is needed.

MODELO: visito/las chicas
Yo visito a las chicas.

1. compramos/un televisor

_____

2. saludan/Julián

_____

3. quiere/pantalones nuevos

_____

4. miras/los estudiantes

_____

5. leo/las novelas de misterio

_____

6. admiramos/el director

_____

7. arregla/el coche de su padre

_____

8. conozco/el policía

_____

9. tocas/el piano

_____

10. tienen/dos hermanas

_____

DIRECT OBJECT PRONOUNS

Direct object pronouns replace nouns that are the direct object of a verb. They can replace people or things.

DIRECT OBJECT PRONOUNS	
SINGULAR	PLURAL
me—me	nos—us
te—you informal	os—you, informal
lo—him	los—them, masc.
lo—it, masc.	los—them, masc.
lo—you, formal, masc.	los—you, formal masc.
la—her	las—them, fem.
la—it, fem.	las—them, fem.
la—you, formal, fem.	las—you, formal, fem.

¿Conoces al señor Díaz? Sí, lo conozco. *Or,* No, no lo conozco.
Do you know Mr. Díaz? Yes, I know him. *Or,* No, I do not know him.

Notice that in Spanish, the direct object pronoun:

- Is placed directly before a conjugated verb
- Replaces the *personal a* as well as the direct object noun
- Must be preceded by *no* in a negative sentence

María no lo compró.
Maria did not buy it.

EXERCISES

A. Answer the following questions about your activities and those of your friends. Use object pronouns to express your ideas in fewer words.

> **MODELO:** ¿Lees el periódico?
> *Sí, lo leo.*

1. ¿Cuándo haces las tareas?

   _____

2. ¿Dónde escribes los apuntes (*notes*) de tus clases?

   _____

3. ¿Por qué prefieres la música rock?

   _____

4. ¿Miras los programas de ciencia ficción?

   _____

5. Tus amigos, ¿usan las computadoras de la escuela?

   _____

6. ¿Preparas tú el almuerzo en casa?

   _____

7. Tú y tus amigos, ¿discuten la política?

   _____

8. ¿Explican bien las lecciones tus profesores?

_____

B. Geronimo is talking about someone he greeted in the street. Express what he says about this person and his family in Spanish.

1. He knows me well.

_____

2. I always greet _(saludar)_ him when I see him.

_____

3. He and his wife visit us.

_____

4. I see her at the market.

_____

5. He has two daughters, Andrea and Celia. I do not see them often.

_____

6. When Celia has problems with her homework, my son says to her "I will help (use the present tense) you (fam.)."

_____

7. He calls me if he needs me when they need to practice the vocabulary.

_____

8. Do you (pl.) practice it too?

_____

INDIRECT OBJECT PRONOUNS

Indirect object pronouns replace nouns that are the indirect object of a verb. The indirect object pronoun replaces the person that benefits (or is harmed) by the action of the verb.

INDIRECT OBJECT PRONOUNS	
SINGULAR	PLURAL
me—to/for me	nos—to/for us
te—to/for you, informal, masc.	os—to/for you, informal, masc.
te—to/for you, informal, fem.	os—to/for you, informal, fem.
le—to/for him	les—to/for them, masc.
le—to/for her	les—to/for them, fem.
le—to /for you, formal, masc.	les—to/for you, formal, masc.
le—to/for you, formal, fem.	les—to/for you, formal, fem.

¿Quién te prepara el almuerzo? Mi padre me prepara el almuerzo.
Who prepares lunch for you? My father prepares lunch for me.

La profesora no les explica la lección.
The teacher does not explain the lesson to them.

In addition to using the indirect object pronoun, the person for whom or to whom something is done may be included by adding *a + person* either at the beginning or at the end of the sentence. In English only one of the two is used.

La profesora no les explica la lección a María y a Juan.
The teacher does not explain the lesson to María and Juan.

It is also possible to clarify or emphasize the indirect object by adding *a* + pronoun to the sentence. The following are the only pronouns that can be used after *a*.

TO STRESS . . .	USE . . .
me	a mí
te	a ti
nos	a nosotros
os	a vosotros

TO CLARIFY . . .	USE . . .
le	a él
	a ella
	a Ud.
les	a ellos
	a ellas
	a Uds.

Notice that in Spanish the indirect object pronoun:

- Differs in form from the direct object pronoun only in the third person
- Is placed directly before a conjugated verb
- Must be preceded by *no* in a negative sentence

  La profesora no les explica la lección a ellos.
  The teacher does not explain the lesson to them.

EXERCISES

A. Use the following words to write complete sentences about the different activities and chores in which Julia and her family are involved. Do not forget to include the indirect object pronouns.

> **MODELO:** tú/lavar los zapatos/a tu hermana
>
> *Tú le lavas los zapatos a tu hermana.*

1. yo/leer los cuentos/a mis hermanos

   _____

2. mi papá/lavar la ropa/a mí

   _____

3. nosotros/pedir dinero/a mis padres

   _____

4. ustedes/escribir una carta/al director

   _____

5. tú/dar las recetas/a nosotros

   _____

6. tu madre/limpiar el cuarto/a ti

   _____

7. yo/hacer la cama/a ustedes

   _____

8. ella/preparar el desayuno/a su hermano

   _____

B. Preferences. Write complete sentences expressing what you and the following people like. Remember that if the thing someone likes is singular you use *gusta,* and if it is plural you use *gustan.*

> **MODELO:** tú/los vegetales
>
> *Te gustan los vegetales.*

1. yo/las frutas

_____

2. nosotros/el pescado

_____

3. tú/los dulces

_____

4. ella/las papas fritas

_____

5. Uds./el arroz con pollo

_____

6. ellas/los tacos

_____

7. Ud./la comida italiana

_____

8. él/el queso

_____

DOUBLE OBJECT PRONOUNS

The following sentences contain both a direct object noun and an indirect object pronoun.

Alberto <u>me</u> presta <u>su raqueta de tenis</u>.
     I.O.   D.O.

Alberto lends <u>me</u> <u>his tennis racket</u>.
           I.O.   D.O.

Nuestros abuelos <u>nos</u> dan <u>regalos</u>.
            I.O.   D.O.

Our grandparents give <u>us</u> <u>gifts</u>.
                I.O. D.O.

<u>Les</u> llevo <u>la comida</u>.
I.O.   D.O.

I take <u>the food</u> <u>to them</u>.
    D.O.   I.O.

Now look at the same sentences when the direct object noun is replaced by a pronoun.

Alberto <u>me</u> <u>la</u> presta.
I.O. D.O.

Alberto lends <u>it</u> <u>to me</u>.
D.O. I.O.

Nuestros abuelos <u>nos</u> <u>los</u> dan.
I.O. D.O.

Our grandparents give <u>them</u> <u>to us</u>.
D.O. I.O.

<u>Se</u> <u>la</u> llevo (a ellos).
I.O.D.O.

I take <u>it</u> <u>to them</u>.
D.O. I.O.

When the direct and indirect object pronouns are used in the same sentence:

- The indirect object pronoun always apppears first
- The pronoun *se* replaces the indirect object pronouns *le* and *les* if both the direct and the indirect object pronoun start with the letter *l*
- Since the meaning of *se* is unclear, *a él, a ella, a Ud., a Uds., a ellos,* or *a ellas* is often added

EXERCISES

A. While in the store you hear the following comments. Read the comments, then shorten them by using pronouns.

> **MODELO:** Yo le compro la camisa a Ricardo.
> *Yo se la compro.*

1. Yolanda me regala las camisetas.

   _____

2. Tú te pones los zapatos.

   _____

3. Ellos le compran los guantes a su madre.

   _____

4. Nosotros le pagamos el total al dependiente.

   _____

5. El le recomienda los pantalones azules a su novia.

_____

6. Tú nos pides el dinero a nosotros.

_____

7. Yo le pregunto el precio a la dependiente.

_____

8. Ella le da los paquetes a sus amigos.

_____

B. You take your friend to the airport. He is going to Buenos Aires for the first time and he is a little nervous. Answer his questions using the information in parentheses. Use pronouns in your responses.

> **MODELO:** ¿A quién le doy la propina *(tip)?* (al taxista)
> *Se la das al taxista.*

1. ¿A quién le doy el pasaporte? (al aduanero)

_____

2. ¿A quiénes les damos los billetes? (a los asistentes de vuelo)

_____

3. ¿A quién le muestro la visa? (al policía)

_____

4. ¿A quiénes les preguntamos la hora de salida? (a las señoras)

_____

5. ¿A quién le doy la dirección del hotel? (a mí)

_____

PART J: Pointing Out Specific Objects, People, Occasions, and Things

DEMONSTRATIVE ADJECTIVES

Demonstrative adjectives point out specific people and things. In Spanish, which demonstrative adjective you use depends on:

- The location (near or far?)
- The gender (feminine or masculine?) and number (singular or plural?) of the noun being pointed out

To talk about something or someone near the speaker, use:

este—this + masculine noun   *estos*—these + masculine noun

esta—this + feminine noun   *estas*—these + feminine noun

To talk about something or someone near the listener, use:

ese—that + masculine noun   *esos*—those + masculine noun

esa—that + feminine noun   *esas*—those + feminine noun

To talk about something or someone far from both, use:

aquel—that + masculine noun   *aquellos*—those + masculine noun

aquella—that + feminine noun   *aquellas*—those + feminine noun

Ese libro es interesante pero esta revista es muy aburrida.
That book is interesting but this magazine is very boring.

Esa casa es muy vieja pero aquel edificio es del siglo pasado.
That house is very old, but that building (over there) is from the last century.

Notice that demonstrative adjectives are generally placed before the noun they modify.

EXERCISES

A. Gilberto doesn't like to go shopping with his friend Rosaura. Any time he suggests something, she responds that she likes something different. Follow the model and respond as if you were his friend.

> **MODELO:** ¿Te gusta este pañuelo rojo?
>
> *No, me gusta ese pañuelo verde.*

1. ¿Vas a comprar aquellos zapatos?

   _____

2. ¿Prefieres esa blusa?

_____

3. ¿Te gusta aquella camiseta?

_____

4. ¿Quieres estos calcetines para tu hermano?

_____

5. ¿Y aquel sombrero? ¿Lo compras?

_____

6. ¿No te gusta esta blusa?

_____

B. Eliseo and his father go shopping. He tries to help by pointing to things that he needs to buy. Complete the questions with the word in parentheses in Spanish.

1. ¿Compramos _____ (these) tomates o _____

(that over there) lechuga?

2. ¿Pongo _____ (those) manzanas en la bolsa o

_____ (these) fresas?

3. ¿Te gustan _____ (those, over there) melones o

_____ (those) melocotones?

4. ¿Quieres _____ (this) pollo o _____ (these)

paquetes de carne?

5. ¿Vas a comprar _____ (that) cereal o _____

(this) botella de leche?

DEMONSTRATIVE PRONOUNS
Demonstrative pronouns point out the noun they are replacing and agree with it in gender and number.

To talk about something or someone near the speaker, use:

éste—this (one)   *éstos*—these

ésta—this (one)   *éstas*—these

To talk about something or someone near the listener, use:

ése—that (one)   *ésos*—those

ésa—that (one)   *ésas*—those

To talk about something or someone far from both, use:

aquél—that (one)   *aquéllos*—those

aquélla—that (one)   *aquéllas*—those

> ¿Qué manzanas quieres? ¿Éstas o aquéllas?
> What apples do you want? These or those?

> Éstas están maduras pero ésas están verdes.
> These are ripe but those are green.

> Quiero ésta.
> I want this one.

To talk about an abstract idea or something which has not been identified, use:

esto—this   *eso*—that   *aquello*—that

> La profesora está gritando. Esto no me gusta.
> The teacher is yelling. I don't like this.

> —¿Qué es aquello?
> —What is that?

> —¿Eso? Es un programa para la computadora.
> —That? It is a program for the computer.

EXERCISES

A. While in the furniture store you hear several conversations. Translate the word in parentheses to complete the sentence.

1. Me gusta _____ (that) silla pero no _____

   (this one).

2. _____ (These) estantes son más bonitos que

   _____ (those, over there).

3. ¿Debo comprar _____ (this) cama o _____
(that one)?

4. ¿Qué alfombras prefieres? ¿_____ (those) o
_____ (these)?

5. _____ (This) televisor es mejor que _____
(that one).

6. Papá, ¿quieres _____ (that) sillón o _____
(that one, over there)?

7. —Juan es un mentiroso.

—_____ (That) no es verdad.

8. —¿Quieres _____ (this)?

—No sé. ¿Qué es _____ (that)?

B. Which is better? Mirna takes her little brother shopping for school supplies. He asks her about certain things and she reponds with a comparison. Follow the model.

> **MODELO:** ¿Es bueno este bolígrafo?
> *No, éste es más bonito que ése. O,*
> *No, éste es mejor que ése.*

1. ¿Compro esta mochila?

_____

2. ¿Necesito aquel cuaderno?

_____

3. ¿Te gustan esos lápices?

_____

4. ¿Debo comprar aquellos libros?

_____

5. ¿Compro esa goma de borrar?

---

6. Necesito una calculadora. ¿Compro ésta?

PART K: Indicating the Presence and Absence of People and Things

INDEFINITE AND NEGATIVE WORDS

The following expressions can be used when indicating the presence and absence of people and things in Spanish.

AFFIRMATIVE	NEGATIVE
algo—something, anything	nada—nothing, not . . . anything
alguien—someone, somebody, anyone, anybody	nadie—no one, nobody, not . . . anyone, not . . . anybody
alguno(a)—some, someone, any	ninguno(a)—no, no one, none, not . . . any, not . . . anybody
algunos(as)—some, any, several	
siempre—always	nunca—never, not . . . ever
también—also, too	tampoco—neither, not . . . either
o . . . o—either . . . or	ni . . . ni—neither . . . nor

Remember that, in Spanish:

- In a negative sentence, a negative word (usually *no*) must be placed before the verb

  Mi mejor amigo no viaja en avión nunca. Or,
  Mi mejor amigo nunca viaja en avión.
  My best friend never travels by plane.

- *Alguno* and *ninguno* drop the *-o* before a masculine singular noun. Remember that *algún* and *ningún* carry a written accent

  ¿Hay algún dinero en la cartera? No, no tengo ningún dinero.
  Is there any money in the wallet? No, I don't have any money.

- Ninguno(a) is used only in the singular form

  ¿Le prestas algunos discos a Juan?
  No, no le presto ninguno.

- Double and even triple negatives are frequent in Spanish

No voy al cine con nadie tampoco.

I don't go to the movies with anyone either.

EXERCISES

A. Dora's brother is being very contradictory. Any time Dora says something, he has to change what she says to a negative statement. Write the following statements as he might say them.

> **MODELO:** Allí hay algo extraño.
>
> *Allí no hay nada extraño.*

1. Tengo algo en el bolsillo.

_____

2. Ves a alguien en el laboratorio.

_____

3. Hablan con algunos estudiantes.

_____

4. Siempre llego a tiempo.

_____

5. Ayudamos a Cecilia y a Oscar.

_____

6. Limpian los escritorios también.

_____

7. ¿Los experimentos? ¿Preparaste alguno?

_____

8. Les explicas la lección a algunas chicas.

_____

B. Today you are very negative. Any time someone asks you a question you answer in the negative. Answer the following questions using as many negative words as possible.

> **MODELO:** ¿Hay algo extraño allí siempre?
>
> *No, no hay nada extraño allí nunca.*

1. ¿Aprendes algo interesante de vez en cuando?

   _____

2. ¿Estás de buen humor siempre?

   _____

3. ¿Están ocupados tus amigos siempre?

   _____

4. ¿Siempre estás ocupado(a) tú también?

   _____

5. ¿Conoces a alguien antipático?

   _____

6. ¿Vas a la playa o a la piscina?

   _____

7. ¿Eres amable con algunos de tus amigos?

   _____

8. ¿Sales de compras con alguien siempre?

   _____

LESSON 3
Providing and Obtaining Information About Events

PART A: Talking About Everyday Activities and Ongoing Situations and Actions

PRESENT TENSE OF REGULAR VERBS

The present tense of regular verbs is formed by dropping the infinitive ending *(-ar, -er, -ir)* and adding the following endings to the stem:

- For *-ar* verbs, add *(-o, -as, -a, -amos, -áis, -an)*

HABLAR (TO SPEAK)	
yo hablo	nosotros(as) hablamos
tú hablas	vosotros(as) habláis
él habla	ellos hablan
ella habla	ellas hablan
Ud. habla	Uds. hablan

- For *-er* verbs, add *(-o, -es, -e, -emos, -éis, -en)*

APRENDER (TO LEARN)	
yo aprendo	nosotros(as) aprendemos
tú aprendes	vosotros(as) aprendéis
él aprende	ellos aprenden
ella aprende	ellas aprenden
Ud. aprende	Uds. aprenden

- For *-ir* verbs, add *(-o, -es, -e, -imos, -ís, -en)*

RECIBIR (TO RECEIVE)	
yo recibo	nosotros(as) recibimos
tú recibes	vosotros(as) recibís
él recibe	ellos reciben
ella recibe	ellas reciben
Ud. recibe	Uds. reciben

Remember that in Spanish:

* The subject pronoun is often omitted
* The present tense is equivalent to three forms in English

For example, the Spanish sentence, *Aprendemos español,* can be translated as *We learn Spanish,* or *We are learning Spanish,* or *We do learn Spanish.*

USES OF THE PRESENT TENSE

The most commonly used tense in Spanish is the present indicative. It is used to express:

* Actions or states of being at the present time

  ¿Qué hacen Uds.?
  What are you doing?

  Descansamos.
  We are resting.

  Estamos muy cansados.
  We are very tired.

* Actions that are habitual

  Tomo el tren cada mañana.
  I take the train each morning.

* Actions in the near future

  Las clases empiezan mañana.
  Classes begin tomorrow.

* Actions or states of being in the past in a more vivid way

  Felipe entra en la sala, saluda y todos aplauden.
  Felipe enters the living room, greets everyone, and they all applaud.

EXERCISES

A. Practice. While walking in the halls of your school, you hear teachers and students making comments. Complete what you hear with the correct form of the verb in parentheses in the present tense. Then, substitute the underlined subject of the original sentence with the subjects in parentheses and make the necessary changes.

1. Los estudiantes _____ (prometer) hacer todo el trabajo.
(mi hermano, nosotros, tú)

2. Nosotros _____ (prestar) mucha atención en clase.
(yo, Graciela, Uds.)

3. Yo _____ (sufrir) cuando tengo un examen.
   (ella, nosotros, tú)

4. Mi prima _____ (recibir) una beca (*scholarship*). (Uds.,
   Ud., yo)

5. Tú _____ (sacar) buenas notas siempre. (nosotros, Ud.,
   ellos)

6. Yo _____ (aprender) muchas cosas en esa clase. (Uds.,
   ella, nosotras)

B. Oscar is telling his friends what he, his friends, and family do when
they have free time. Complete what he says with the correct form of the
verb in parentheses.

1. Mis padres _____ (asistir) a conferencias sobre arte.

2. Yo _____ (ayudar) a mis padres.

3. Mi mamá les _____ (escribir) correo electrónico a sus
   parientes.

4. Nosotros _____ (aprender) a patinar.

5. Mis amigos y yo _____ (cenar) en un restaurante.

6. Tú _____ (decidir) qué hacer en ese momento.

7. Mi amiga Lourdes _____ (bailar) en el club.

8. Yo también _____ (subir) a una montaña cerca de mi
   casa.

9. Alejandro _____ (correr) en el parque.

10. La familia de Andrés _____ (partir) para la playa.

C. Using the list of verbs below write complete sentences telling which
activities the following people do during the week and which activities
they do on weekends. Remember that you must add some words to
make the statements complete.

bailar/desayunar/abrir/escuchar/estudiar/correr/beber/asistir

1. Durante la semana yo . . .

2. Durante la semana el (la) profesor(a) de español . . .

3. Durante la semana mis padres y yo . . .

4. Los fines de semana el dueño *(owner)* de la florería . . .

5. Durante los fines de semana mis amigos . . .

6. Los fines de semana tú . . .

PRESENT TENSE OF IRREGULAR VERBS

In the present tense, the following verbs are irregular only in the first person singular:

CAER (TO FALL)	
caigo	caemos
caes	caéis
cae	caen

CONOCER (TO KNOW)	
conozco	conocemos
conoces	conocéis
conoce	conocen

Verbs like *conocer:*

agradecer—to thank, be grateful for
complacer—to please
crecer—to grow
desaparecer—to disappear
enorgullecerse de—to take pride in
entristecerse—to become sad
merecer—to deserve, merit

nacer—to be born
obedecer—to obey
ofrecer—to offer
parecerse a—to resemble, look like
pertenecer—to belong
reconocer—to recognize

DAR (TO GIVE)	
doy	damos
das	dáis
da	dan

HACER (TO DO, MAKE)	
hago	hacemos
haces	hacéis
hace	hacen

PONER (TO PUT, PLACE)	
pongo	ponemos
pones	ponéis
pone	ponen

Verbs like *poner:*

componer—to fix, repair

oponerse a—to be against, opposed to

ponerse—to put on; (+ adjective) to become
(change in physical or emotional state)

proponer—to propose

imponer—to impose

suponer—to suppose

CONDUCIR (TO DRIVE, TO LEAD, TO CONDUCT)	
conduzco	conducimos
conduces	conducís
conduce	conducen

Verbs like *conducir:*

producir—to produce

reducir—to reduce

traducir—to translate

SABER (TO KNOW)		SALIR (TO GO OUT, LEAVE)	
sé	sabemos	**salgo**	salimos
sabes	sabéis	sales	salís
sabe	saben	sale	salen

TRAER (TO BRING)	
traigo	traemos
traes	traéis
trae	traen

Verbs like *traer:*

atraer—to attract

VALER (TO BE WORTH)		VER (TO SEE)	
valgo	valemos	**veo**	vemos
vales	valéis	ves	veis
vale	valen	ve	ven

EXERCISES

A. Practice. Dolores and Patricia are talking about shopping and fashion. Complete what they say with the correct form of the verb in parentheses in the present tense. Then, substitute the subject of the original sentence with the subjects in parentheses and make the necessary changes.

1. <u>Yo</u> les _____ (dar) muchas ideas a mis amigos sobre la última moda *(fashion)*. (mi mamá, ellos, tú)

2. ¿Qué _____ (hacer) <u>tú</u> para encontrar buenos precios? (nosotros, ellos, yo)

3. <u>Tú</u> no _____ (conocer) a ese diseñador. (yo, Uds., Jacinto)

4. ¿Dónde _____ (poner-<u>yo</u>) las revistas de moda? (tú, nosotras, él)

5. <u>Mi padre</u> _____ (conducir) su coche al centro comercial. (tú, Uds., yo)

6. <u>Tú</u> _____ (saber) donde venden esas camisetas. (nosotros, ellas, yo)

7. <u>Ella</u> _____ (ver) a sus amigas cuando ella va de compras. (yo, Ud., nosotros)

8. <u>Tú</u> siempre _____ (traer) algo para los parientes. (yo, Uds., nosotros)

9. <u>Nosotros</u> _____ (salir) de compras todos los fines de semana. (tú, yo, él)

10. <u>Yo</u> _____ (traducir) las instrucciones al inglés cuando yo traigo regalos de México. (ella, tú, nosotros)

B. One of your classmates is gathering information about the habits of the students in your school for a newspaper article. Answer the questions she asks you according to your personal experience.

1. ¿Haces la tarea temprano o tarde?

_____

2. ¿Traes mucho trabajo de la escuela a casa?

_____

3. ¿Sabes hacer apuntes *(take notes)* en las clases?

_____

4. ¿Ves a tus amigos durante la semana después de las clases?

_____

5. ¿Sales con tus amigos los fines de semana?

_____

6. ¿Pones música cuando estudias?

_____

7. ¿Les das apoyo *(support)* a tus amigos?

_____

8. ¿Conoces a muchas personas en tu escuela?

_____

The following verbs have irregular forms in the present tense:

DECIR (TO SAY, TELL)	
digo	decimos
dices	decís
dice	**dicen**

ESTAR (TO BE)	
estoy	estamos
estás	estáis
está	**están**

IR (TO GO)	
voy	**vamos**
vas	**vais**
va	**van**

OÍR (TO HEAR)	
oigo	oímos
oyes	oís
oye	**oyen**

SER (TO BE)	
soy	**somos**
eres	**sois**
es	**son**

TENER (TO HAVE)	
tengo	tenemos
tienes	tenéis
tiene	**tienen**

Verbs like *tener:*

contener—to contain

detener—to detain

detenerse—to stop

entretener—to entertain

mantener—to maintain, support

obtener—to obtain, get

VENIR (TO COME)	
vengo	venimos
vienes	venís
viene	**vienen**

Verbs like *venir:*

convenir—to agree, be suitable, good for   intervenir—to intervene

EXERCISES

A. Practice. Georgina and her friends are talking about the news. Complete the sentences with the correct form of the verb in parentheses in the present tense. Then, substitute the subject of the original sentence with the subjects in parentheses and make the necessary changes.

1. ¿_____ (Decir) <u>los programas de noticias</u> la verdad siempre? (nosotros, ellos, Ud.)

2. <u>Esos reporteros</u> _____ (estar) en la corte hoy. (yo, Uds., Eduardo)

3. <u>Estos reporteros</u> _____ (venir) a entrevistar al presidente cuando él visita nuestra ciudad. (Ud., nosotros, ellas)

4. <u>Yo</u> no _____ (oír) las noticias en la radio. (ellas, nosotros, él)

5. ¿A dónde _____ (ir) <u>tú</u> a comprar los periódicos? (nosotros, Ud., ella)

6. <u>Nosotros</u> no _____ (tener) mucho tiempo para leer las noticias. (yo, Uds., tú)

7. <u>Yo</u> _____ (ser) experto en las actividades de las Naciones Unidas. (él, tú, Ud.)

B. Dolores is writing a note to one of her friends. Help her complete the note by supplying the correct form of the verbs in parentheses.

Mis amigos _____ (venir) a mi casa todas las tardes.

Generalmente nosotros _____ (ir) al patio de mi casa. Allí

siempre _____ (estar) mis dos hermanitos. Yo les

_____ (decir) a ellos lo que hacemos en la escuela. Ellos

_____ (ser) muy inteligentes. A las cuatro yo siempre

_____ (oír) el coche de mi madre. Nosotros

_____ (ir) a saludarla. Cuando yo _____ (tener)

mucha tarea, entro a mi casa y la hago. A veces Juan, mi mejor amigo,

_____ (venir) a cenar con nosotros. Mis padres

_____ (decir) que yo _____ (ser) la hija ideal.

Ellos _____ (estar) muy orgullosos *(proud)* de mí. ¿Y tú?

¿_____ (Ser) el hijo ideal de tus padres? Yo

_____ (estar) segura de que tú _____ (tener)

buenas cualidades.

HAY

The verb *haber* (to have) is used impersonally (without a subject) only in the third person singular: *hay. Hay* means *there is* or *there are*.

Hay muchas oportunidades de trabajo en el periódico.
There are many job opportunities in the newspaper.

EXERCISES

One of your neighbors' sons is thinking about attending your school. Answer his questions with complete sentences.

1. ¿Cuántos estudiantes hay en tu clase?

_____

2. ¿Hay muchas chicas en tu escuela?

_____

3. ¿Qué hay en las paredes de tu sala de clase?

_____

4. ¿Hay estudiantes de diferentes países en tu escuela?

_____

5. ¿Cuántos profesores de español hay en tu escuela?

VERBS WITH SPELLING CHANGES IN THE PRESENT TENSE

In the present tense of certain verbs, the first person singular has the following spelling changes:

- Verbs ending in -*ger* or -*gir,* change *g* to *j* before *o* and *a*

COGER (TO SEIZE, CATCH, TAKE)	
cojo	cogemos
coges	cogéis
coge	cogen

Verbs like *coger:*

escoger—to choose   proteger—to protect

recoger—to pick up

DIRIGIR (TO DIRECT)	
dirijo	dirigimos
diriges	dirigís
dirige	dirigen

Verbs like *dirigir:*

exigir—to demand   fingir—to pretend

Note that some -*gir* verbs with spelling changes also have stem changes (see page 86). Two such verbs are:

corregir (i, i)*—to correct   elegir (i, i)—to elect

- Verbs ending in -*guir* change *gu* to *g* before *o* and *a*

DISTINGUIR (TO DISTINGUISH)	
distingo	distinguimos
distingues	distinguís
distingue	distinguen

Verbs like *distinguir:*

extinguir—to extinguish

---

*Verbs that have stem changes will be listed followed by changes in parentheses: (ie), (ue), (ue, u), (ie, i). and (i, i)

Some *-guir* verbs with spelling changes that also have stem changes are:

seguir (i, i)—to continue, follow

conseguir (i, i)—to obtain, get

perseguir (i, i)—to pursue, persecute

- Verbs ending in *-cer* or *-cir* preceded by a consonant change *c* to *z* before *a* and *o*

VENCER (TO OVERCOME, CONQUER)	
venzo	vencemos
vences	vencéis
vence	vencen

Verbs like *vencer:*

convencer—to convince

ejercer—to practice a profession, to exercise (exert)

EXERCISES

A. Practice. Ramiro loves to go fishing. Complete what he says with the correct form of the verb in parentheses in the present tense. Then, substitute the subject of the original sentence with the subjects in parentheses and make the necessary changes.

1. Cuando yo quiero ir a pescar, yo _____ (convencer) a mis padres. (nosotros, él, tú)

2. Tú _____ (exigir) mucho de tus amigos cuando ellos van a pescar contigo. (ellas, yo, Ud.)

3. Cuando vamos al lago nosotros _____ (coger) muchos peces. (yo, ella, Uds.)

4. ¿Están frecos esos pescados? Yo no _____ (distinguir) la diferencia. (ellas, Ud., tú)

B. Answer the following questions based on your own experience.

1. ¿Escoges bien a tus amigos?

_____

2. ¿Proteges a las personas que necesitan ayuda?

_____

3. ¿Finges estar enfermo(a) para no ir a la escuela?

_____

4. Cuando tu cuarto no está en orden, ¿quién recoge las cosas?

_____

5. ¿Diriges algún grupo musical en la escuela?

_____

VERBS WITH STEM CHANGES IN THE PRESENT TENSE

In the present tense, certain Spanish verbs have a change in the stem. The stem of these verbs changes in the singular _(yo, tú, él, ella, Ud.)_ and in the third person plural _(ellos, ellas, Uds.),_ but not in the _nosotros_ or _vosotros_ form.

- Verbs that change _e_ to _ie_

CERRAR (TO CLOSE, TO SHUT)	
cierro	cerramos
cierras	cerráis
cierra	**cierran**

Verbs like _cerrar:_

atravesar—to cross

comenzar—to begin

confesar—to confess

despertar—to awaken

*despertarse—to wake up

empezar—to begin

encerrar—to enclose, to lock in

negar—to deny

nevar—to snow

pensar—to think, to plan

recomendar—to recommend

sentar—to seat

*sentarse—to sit down

temblar—to tremble

---

*Note that verbs that are listed with -_se_ attached to the infinitive ending are reflexive. You will review reflexive verbs on page 99–100.

PERDER (TO LOSE)	
pierdo	perdemos
pierdes	perdéis
pierde	**pierden**

Verbs like *perder:*

defender—to defend

encender—to light, to ignite

entender—to understand

querer—to want, to wish, to love (a person)

PREFERIR (TO PREFER)	
prefiero	preferimos
prefieres	preferís
prefiere	**prefieren**

Verbs like *preferir:*

divertir—to amuse

divertirse—to have a good time

mentir—to lie

sentir—to regret, to feel (be) sorry

sentirse—to feel (well, sick, etc.)

- Verbs that change *o* to *ue*

CONTAR (TO COUNT, TO TELL)	
cuento	contamos
cuentas	contáis
cuenta	**cuentan**

Verbs like *contar:*

acordarse (de)—to remember

acostar—to put to bed

acostarse—to go to bed

almorzar—to have lunch

costar—to cost

demostrar—to demonstrate, to show

encontrar—to find

encontrarse (con)—to meet

jugar—to play

mostrar—to show

probar—to try, to taste

probarse—to try on

recordar—to remember

rogar—to beg, to ask, to request

sonar—to ring, to sound

soñar—to dream

volar—to fly

VOLVER (TO RETURN, TO GO BACK)	
vuelvo	volvemos
vuelves	volvéis
vuelve	**vuelven**

Verbs like *volver:*

devolver—to return, to give back

doler—to pain, to ache

envolver—to wrap

llover—to wrap

mover—to move

poder—to be able

DORMIR (TO SLEEP)	
duermo	dormimos
duermes	dormís
duerme	**duermen**

Verbs like *dormir:*

dormirse—to fall asleep

morir—to die

- Verbs that change *e* to *i*

REPETIR (TO REPEAT)	
repito	repetimos
repites	repetís
repite	**repiten**

Verbs like *repetir:*

conseguir—to get, to obtain

despedir—to fire (let go)

despedirse (de)—to say goodbye to

medir—to measure

pedir—to request, to ask for

reír(se)—to laugh

seguir—to follow, to continue

servir—to serve

sonreír(se)—to smile

vestir—to dress

vestirse—to get dressed

Remember that the verbs *seguir* and *conseguir* also have a spelling change (*gu* to *g*) in the first person singular *(yo)*. For example:

SEGUIR (TO FOLLOW)	
sigo	seguimos
sigues	seguís
sigue	**siguen**

EXERCISES

A. Practice. Antonio and his friends are talking about their plans for the future. Complete what they say with the correct form of the verb in parentheses in the present tense. Then, substitute the underlined subject of the original sentence with the subjects in parentheses and make the necessary changes.

1. Yo _____ (querer) ser arquitecto. (nosotros, ellas, tú)

2. Mi amiga _____ (pensar) estudiar en Italia. (él, Uds., nosotras)

3. Mi novia _____ (preferir) estudiar en un país de habla hispana. (tú, Ud., nosotros)

4. Ellos _____ (poder) viajar después de terminar los estudios universitarios. (nosotros, yo, ella)

5. Los estudios _____ (costar) mucho. (la universidad, el viaje a Italia, los cursos)

6. Los consejeros _____ (conseguir) muchas becas *(scholarships)* para los estudiantes. (Ud., el profesor, nosotros)

B. Carolina was working at her computer and something went wrong. Help her by writing complete sentences with words from each list. Make sure you use all the words and phrases from the lists.

MODELO: *Ellos duermen en casa de mi tía.*

ellos	devolver	los intereses de los pobres
nosotros	almorzar	hablar español muy bien
yo	dormir	las clases a las nueve
tú	medir	los libros a la biblioteca
Ud.	seguir	cinco pies, dos pulgadas
ella	poder	ir de viaje durante la primavera
él	preferir	en un café cerca de la escuela
Uds.	defender	en casa de mi tía
nosotras	empezar	los cambios en la bolsa *(stock market)*

C. Actions count! Answer the following questions in complete sentences expressing your opinion about the different topics presented.

1. ¿Qué piensas de los líderes estudiantiles?

   _____

2. ¿Resuelven los políticos los problemas de tu comunidad?

   _____

3. Tus amigos y tú, ¿mienten a veces?

   _____

4. ¿Defienden Uds. a las personas pobres?

   _____

5. ¿Confiesas tus errores a tus padres?

   _____

6. ¿Demuestran Uds. sus sentimientos *(feelings)* libremente?

   _____

7. ¿Consiguen los ciudadanos cambiar las leyes *(laws)* cuando votan?

   _____

8. ¿Recuerdan Uds. las cosas que prometen?

   _____

D. Getting to know you and your friends better. Use the list of verbs and phrases to write six sentences about your feelings and those of your friends.

negar los errores

mentir para no hacer daño *(to hurt)*

entender por qué los padres son estrictos

temblar delante de un artista famoso

resolver los problemas de mis amigos

pedir ayuda a la policía

mostrar los sentimientos

MODELO: *Yo nunca niego mis errores.* Or,
Mis amigos nunca niegan sus errores.

1. _____

2. _____

3. _____

4. _____

5. _____

6. _____

VERBS ENDING IN *-IAR*

Some verbs ending in *-iar* require an accent on the *i* in all the singular forms *(yo, tú, él ella,* and *Ud.)* and in the third person plural *(ellos, ellas,* and *Uds.).*

CONFIAR EN (TO CONFIDE IN, TO RELY ON)	
confío	confiamos
confías	confiáis
confía	**confían**

Verbs like *confiar:*

esquiar—to ski

enviar—to send

guiar—to guide

resfriarse—to catch a cold

VERBS ENDING IN *-UAR*

Verbs ending in *-uar* require an accent on the *u* in the singular *(yo, tú, él, ella,* and *Ud.)* and the third person plural *(ellos, ellas,* and *Uds.).*

CONTINUAR (TO CONTINUE)	
continúo	continuamos
continúas	continuáis
continúa	**continúan**

Verbs like *continuar:*

actuar—to act

graduarse—to graduate

VERBS ENDING IN -UIR

In verbs ending in *-uir* (with the exception of those ending in *-guir*), *y* is inserted after the *u* in the singular *(yo, tú, él, ella,* and *Ud.)* and in the third person plural *(ellos, ellas,* and *Uds.).*

CONSTRUIR (TO CONSTRUCT, BUILD)	
construyo	construimos
construyes	construís
construye	**construyen**

Verbs like *construir:*

concluir—to conclude, to end

contribuir—to contribute

destruir—to destroy

distribuir—to distribute

incluir—to include

influir—to influence

sustituir—to substitute

EXERCISES

A. Practice. Carolina and her family are very involved in their community. Complete what she says with the correct form of the verb in parentheses in the present tense. Then, substitute the underlined subject of the original sentence with the subjects in parentheses and make the necessary changes.

1. Mis padres _____ (confiar) en el gobierno. (nosotros, Uds., yo)

2. Nosotros _____ (contribuir) a muchas organizaciones benéficas (*charities*). (yo, ella, tú)

3. Ese señor _____ (actuar) como un payaso *(clown)* para divertir a los niños enfermos. (Ud., yo, nosotras)

B. Imagine that you are asked to respond to a survey about your values. Answer the following questions as fully as possible.

1. ¿Confías en tus amigos?

   _____

2. ¿Influyen tus padres en tus decisiones?

   _____

3. ¿Actúas con madurez (*maturity*) siempre?

_____

4. ¿Incluyen Uds. a todos sus amigos en todas sus fiestas?

_____

5. ¿Qué destruye muchas relaciones personales?

_____

6. ¿Contribuyes a las discusiones sobre los problemas de tu comunidad?

_____

PART B: Talking About Situations and Actions that Have Been Going on for a While

HACE AND *DESDE HACE*

When talking about an action or state of being that began in the past and continues up to the present, Spanish speakers use the present tense in two equivalent constructions:

> *Hace* + length of time + *que* + present tense

Or,

> Present tense + *hace* + length of time
>
> Hace un mes que llueve.

Or,

> Llueve hace un mes.
> It has been raining for a month.

In order to ask questions about actions that began in the past and are still going on in the present, use the construction:

> *¿Cuánto [tiempo] hace que* + present tense?
>
> ¿Cuánto [tiempo] hace que llueve?
> How long has it been raining?

It is also possible to use the present tense to refer to actions or states of being that began in the past and are still going on in the present by using the construction:

> Present tense + *desde hace* + length of time
>
> Nieva desde hace tres horas.
> It has been snowing for three hours.

Notice the construction for this type of question:

¿Desde cuándo + present tense?

¿Desde cuándo nieva?

How long has it been snowing?

EXERCISES

A. How long have you been involved in the following activities? Use the list of phrases below to talk about the length of time you have been doing or not doing the following activities.

> **MODELO:** practicar el piano
>
> *Hace una semana que no practico el piano.* Or,
>
> *No practico el piano hace una semana.*

1. aprender español

_____

2. asistir a esta escuela

_____

3. salir con tus amigos por la noche

_____

4. patinar (*skate*)

_____

5. leer el periódico regularmente

_____

6. ir a acampar en las montañas

_____

7. nadar en la piscina pública

_____

8. recoger manzanas en el campo

_____

9. dormir en casa de tus amigos

_____

10. jugar al béisbol

_____

B. Your Spanish teacher wants to find out since when you have been doing certain activities. Use the information below to tell him/her how long you have been doing them.

1. estudiar español

_____

2. no hacer la tarea

_____

3. no salir a cenar a un restaurante

_____

4. ir a los partidos de fútbol

_____

5. no visitar a tus parientes

_____

6. comer en la cafetería

_____

7. servir la cena en casa

_____

8. no devolver un libro a la biblioteca

_____

9. distribuir los libros en clase

_____

10. venir a la escuela en autobús

_____

C. It's your turn. Imagine that you want to ask a new student in your school about the activities in which he/she participates. Write five questions asking him/her how long he or she has been doing some activities you enjoy doing.

1. _____

2. _____

3. _____

4. _____

5. _____

PART C: Talking About How Well or How Often We Do Something

ADVERBS

The following are some words and expressions in Spanish that indicate how often or how well we do something.

How often?	
a menudo—frequently	por lo general—generally
frecuentemente—frequently	muchas (pocas) veces—many (few) times
siempre—always	
nunca—never	todos los días (años, meses)— every day (year, month)
a veces—sometimes	todas las semanas—every week
de vez en cuando—from time to time	todos los domingos (lunes, etc.)—every Sunday (Monday, etc.)
rara vez—rarely	
generalmente—generally	

How well?	
(muy) bien—(very) well	(muy) mal—(very) badly

EXERCISES

A. Your friend asks you several questions about your habits. Use the list of adverbs below to express how often you do these activities.

a menudo/a veces/rara vez/siempre/pocas veces/de vez en cuando/nunca

1. ¿Vas a las tiendas?

_____

2. ¿Visitas a tus parientes?

_____

3. ¿Practicas algún deporte?

_____

4. ¿Lees novelas de aventura?

_____

5. ¿Cuándo vas a esquiar?

_____

6. A mí me gusta patinar. ¿Tú patinas?

_____

7. ¿Haces un viaje durante las vacaciones?

_____

8. ¿Das un paseo por el parque?

_____

9. ¿Pones la mesa para la cena?

_____

10. ¿Almuerzas en un restaurante?

_____

11. ¿Oyes música rock?

_____

12. ¿Cuándo llamas a los amigos por teléfono?

_____

B. Don't be modest! Use the list of activities below to say how well you do these activities.

1. construir modelos de puentes *(bridges)*

_____

2. esquiar

_____

3. contar chistes

_____

4. vencer a mis enemigos en los juegos electrónicos

_____

5. escoger novelas interesantes

_____

6. jugar al ajedrez *(chess)*

_____

7. pintar

_____

8. montar en bicicleta

_____

PART D: Talking About Everyday Activities, Situations, and Actions

REFLEXIVE SENTENCES
When the direct or the indirect object of a sentence is the same person (or thing) as the subject, the sentence is called reflexive.

Reflexive pronouns must be used in reflexive sentences:

REFLEXIVE PRONOUNS	
me—myself, to (for) myself	nos—ourselves, to (for) ourselves
te—yourself, to (for) yourself (fam.)	os—yourselves, to (for) yourselves (fam.)
se—himself, to (for) himself, itself	se—themselves, to (for) themselves
se—herself, to (for) herself, itself	se—themselves, to (for) themselves
se—yourself, to (for) yourself (for.)	se—yourselves, to (for) yourselves (for.)

The infinitive of reflexive verbs is recognized by the *-se* attached to it. Many daily activities are reflexive. For example: *despertarse (ie)*—to wake up, *levantarse*—to get up, *lavarse*—to wash (oneself), *cepillarse*—to brush, *afeitarse*—to shave, *vestirse (i, i)*—to get dressed, etc.

BAÑARSE (TO BATHE ONESELF)			
me baño	I bathe (myself)	nos bañamos	we bathe (ourselves)
te bañas	you bathe (yourself)	os bañáis	you bathe (yourselves)
se baña	he, she, it bathes (himself, herself, itself)	se bañan	they bathe (themselves)
se baña	you bathe (yourself)	se bañan	you bathe (yourselves)

Note that:

- In most cases reflexive pronouns (*myself, yourself,* etc.) are understood, but not stated in English
- The pronoun *se* is both singular and plural and has several meanings
- With the exception of the affirmative commands, the reflexive pronouns are placed immediately before a conjugated verb

  ¿A qué hora se acuestan Uds.? Nos acostamos a las once.
  At what time do you go to bed? We go to bed at eleven.

Remember that the possessive pronouns are not used with parts of the body.

  Primero, nos cepillamos los dientes.
  First, we brush our teeth.

Reflexive verbs are often used to express a mental, social, or physical change. In English this is often expressed by *to get* or *to become.* Some Spanish verbs of this type are:

asustarse—to become afraid, get scared

aburrirse—to get (become) bored

casarse—to get married

cansarse—to get (become) tired

desmayarse—to faint (become faint)

enfadarse—to get (become) angry

enojarse—to get (become) angry

resfriarse—to become cold, get a cold

mojarse—to get wet

Some reflexive verbs are idiomatic. In such cases, they are always used reflexively in Spanish but not in English. The most common verb of this type is *irse*—to leave, to go away. Other common verbs of this type are:

acordarse (ue) de—to remember

apresurarse—to hurry

arrepentirse (ie) de—to repent, be sorry

atreverse a—to dare

burlarse de—to make fun of

negarse (ie) a—to refuse to

olvidarse de—to forget

parecerse a—to resemble, look like

quejarse—to complain

reírse (i, i) de—to laugh at

tratarse de—to be concerned with, be about (a question of)

EXERCISES

A. Practice. Inés and her friends are talking about sports and their physical education class. Complete what they say with the correct form of the verb in parentheses in the present tense. Then, substitute the subject of the original sentence with the subjects in parentheses and make the necessary changes.

1. Yo _____ (cansarse) mucho en la clase de educación física. (nosotros, Uds., él)

2. Ese chico _____ (quejarse) del entrenador *(coach)*. (yo, tú, ellas)

3. Nosotros no _____ (acordarse) del resultado final del partido. (Ud., yo, ella)

4. ¿Por qué _____ (burlarse-tú) de esos jugadores? (él, Uds., nosotros)

5. Uds. _____ (aburrirse) en los partidos de fútbol americano. (yo, Ud., tú)

B. A group of students from Chile comes to visit your school and they want to know about you and your life. Answer their questions with a complete sentence in Spanish.

1. Cuando tienes una cita, ¿dónde te encuentras con tus amigos?

_____

2. ¿Qué ropa te pones cuando vas a una fiesta?

_____

3. ¿Por qué se entristecen tus padres?

_____

4. ¿Te acuerdas del cumpleaños de tus amigos siempre?

_____

5. ¿Cuándo se enfadan tus amigos y tú?

_____

6. ¿Te pareces tú a alguien en tu familia?

_____

7. ¿Se quejan mucho los profesores de los estudiantes?

_____

8. ¿Qué hacen Uds. cuando se aburren?

_____

C. You are expecting an exchange student to stay with you and your family. You want to let him/her know about your daily routine. Use the following list of verbs to talk about a typical day in your life. Make sure that you include as much information as possible.

> despertarse/levantarse/bañarse/lavarse/vestirse/despedirse/
> acostarse/dormirse

Por la mañana . . .

_____

_____

_____

Luego . . .

_____

_____

Por la noche . . .

_____

_____

D. Use the following verbs to talk about your parents' morning routine. There may be some activities that they do not do, and others that are not listed. Try to be as thorough as possible.

> levantarse/bañarse/lavarse/vestirse/maquillarse/afeitarse/ desayunarse

_____

_____

_____

_____

_____

E. In complete sentences, tell how often you do the following activities. Include one of the following expressions in your answer.

> siempre/a menudo/de vez en cuando/rara vez/nunca

> **MODELO:** enamorarse del actor (de la actriz) de una película
> *Nunca me enamoro del actor de una película.*

1. olvidarse de un examen

_____

2. quejarse de las notas que recibe

_____

3. enojarse con su mejor amigo

_____

4. burlarse de otra persona

_____

5. negarse a ayudar a un amigo

_____

6. acordarse del cumpleaños de sus padres

_____

F. Changes. Read the following situations and then use a reflexive verb to express the mental or physical change resulting from the circumstances described.

> apresurarse/arrepentirse/asustarse/aburrirse/cansarse/desmayarse/ enfadarse/enojarse/mojarse/olvidarse/reírse/resfriarse

MODELO: Hace mucho frío y no llevas un abrigo.
Me resfrío.

1. Caminas por el bosque y ves un oso _(bear)._

_____

2. La conferencia es larga y no comprendes nada.

_____

3. Son las tres de la tarde y no has comido nada.

_____

4. Llueve y sales sin paraguas.

_____

5. Le haces un favor a tu amigo y él no te da las gracias.

_____

6. Trabajas todo el día y luego haces ejercicios.

_____

7. Tienes una cita a las dos y son las dos menos cinco.

_____

8. Le gritas a tu mejor amigo sin razón _(without a reason)._

_____

9. Oyes un chiste muy gracioso.

_____

10. Es tarde y tienes que estar en la parada del autobús *(bus stop)* en cinco minutos.

_____

IMPERSONAL *SE*

In the passive voice, the subject is acted upon, i.e. *Spanish is spoken in this classroom.*

When a passive sentence is impersonal (the doer is not mentioned), the third person singular *(él, ella, Ud.)* or plural *(ellos, ellas, Uds.)* of reflexive verbs is used to express the passive voice (i.e. *Se habla español en esta clase*—Spanish is spoken in this class).

Note that in a passive sentence in Spanish:

- The subject usually follows the verb
- The verb agrees with the subject (as always)

 Se venden computadoras de segunda mano en esa tienda.
 Second-hand computers are sold in that store.

In general, the active voice (where the subject acts upon an object) is preferred in Spanish.

INDEFINITE SUBJECT

The pronoun *se* is also used with the third person singular of the verb in order to express an indefinite subject (one, people, we, they, you, etc.).

 Se come bien en este restaurante.
 One eats well in this restaurant.

When not stating the indefinite subject might lead to confusion (i.e. with reflexive verbs), the word *uno* is used in addition to *se*.

 ¿Qué se hace los domingos? Uno se levanta tarde.
 What does one do on Sundays? One gets up late.

EXERCISES

A. Imagine that you are working for a newspaper and that you are in charge of the "Help Wanted" section. Use the information below to write the headings for different ads.

> **MODELO:** comprar/primeras ediciones de libros
>
> *Se compran primeras ediciones de libros.*

1. vender/un coche del año

_____

2. comprar/sellos de España

_____

3. buscar/secretarias bilingües

_____

4. alquilar/un apartamento de cinco cuartos

_____

5. necesitar/traductores e intérpretes

_____

B. Generalizations. Think about your school and what goes on there. Write five sentences expressing general statements about it. Do not use a particular person as the subject; use "indefinite" subjects.

> **MODELO:** (no) jugar mucho vólibol
> _Se juega mucho vólibol._ Or,
> _No se juega mucho vólibol._

1. (no) practicar muchos deportes

_____

2. (no) estudiar mucho

_____

3. (no) conocer a mucha gente

_____

4. (no) discutir muchos temas interesantes

_____

5. (no) comer muy mal en la cafetería

_____

PART E: Talking About Actions that Are in Progress at the Moment We Are Talking

PRESENT PROGRESSIVE

When stressing the fact that actions are in progress at the moment they are talking, Spanish speakers use the present progressive. The present progressive is formed with the present tense of the verb *estar* + the present participle of the verb describing the action.

> ¿Qué estás haciendo? Estoy escribiendo una carta.
> What are you doing? I am writing a letter.

The present participle is formed by adding:

* *-ando* to the stem of *-ar* verbs (i.e. *hablar—hablando*)
* *-iendo* to the stem of *-er* and *-ir* verbs (i.e. *comer—comiendo, escribir—escribiendo*)

The present participle is equivalent to the *-ing* form in English (*hablando*—talking, *comiendo*—eating, *escribiendo*—writing).

Some irregular forms are:

decir—diciendo (saying)	reír—riendo (laughing)
divertirse—divirtiendo (enjoying)	leer—leyendo (reading)
dormir—durmiendo (sleeping)	caer—cayendo (falling)
pedir—pidiendo (asking for)	traer—trayendo (bringing)
servir—sirviendo (serving)	oír—oyendo (hearing)
mentir—mintiendo (lying)	

When using an object pronoun or a reflexive pronoun with the present progressive, the pronouns can be placed before the verb *estar* or after and attached to the present participle.

> Lo estoy comprando. Or, Estoy comprándolo.
> I am writing it.

> Me estoy divirtiendo. Or, Estoy divirtiéndome.
> I am having fun (enjoying myself).

Notice that when a pronoun is attached, a written accent is used *(comprándolo, divirtiéndome)*.

Also, please remember that the present progressive:

* Is used to describe and/or stress actions in progress

  Estoy comiendo (ahora mismo).
  I am eating (right now).

* Can never be used to refer to the future. (See p. 108 for talking about the future)

EXERCISES

A. Use the information below to write sentences in which the people do (or don't do) what they should be doing.

> **MODELO:** Alfredo/practicar el violín
> *Alfredo (no) está practicando el violín.*

1. nosotros/prestarle atención al (a la) profesor(a)

_____

2. el director/divertirse

_____

3. mi amigo/dormirse

_____

4. la clase/leer el cuento

_____

5. tú/repetir las frases

_____

6. yo/bailar

_____

B. If you want to be successful in the future you must prepare by doing certain things now. Use the information below to write phrases that stress what you are doing to be prepared. Use the present progressive in your responses.

> **MODELO:** trabajar en un laboratorio
> Para prepararme para el futuro, yo
> *estoy trabajando en un laboratorio.*

Para prepararme para el futuro, yo . . .

1. estudiar todo lo posible *(as much as possible)*

_____

2. leer mucho

_____

3. aprender a usar una computadora

_____

4. ahorrar dinero

_____

5. aprender un idioma extranjero

_____

Now write three more things you are doing that are not included in the list above.

1. _____

2. _____

3. _____

PART F: Talking About Future Actions

IR A + INFINITIVE
When talking about what you are going to do, Spanish generally uses the following construction:

> present tense of *ir* + *a* + infinitive

> ¿Qué vas a hacer este verano? Voy a ir a un campamento.
> What are you going to do this summer? I am going to go to a camp.

ADVERBIAL EXPRESSIONS OF FUTURE TIME
There are many words and expressions that indicate future time. Some useful ones are:

hoy—today

esta mañana—this morning

esta tarde—this afternoon

esta noche—this evening, tonight

mañana—tomorrow

pasado mañana—the day after tomorrow

el lunes (martes, etc.)—on Monday (Tuesday, etc.)

los lunes (martes, etc.)—on Mondays (Tuesdays, etc.)

este fin de semana—this weekend

este verano (invierno, etc.)—this summer (winter, etc.)

el mes (año, etc.) próximo—next month (year, etc.)

el mes (año, etc.) que viene— next month (year, etc.)

la semana próxima (que viene)— next week

EXERCISES

A. What are you and your friends doing this weekend? Use the following verbs to express the activities you are going to do or not going to do this weekend.

> **MODELO:** mi amigo . . . (dar un paseo)
>
> *Mi amigo va a dar un paseo.* Or,
>
> *Mi amigo no va a dar un paseo.*

1. nosotros . . . (practicar un deporte)

2. mi amiga . . . (ver una película)

3. mis amigos . . . (dormir)

4. yo . . . (visitar a amigos)

5. mi amigo y yo . . . (estudiar)

6. mi padre . . . (preparar un informe)

7. tú . . . (escribir un ensayo)

8. mis padres . . . (descansar)

B. When are you going to do the following activities? Use the list of verbs below to write sentences expressing when you are going to do these activities. You may want to refer to the list of expressions that indicate future time.

> **MODELO:** esquiar
>
> *Voy a esquiar el invierno próximo.*

1. hacer ejercicio

   _____

2. escribir unas tarjetas postales

   _____

3. comprar unas revistas

   _____

4. divertirse

   _____

5. graduarse

   _____

6. ir a la heladería

   _____

7. prepararse para un examen

   _____

8. discutir política

   _____

9. hacer la cama

   _____

10. terminar un proyecto

   _____

LESSON 4
Providing and Obtaining Information About the Past

PART A: Talking About Events in the Near Past

***ACABAR DE* + INFINITIVE**

When you want to talk about something that has just taken place, use the following construction:

> present tense of *acabar* + *de* + infinitive

> El programa acaba de empezar.
> The program has just started.

Notice that in English this concept is expressed by using *have just* + past participle.

EXERCISES

Any time someone asks you to do something, you and your friends respond that you have just done it. Use the information below to write complete sentences. Answer the following questions using *acabar de* + infinitive.

> **MODELO:** ¿Quieres practicar el piano?
>
> *No, acabo de practicar el piano.*

1. ¿Piensas almorzar ahora?

_____

2. ¿Quieren Uds. ir al café?

_____

3. ¿Vas a saludar al nuevo estudiante?

_____

4. ¿Quiere tu amiga jugar al ajedrez?

_____

5. Tus padres, ¿piensan ir al cine esta noche?

_____

6. ¿Los profesores van a ayudar a los estudiantes?

_____

7. ¿Deseas ir al centro?

_____

8. ¿Tienen Uds. planes para ir de vacaciones pronto?

_____

PART B: Talking About the Past

PRETERITE OF REGULAR VERBS

When talking about past events, actions, or states completed or finished within a definite period of time, use the preterite tense.

The preterite of regular verbs is formed by dropping the infinite ending and adding the following endings:

- For -ar verbs, add *(-é, -aste, -ó, -amos, -asteis, -aron)*

CANTAR (TO SING)	
canté	cantamos
cantaste	cantasteis
cantó	cantaron

- For -er verbs, add *(-í, -iste, -ió, -imos, -isteis, -ieron)*

CORRER (TO RUN)	
corrí	corrimos
corriste	corristeis
corrió	corrieron

- For -ir verbs, add *(-í, -iste, -ió, -imos, -isteis, -ieron)*

RECIBIR (TO RECEIVE)	
recibí	recibimos
recibiste	recibisteis
recibió	recibieron

EXERCISES

A. Practice. Justino is talking about a letter he received from his friend Jorge. Complete what he says with the correct form of the verb in parentheses in the preterite tense. Then, substitute the underlined subject of the original sentence with the subjects in parentheses and make the necessary changes.

1. Ayer <u>yo</u> _____ (recibir) una carta de Jorge. (ella, nosotros, Uds.)

2. La semana pasada <u>él</u> _____ (correr) en un maratón. (yo, ellos, tú)

3. <u>El y su hermana</u> _____ (terminar) el maratón por primera vez. (nosotros, Ud., yo)

B. Last year was very exciting for many of the people that Alejandro knows. Use the words below to tell what they did last year.

> **MODELO:** Rosario/participar/en los Juegos Olímpicos
> *Rosario participó en los Juegos Olímpicos.*

1. Gilda/terminar/los estudios universitarios

   _____

2. Diego y Ricardo/recibir/una beca para estudiar en Madrid

   _____

3. Nosotros/viajar/por cuatro países latinoamericanos

   _____

4. Un ladrón *(thief)*/entrar/en el apartamento de Dora/y llevarse/ muchas cosas

   _____

5. Yo/prometer/casarme con Susana

   _____

6. Tú/vender/la casa de tus abuelos

   _____

7. Uds./descubrir/unos programas de computadora interesantísimos

_____

8. Yo/visitar/las famosas cuevas de Altamira

_____

C. What did you do yesterday? Answer the following questions truthfully.

1. ¿Cenaste en la cafetería de la escuela?

_____

2. ¿Corriste en el parque?

_____

3. ¿Miraste las noticias internacionales en la televisión?

_____

4. ¿Asististe a una fiesta?

_____

5. ¿Ayudaste a tus padres con los quehaceres _(chores)_ de la casa?

_____

D. Alicia had a bad day today. Complete her own description of what happened to her with the _yo_ form of the verb in parentheses in the preterite tense.

Esta mañana yo _____ (despertarse) tarde. _____

(Levantarse), _____ (lavarse) y _____ (cepillarse)

los dientes rápidamente. _____ (Mirarse) en el espejo y

_____ (peinarse). No _____ (desayunarse).

_____ (Salir) de casa y _____ (tomar) el autobús.

_____ (Bajarse) cerca de la escuela y _____

(correr) a la clase. _____ (Tomar) el examen de historia pero

_____ (salir) mal.

Some Spanish verbs that have an irregular stem in the preterite share common endings. The following are some of the most common ones.

The endings for the following verbs are *(-e, -iste, -o, -imos, -isteis, -ieron)*:

ANDAR (TO WALK, GO AROUND) (ANDUV-)	
anduve	anduvimos
anduviste	anduvisteis
anduvo	anduvieron

ESTAR (TO BE) (ESTUV-)	
estuve	estuvimos
estuviste	estuvisteis
estuvo	estuvieron

HACER (TO DO, MAKE) (HIC-)	
hice	hicimos
hiciste	hicisteis
hizo*	hicieron

*Note spelling change

PONER (TO PUT) (PUS-)	
puse	pusimos
pusiste	pusisteis
puso	pusieron

VENIR (TO COME) (VIN-)	
vine	vinimos
viniste	vinisteis
vino	vinieron

The endings for the following verbs are *(-e, -iste, -o, -imos, -isteis, -eron)*. Notice that the stem of these verbs ends in *j*.

CONDUCIR (TO DRIVE) (CONDUJ-)	
conduje	condujimos
condujiste	condujisteis
condujo	condujeron

DECIR (TO SAY, TELL) (DIJ-)	
dije	dijimos
dijiste	dijisteis
dijo	dijeron

TRADUCIR (TO TRANSLATE) (TRADUJ-)	
traduje	tradujimos
tradujiste	tradujisteis
tradujo	tradujeron

TRAER (TO BRING) (TRAJ-)	
traje	trajimos
trajiste	trajisteis
trajo	trajeron

EXERCISES

A. Practice. Ernesto and his friends are talking about the last party they had. Complete what they say with the correct form of the verb in parentheses in the preterite tense. Then, substitute the underlined subject of the original sentence with the subjects in parentheses and make the necessary changes.

1. ¿Qué _____ (traer) tú para la fiesta? (Uds., él, ellas)

2. Yolanda _____ (hacer) todas las decoraciones. (nosotros, yo, él)

3. Yo le _____ (decir) la hora de la fiesta a Roberto. (nosotros, tú, Ud.)

4. ¿Dónde _____ (poner) Uds. los refrescos? (ella, tú, ellos)

5. Mis tíos _____ (conducir) a la fiesta con nosotros. (tú, ella, Uds.)

6. Nosotros _____ (andar) buscando los discos por el centro. (yo, Uds., él)

7. ¿_____ (Venir) tus primos a la fiesta? (ella, tú, Ud.)

8. Yo _____ (traducir) la invitación para los estudiantes extranjeros. (nosotros, Uds., tú)

9. Tú _____ (estar) en la tienda para recoger los bocadillos. (Ud., yo, nosotros)

B. Tomás and some of his friends are in the mountains skiing. Tomás begins to reminisce about last winter when his friend, Ricardo, from El Salvador, came to visit him. Here are some of the things he says. Complete the description with the correct form of the verb in the preterite.

Mi amigo Ricardo _____ (estar) con nosotros por un mes. Un

fin de semana mis padres y yo _____ (conducir) a las

montañas con él para ver la nieve. El y yo _____ (andar) por

los bosques cubiertos de nieve. Yo _____ (traducir) todos los avisos *(warnings)*. El _____ (ponerse) un poco nervioso

cuando yo le _____ (decir) la temperatura. Mi madre

_____ (traer) chocolate caliente. Cuando nosotros

_____ (venir) de las montañas, Ricardo _____

(llamar) a su familia inmediatamente. "¡Qué maravilloso!"

_____ (decir) él varias veces durante la conversación. Mis

padres y yo _____ (hacer) todo lo posible para divertirnos en

ese viaje de descubrimiento.

C. After a friend of Tomás heard about Ricardo's visit, he had some questions for Tomás. Read the questions and answer them as you think Tomás would have answered them.

1. ¿Se pusieron botas Uds.?

_____

2. ¿Quién tradujo las conversaciones?

_____

3. ¿Condujiste el coche tú?

_____

4. ¿Trajeron Uds. los esquíes?

_____

5. ¿Vinieron tus hermanos también?

_____

6. ¿Estuvieron Uds. aquí mucho tiempo?

_____

7. ¿Qué hizo Ricardo cuando vio la nieve por primera vez?

_____

8. ¿Anduvieron Uds. por aquella montaña?

VERBS WITH SPECIAL MEANING IN THE PRETERITE TENSE

In addition to their regular meaning, the following verbs usually have a special meaning in the preterite.

PODER (TO BE ABLE) (PUD-)*	
pude	pudimos
pudiste	pudisteis
pudo	pudieron
*Special meaning in the preterite: *succeeded in*	

Por fin pudimos abrir la puerta.
We finally succeeded in opening the door.

QUERER (TO WANT) (QUIS-)*	
quise	quisimos
quisiste	quisisteis
quiso	quisieron
*Special meaning in the preterite: *tried to*	

Quise hacer la tarea.
I tried to do the homework.

Note that *no querer* in the preterite has the special meaning of *refused to*.

El bebé no quiso abrir la boca.
The baby refused to open his mouth.

SABER (TO KNOW) (SUP-)*	
supe	supimos
supiste	supisteis
supo	supieron
*Special meaning in the preterite: *found out*	

Supimos eso la semana pasada.
We found out last week.

CONOCER* (TO KNOW, TO BE ACQUAINTED WITH) (REGULAR VERB IN THE PRETERITE)	
conocí	conocimos
conociste	conocisteis
conoció	conocieron

*Special meaning in the preterite: *met a person* "for the first time"

Conocí al hermano de Cristóbal en la fiesta.
I met Cristóbal's brother at the party.

TENER (TO HAVE) (TUV-)*	
tuve	tuvimos
tuviste	tuvisteis
tuvo	tuvieron

*Special meaning in the preterite: *received, got*

No tuvimos carta hoy.
We did not get a letter today.

Note that *tener que* (meaning *to have to*) has a special meaning in the preterite: *was/were compelled*.

La señora Pérez tuvo que hacer un viaje de negocios.
Mrs. Pérez was compelled to take a business trip.

EXERCISES

A. Read the conversation Pedro had with his friend Adolfo about Ricardo and Tina and translate the verbs in parentheses using the list of verbs given. Remember that the verbs you will be using have a special meaning in the preterite.

tener/saber/conocer/no querer/poder

1. ¿_____ *(received)* Ricardo noticias de Tina? Sí, él _____
(received) noticias de ella. Ella tuvo un accidente.

2. ¿Cuándo _____ *(did he find out)* la noticia? El la _____
   (found out) ayer.

3. ¿Tú la _____ *(met)* aquí o en la Argentina? Yo la _____
   (met) aquí.

4. ¿Por qué _____ *(he refused)* salir para Buenos Aires
   inmediatamente? El _____ *(refused)* salir inmediatamente
   porque quería pensarlo bien.

5. ¿_____ *(Did you succeed in)* tú convencerlo? No, yo _____
   (did not succeed in) convencerlo.

B. Your friend Pam doesn't speak Spanish and she is very eager to find out
what was going on with Tina. Translate the conversation from the previous exercise so that she can find out what happened.

1. _____

2. _____

3. _____

4. _____

5. _____

C. Imagine that you found out about a concert in town and that you and
your friends went because you like the guest artist a lot. One of your
friends wants to find out what happened. Answer his questions in complete sentences.

1. ¿Cuándo supieron Uds. el nombre del artista invitado?

   _____

2. ¿Pudiste tú comprar boletos baratos para el concierto?

   _____

3. ¿Tuvieron Uds. que hacer cola *(stand in line)* por mucho tiempo?

   _____

4. ¿Tuviste que pedirles permiso a tus padres?

_____

5. ¿Conocieron al artista después del concierto?

_____

OTHER IRREGULAR VERBS IN THE PRETERITE TENSE

Some other common verbs that are irregular in the preterite are:

DAR (TO GIVE)	
di	dimos
diste	disteis
dio	dieron

VER (TO SEE)	
vi	vimos
viste	visteis
vio	vieron

SER (TO BE)	
fui	fuimos
fuiste	fuisteis
fue	fueron

IR (TO GO)	
fui	fuimos
fuiste	fuisteis
fue	fueron

Notice that in the preterite:

- There are no written accents on any of the irregular forms
- _Ir_ and _ser_ have the same forms (the context clarifies the meaning)

  Antonio fue presidente del club el año pasado. Fue a todas las reuniones.
  Antonio was president of the club last year. He went to all the meetings.

EXERCISES

A. Practice. Hugo and Felicia went to visit their friend Sebastián in the hospital. Complete what they say with the correct form of the verb in parentheses in the preterite tense. Then, substitute the underlined subject of the original sentence with the subjects in parentheses and make the necessary changes.

1. <u>Nosotros</u> _____ (ir) a visitar a Sebastián en el hospital. (yo, ellas, Ud.)

2. <u>Yo</u> le _____ (dar) las flores que le compramos. (tú, Uds., nosotros)

121

3. ¿_____ (Ver) tú a su madre en el hospital? (Ud., él, Uds.)

4. Ella _____ (ser) muy amable con nosotros. (tú, ellos, él)

B. Victor and Juanita just came back from a trip to the capital. Complete their description of the trip with the correct form of the verb in the preterite.

Nosotros _____ (ir) a visitar a varios congresistas.

_____ (Ver-nosotros) el capitolio y muchos monumentos.

Juanita _____ (ir) a visitar el museo del Holocausto. Yo

_____ (ir) al cementerio Arlington. La experiencia

_____ (ser) muy emocionante. Allí yo _____

(ver) la tumba del presidente Kennedy. Un guía nos _____

(dar) un recorrido *(tour)* por varios lugares de importancia histórica. Yo

le _____ (dar) las gracias al final. Según mis padres, yo

_____ (ser) el primer miembro de mi familia en visitar la

capital.

VERBS THAT CHANGE *I* TO *Y* IN THE PRETERITE TENSE
For the following verbs in the preterite:
- The *Ud.* form ends in *-yo*
- The *Uds.* form ends in *-yeron*
- The *tú, nosotros,* and *vosotros* forms have a written accent on the *-íste, -ímos,* and *-ísteis* endings.

OÍR (TO HEAR)	
oí	oímos
oíste	oísteis
oyó	oyeron

CAER (TO FALL)	
caí	caímos
caíste	caísteis
cayó	cayeron

LEER (TO READ)	
leí	leímos
leíste	leísteis
leyó	leyeron

CREER (TO BELIEVE)	
creí	creímos
creíste	creísteis
creyó	creyeron

For verbs ending in *-uir* (except *-guir*) in the preterite:

• The *Ud.* form ends in *-yo*
• The *Uds.* form ends in *-yeron*

CONSTRUIR (TO BUILD)	
construí	construimos
construiste	construisteis
construyó	construyeron

Verbs like *construir:*

contribuir—to contribute   huir—to flee

distribuir—to distribute   incluir—to include

Verbs ending in *-guir* have regular endings in the preterite, i.e. *distinguir*—to distinguish, *extinguir*—to extinguish. Note however that some verbs ending in *-guir* do have changes in their stems, i.e. *seguir*—to follow, continue, *conseguir*—to obtain, get, succeed in, *perseguir*—to pursue, persecute.

EXERCISES

A. Tito is talking about the biggest snowstorm in the western region of the country. Complete what he says with the correct form of the verb in parentheses.

Anoche _____ (caer) mucha nieve en el oeste del país. Yo

_____ (leer) la noticia en el periódico pero mi amigo Jacinto

no la _____ (leer). El _____ (oír) en la radio que

_____ (caer) más de treinta pulgadas. Cuando se lo dijimos a

Beatriz, ella no lo _____ (creer). Muchos de los oficiales del

gobierno municipal _____ (distribuir) palas *(shovels).* Unas

mil personas _____ (huir) de la región montañosa. En los

reportes no _____ (incluir-ellos) el número de personas que

123

murió pero estoy seguro de que no murieron muchas. Los avisos

(warnings) _____ (contribuir) a la cuidadosa preparación de

los ciudadanos.

B. Your friends are talking with Francisco about the last elections. You hear them ask each other questions. Use the cues to write the answers in the space provided.

1. ¿Quiénes contribuyeron a la campaña del Sr. Mederos? (los sindicatos *[unions]*)

   _____

2. ¿Qué distribuyeron Uds. sobre el candidato? (panfletos)

   _____

3. ¿Qué leyó Francisco en el periódico sobre su candidato favorito? (datos políticos)

   _____

4. ¿Qué oíste tú en la radio? (los resultados de las encuestas *[polls]*)

   _____

5. ¿Qué oyeron Uds. en la calle? (comentarios positivos)

   _____

6. ¿Qué día cayó el debate? (el sábado por la noche)

   _____

7. ¿Creyó Francisco lo que dijo el Sr. Mederos? (sí)

   _____

8. ¿Construyeron muchas escuelas después de las últimas elecciones? (no)

   _____

Verbs ending in *-car, -gar,* and *-zar* have spelling changes in the first person singular of the preterite.

- Verbs ending in *-car* change *c* to *qu* before *-é*

TOCAR (TO TOUCH, PLAY MUSIC)	
toqué	tocamos
tocaste	tocasteis
tocó	tocaron

Verbs like *tocar:*

acercarse—to come near, approach

buscar—to look for

chocar—to crash

colocar—to place, put

complicar—to complicate

comunicar—to communicate

criticar—to criticize, critique

dedicar—to dedicate, devote

educar—to educate

equivocarse—to make a mistake

explicar—to explain

pescar—to fish

practicar—to practice

secar—to dry

- Verbs ending in *-gar* change *g* to *gu* before *-é*

PAGAR (TO PAY)	
pagué	pagamos
pagaste	pagasteis
pagó	pagaron

Verbs like *pagar:*

ahogarse—to drown

apagar—to turn off

cargar—to carry, load

castigar—to punish

despegar—to take off

encargar—to put in charge, to order (goods)

encargarse de—to be in charge

entregar—to hand over, deliver

llegar—to arrive

In the preterite, the following verbs do not have the stem change they have in the present tense. (They do have the spelling change from *g* to *gu* in the first person singular *[yo].*)

JUGAR (TO PLAY A GAME, SPORTS) (UE)	
jugué	jugamos
jugaste	jugasteis
jugó	jugaron

Verbs like *jugar:*

colgar (ue)—to hang up (colgué . . .)   regar (ie)—to water plants (regué . . .)

negar (ie)—to deny (negué . . .)   rogar (ue)—to beg (rogué . . .)

- Verbs ending in -*zar* change *z* to *c* before -*é*

CRUZAR (TO CROSS)	
crucé	cruzamos
cruzaste	cruzasteis
cruzó	cruzaron

Verbs like *cruzar:*

abrazar—to hug	realizar—to carry out, attain, realize
alcanzar—to reach, catch up with	rezar—to pray
aterrizar—to land	tranquilizar(se)—to calm down
garantizar—to guarantee	tropezar—to trip, stumble
gozar (de)—to enjoy	utilizar—to use, make use of

In the preterite, the following verbs do not have the stem change they have in the present tense. (They do have the spelling change from *z* to *c* in the first person singular [*yo*].)

ALMORZAR (TO HAVE LUNCH) (UE)	
almorcé	almorzamos
almorzaste	almorzasteis
almorzó	almorzaron

Verbs like *almorzar:*

comenzar (ie)—to begin empezar (ie)—to begin

EXERCISES

A. Practice. Ricardo and his friends are talking about the procedures to enter an university. Complete what they say with the correct form of the verb in parentheses in the preterite tense. Then, substitute the subject of the original sentence with the subjects in parentheses and make the necessary changes.

1. Anoche yo _____ (buscar) la copia del ensayo para la universidad. (nosotros, Uds., Teresa)

2. La universidad le _____ (negar) la entrada a Bernardo. (tú, él, yo)

3. Yo _____ (entregar) todas las recomendaciones de los profesores el semestre pasado. (Ud., tú, ella)

4. El consejero no le _____ (garantizar) la entrada a esa universidad. (yo, Uds., Ud.)

5. Cuando yo recibí la carta de aceptación yo _____ (empezar) a gritar. (ellos, nosotros, tú)

6. Yo le _____ (comunicar) la noticia a la familia en seguida. (ella, tú, ellos)

B. One of your friends is very curious. He asks you many questions about what you did yesterday. Answer the questions truthfully.

1. ¿Dónde almorzaste ayer?

_____

2. ¿Te equivocaste mucho en las tareas?

_____

3. ¿Abrazaste a tus padres cuando llegaste a tu casa?

_____

4. ¿Sacaste la basura?

_____

5. ¿A qué hora comenzaste a estudiar anoche?

_____

6. ¿Regaste las plantas?

_____

C. Rodolfo is very proud because in 1997 he was able to play the piano in one of the most famous concert halls in the world. Complete his description with the correct form of the verb in the preterite.

En 1997 yo _____ (tocar) el piano en Carnegie Hall. Durante

el año _____ (practicar-yo) mucho. Algunas veces fue difícil

tener la motivación necesaria, pero yo seguí pensando en mis padres.

Ese día _____ (llegar-yo) a la sala de conciertos temprano.

¡Los nervios! ¡Qué horror! Mi profesora de piano me _____

(hablar) con mucha calma y después de unos minutos yo

_____ (tranquilizarse). _____ (Rogar-yo) mucho

para no cometer ningún error. No _____ (equivocarse-yo).

Cuando _____ (terminar-yo) de tocar, _____

(abrazar) a mi familia y les _____ (dar) las gracias por su

apoyo *(support)*.

VERBS WITH STEM CHANGES IN THE PRETERITE TENSE

All stem-changing -*ar* verbs are regular in the preterite.

Stem-changing verbs ending in -*ir* also have a stem change in the preterite. In the preterite, the stem vowel changes in the third person singular and plural from:

- (a) *e* to *i* (*e* to *ie* in the present tense)

PREFERIR (TO PREFER) (IE, I)	
preferí	preferimos
preferiste	preferisteis
prefirió	**prefirieron**

Verbs like *preferir:*

divertir (ie, i)—to amuse

divertirse (ie, i)—to amuse oneself

mentir (ie, i)—to lie

sentir (ie, i)—to feel, to be sorry

sentirse (ie, i)—to feel

- (b) *o* to *u* (*o* to *ue* in the present tense)

DORMIR (TO SLEEP) (UE, U)	
dormí	dormimos
dormiste	dormisteis
durmió	**durmieron**

Verbs like *dormir:*

dormirse (ue, u)—to fall asleep   morir (ue, u)—to die

- (c) *e* to *i* (*e* to *i* in the present tense)

REPETIR (TO REPEAT) (I, I)	
repetí	repetimos
repetiste	repetisteis
repitió	**repitieron**

Verbs like *repetir:*

conseguir (i, i)—to get, to obtain

despedir (i, i)—to fire (let go)

despedirse (i, i)—to say good-bye to

medir (i, i)—to measure

pedir (i, i)—to request, to ask for

reír (i, i)—to laugh

reírse (i, i)—to laugh

sonreír (i, i)—to smile

sonreírse (i, i)—to smile

seguir (i, i)—to follow, to continue

servir (i, i)—to serve

vestir (i, i)—to dress

vestirse (i, i)—to get dressed

Note that in addition to the regular accents on the *yo* and the *él, ella,* and *Ud.* forms, the verbs *reír* (i, i) and *sonreír* (i, i) have accents on the *tú, nosotros,* and *vosotros* forms.

SONREÍR (TO SMILE) (I, I)	
sonreí	sonreímos
sonreíste	sonreísteis
sonrió	**sonrieron**

EXERCISES

A. Practice. Micaela and her friends are talking about the party they attended this past weekend. Complete what they say with the correct form of the verb in parentheses in the preterite tense. Then, substitute the underlined subject of the original sentence with the subjects in parentheses and make the necessary changes.

1. ¡Qué fiesta! <u>Nosotros</u> _____ (divertirse) muchísimo. (yo, ellos, tú)

2. <u>Tú</u> _____ (reírse) mucho. (nosotros, ella, yo)

3. ¿_____ (dormir-tú) bien la noche antes? (Uds., él, Ud.)

4. Al día siguiente <u>Carmelo</u> _____ (sentirse) muy bien. (ellas, Ud., nosotros)

5. <u>Rosalía</u> _____ (vestir) bien como siempre. (yo, Uds., nosotros)

6. <u>Ellos</u> _____ (servir) unos aperitivos deliciosos. (ella, nosotros, tú)

B. Read the following paragraph about Consuelo's trip to Barcelona, then write the correct form of the verbs in parentheses in the preterite form.

El año pasado Consuelo _____ (decidir) pasar el verano en

Barcelona. Ella _____ (hacer) sus planes y un día

_____ (despedirse) de sus amigos y _____ (irse)

al aeropuerto. Ella _____ (llegar) a Barcelona sola. Los

primeros días _____ (sentirse-ella) un poco triste pero pronto

_____ (encontrar-ella) a otros chicos norteamericanos.

Cuando la _____ (conocer) ellos _____ (sentirse)

alegres también porque Consuelo es una chica muy divertida. Durante

dos meses ellos _____ (divertirse) mucho. En julio ellos

_____ (ir) a las montañas. Ellos _____ (dormir) al

aire libre y _____ (conseguir) observar el cielo con el

telescopio de Eloisa.

PART C: Talking About How Long Ago Something Took Place

HACE + LENGTH OF TIME + *QUE* + PRETERITE

In order to express *how long ago* an action or state took place, you can use one of the following constructions:

Hace + length of time + *que* + preterite. Or,
Preterite + *hace* + length of time.

Hace dos meses que conocí a Pedro. Or,
Conocí a Pedro hace dos meses.
I met Pedro two months ago.

The following construction is used to ask the question *How long ago?*

¿Cuánto [tiempo] hace que + preterite?

¿Cuánto [tiempo] hace que conociste a Pedro?
How long ago did you meet Pedro?

EXERCISES

A. How long has it been that you and your friends or family did something exciting? Use the following phrases to write complete sentences and express how long ago you or the people mentioned did the following activities.

> **MODELO:** esquiar en los Andes/nosotros
>
> *Hace diez años que nosotros esquiamos en los Andes.*

1. viajar por avión/yo

   _____

2. dar un paseo con su novio(a) por la noche en la playa/mi amigo(a)

   _____

3. hacer una fogata (*bonfire*) en el campo/mis amigos y yo

   _____

4. subir a la antorcha (*torch*) de la estatua de la Libertad/yo

   _____

5. ir a un baile de fin de año/mis padres

_____

B. Now it is your turn to ask your friends how long ago they did certain activities. Use the list below to ask them three questions and add at least two activities you would like to ask them about.

> leer un buen libro/montar a caballo/patinar en el parque/
> ir de vacaciones/vestirse elegantemente/
> hacer alguna locura *(crazy thing)*

> **MODELO:** *¿Cuánto tiempo hace que tú leíste/Uds.*
> *leyeron un buen libro?*

1. _____

2. _____

3. _____

4. _____

5. _____

ADVERBIAL EXPRESSIONS OF PAST TIME (PRETERITE)

The following words and expressions are useful when talking about past events, actions, or states that are completed or finished within a definite period of time.

ayer—yesterday

anteayer—the day before yesterday

anoche—last night

anteanoche—the night before last

el lunes pasado (martes, etc.)—last Monday (Tuesday, etc.)

el fin de semana pasado—last weekend

el verano (invierno, etc.) pasado—last summer (winter, etc.)

el mes (año, etc.) pasado—last month (year, etc.)

la semana pasada—last week

EXERCISES

Tell your teacher about the things you and the members of your family or friends have done. Use the expressions below to tell at least two things for each expression. Remember to use the preterite tense.

> **MODELO:** el mes pasado/mi hermana
>
> *El mes pasado mi hermana fue a Boston y corrió*
> *en el maratón.*

1. el fin de semana pasado/yo

_____

2. el año pasado/mis padres

_____

3. la semana pasada/mi mejor amigo

_____

4. anteayer/yo

_____

5. anoche/nosotros

_____

PART D: Describing Habitual Actions, Situations, or Conditions, and Ongoing Actions in the Past

IMPERFECT TENSE OF REGULAR VERBS

The imperfect tense is formed as follows:

- For *-ar* verbs add the endings *(-aba, -abas, -aba, -ábamos, -abais, -aban)* to the infinitive stem

CAMINAR (TO WALK)	
caminaba	caminábamos
caminabas	caminabais
caminaba	caminaban

- For *-er* and *-ir* verbs add the endings *(-ía, -ías, -ía, -íamos, -íais, -ían)* to the infinitive stem

CORRER (TO RUN)	
corría	corríamos
corrías	corríais
corría	corrían

RECIBIR (TO RECEIVE)	
recibía	recibíamos
recibías	recibíais
recibía	recibían

IMPERFECT TENSE OF IRREGULAR VERBS

All verbs in Spanish have regular forms in the imperfect except *ir, ser,* and *ver.*

IR (TO GO)	
iba	íbamos
ibas	ibais
iba	iban

SER (TO BE)	
era	éramos
eras	erais
era	eran

VER (TO SEE)	
veía	veíamos
veías	veíais
veía	veían

USES OF THE IMPERFECT TENSE

When describing habitual past actions or actions that were repeated an unspecified number of times, Spanish speakers do not use the preterite, they use another past tense called the *imperfect tense.*

Mi hermana practicaba el piano todas las noches.
My sister used to practice the piano every night.

Notice that English often uses the expression *used to* + verb when describing habitual past actions.

The imperfect tense is also used to:

- Describe physical, mental, or emotional states or conditions in the past

Cuando éramos más jóvenes, no nos gustaba estudiar.
When we were younger, we did not like to study.

Cuando tenía diez años, mi hermana era más alta que yo.
When I was ten, my sister was taller than I.

- Describe an action in progress at a certain time in the past when something else happened (the preterite states what happened)

Mientras discutíamos (imperfect), mi padre llegó (preterite).
While we were arguing, my father arrived.

ADVERBIAL EXPRESSIONS OF PAST TIME (IMPERFECT)

The following words and expressions are useful when talking about events, actions or states that are repetitive, ongoing, or continued over a period of time.

a menudo—frequently, often

frecuentemente—frequently

siempre—always

a veces—sometimes

de vez en cuando—from time to time

rara vez—rarely

generalmente—generally

por lo general—generally

todos los días (años, meses)—every day (year, month)

todos los veranos (inviernos, etc.)— every summer (winter, etc.)

todas las semanas—every week

todos los domingos (lunes, etc.)— every Sunday (Monday, etc.)

los fines de semana—on weekends

EXERCISES

A. Practice. Sandra and her friends are reminiscing about their childhood. Complete what they say with the correct form of the verb in parentheses in the imperfect tense. Then, substitute the underlined subject of the original sentence with the subjects in parentheses and make the necessary changes.

1. Cuando <u>yo</u> _____ (estar) en la escuela primaria, <u>yo</u>

   _____ (hacer) dibujos con los dedos a menudo.

   (nosotros, ellas, tú)

2. Cuando <u>Gilda</u> _____ (ser) pequeña <u>ella</u>

   _____ (tener) un perro y un gato. (tú, nosotros, Uds.)

3. Durante el verano <u>mis parientes</u> _____ (venir) a

   visitarnos. (Ud., tú, ellos)

B. Bárbara is telling her friend Guillermo about her daily activities when she was younger. Complete her description with the correct form of the verb in the imperfect tense.

Cuando yo _____ (ser) más pequeña, yo _____

(ir) al parque todos los días. Mi mamá y yo _____ (ir) con

nuestra vecina. Ella _____ (tener) dos hijos. Su hijo

_____ (tener) dos años y su hija _____ (tener)

cinco. Nosotros _____ (jugar) en los columpios *(swings)*.

A su hijo le _____ (gustar) jugar al fútbol. Si nosotros

_____ (ir) a la hora del almuerzo, mi mamá

_____ (llevar) bocadillos. Así nosotros _____

(comer) y _____ (beber) refrescos debajo de un árbol o en

uno de los bancos. Luego mi vecina _____ (comprar)

helados de un señor que _____ (venir) todos los días a

vender refrescos y helados. Yo siempre _____ (comer)

helado de chocolate. Los helados _____ (ser) deliciosos.

Nosotros siempre _____ (pasar) un día maravilloso.

C. One of your friends is talking about what his younger brother does. You reply by saying the things you used to do or did not do when you were younger. Use the imperfect tense in your responses.

> **MODELO:** Generalmente él sale todas las noches.
> *Generalmente yo (no) salía todas las noches.*

1. El juega al ajedrez siempre.

   _____

2. Frecuentemente él y sus amigos comen en un restaurante de comida rápida.

   _____

3. A menudo él pide ayuda cuando no entiende la tarea.

   _____

4. Generalmente él se levanta muy tarde los fines de semana.

   _____

5. Por lo general él hace buenos regalos.

_____

D. Express how often the following people used to do or not do the following activities in the past.

yo	jugar al tenis	rara vez
nosotros	salir por la noche	de vez en cuando
ustedes	dormir hasta muy tarde	frecuentemente
tú	aburrirse en las clases	a menudo
mis amigos	perderse en el metro	a veces
él	limpiar el cuarto	todos los días
ella	estudiar	siempre
		por lo general

MODELO: _Mis amigos no estudiaban todos los días._

_____

_____

_____

_____

_____

_____

_____

_____

E. Interruptions. Complete the following sentences with the correct form of the imperfect in the first part to express what was going on. In the second part of the sentence write the correct form of the preterite to express the actions that interrupted what was going on.

1. Yo _____ (jugar) al baloncesto cuando yo

_____ (caerse).

2. Mi padre _____ (limpiar) la casa cuando mis primos

   _____ (llegar).

3. _____ (Llover) cuando el avión _____

   (aterrizar).

4. Nosotros _____ (escuchar) las noticias cuando las luces

   _____ (apagarse).

5. _____ (Hacer) mucho viento cuando tú _____

   (salir) de mi casa.

6. Los hermanos de Adelaida _____ (dormir) cuando yo

   _____ (llegar).

7. Juan _____ (regar) las plantas cuando _____

   (empezar) a llover.

8. Elena _____ (dormir) cuando la profesora le

   _____ (hacer) una pregunta.

9. Yo _____ (hablar) cuando Ud. _____ (abrir) la

   puerta.

10. Nosotros _____ (dar) un paseo cuando _____

    (ver) a Teresa.

PART E: Talking About Situations and Actions that Had Been Going on for a While at a Certain Time in the Past

HACÍA AND DESDE HACÍA

In order to indicate an action that had been going on for a period of time and was still going on at a certain moment in the past, Spanish uses the construction:

Hacía + length of time + *que* + imperfect tense

Or,

Imperfect tense + *hacía* + length of time

Or,

Imperfect tense + *desde hacía* + length of time

Hacía dos horas que practicaba (cuando el teléfono sonó).
Practicaba hacía dos horas (cuando el teléfono sonó).
Practicaba desde hacía dos horas (cuando el teléfono sonó).
I had been practicing for two hours (when the phone rang).

When the context helps you to understand the moment in time, it is not necessary to state it.

Notice the constructions used for questions:

¿Cuánto [tiempo] + *hacía* + *que* + imperfect?

¿Cuánto [tiempo] hacía que practicabas?

Or,

¿Desde cuándo + imperfect?

¿Desde cuándo practicabas?

How long had you been practicing?

EXERCISES

A. Conclusions. Last night Andrés' parents had guests for dinner. During the course of the dinner, he heard several conversations and came to some conclusions. Read the following statements, then write sentences summarizing the information. Follow the model.

> **MODELO:** Carlos terminó el informe para la compañía.
>
> Trabajó en el informe por dos semanas.
>
> Cuando terminó hacía *dos semanas que Carlos*
>
> *trabajaba en el informe.*

1. Juan regresó a la escuela ayer. Estuvo ausente por diez días.

Cuando regresó a la escuela hacía _____

2. A las ocho fui a buscar a Alberto. El estudiaba desde las tres.

   Cuando fui a buscar a Alberto hacía _____

3. El carpintero terminó todas las puertas este sábado. Las arreglaba (*fix*) desde el sábado pasado.

   Cuando terminó las puertas hacía _____

4. Yolanda volvió a Nueva York anteayer. Ella vivía en Medellín desde el año 1994.

   Cuando volvió a Nueva York hacía _____

5. Mis abuelos vendieron su casa. Vivieron allí por treinta años.

   Cuando vendieron su casa hacía _____

B. How long had they been doing the following activities? Read the following statement, then write a question to find out how long the following people had been doing the activities described.

> **MODELO:** Yo me preparaba cuando el timbre sonó.
> *¿Cuánto hacía que te preparabas?* Or,
> *¿Desde cuándo te preparabas?*

1. Diego terminó de leer el periódico a las once.

   _____

2. Tomás corría cuando se cayó.

   _____

3. Yo hablaba con Genaro cuando el teléfono sonó.

   _____

4. Condujimos mucho. Ya eran las ocho cuando encontramos la casa de los Domínguez.

   _____

5. A las diez y media Ignacio me despertó.

   _____

PART F: Narrating and Describing in the Past

PRETERITE VS. IMPERFECT TENSE

When you are talking or writing about something that happened in the past, your narration will be much more interesting if you include some background information and some of the circumstances surrounding what happened, i.e. what time it was, what the weather was like, what people were wearing.

In a narration:

• The preterite reports the events that took place in the past

• The imperfect is used to describe the background and circumstances surrounding what happened

Imagine that what happened is the following:

Mrs. Soler went out.
La señora Soler salió.

What background information can relate to this action?
Imagine:

It was one o'clock in the afternoon.
It was raining.
She was wearing a raincoat.
She was carrying her pocketbook.
There were fifty dollars in the pocketbook.
She was happy.
She wanted to buy a pair of shoes.

In Spanish, these surrounding circumstances would be stated in the imperfect:

Era la una de la tarde. (Time is always background information.)
Llovía.
Ella llevaba un impermeable.
Llevaba una cartera.
Había cincuenta dólares en la cartera.
Estaba contenta.
Quería comprar un par de zapatos.

Please notice that the important thing about these circumstances is that they were ongoing at the time Mrs. Soler went out, and not when they began or ended. Therefore, all the verbs are in the imperfect tense.

EXERCISES

A. Cecilia had a very busy day yesterday. Read her description to get an idea of the things she did and the circumstances surrounding her actions. Then, complete her narrative with the correct form of the verb in the preterite or the imperfect.

Ayer yo _____ (ir) de compras. Yo _____

(comprar) tres vestidos. _____ (Haber) mucha gente en las

tiendas. Yo _____ (tener) que esperar mucho para pagar por

mis compras. En el segundo piso _____ (encontrarse) con mi

amiga Lourdes. Ella _____ (estar) con su mamá. Ella me

_____ (mostrar) el abrigo que había comprado *(had bought)*.

_____ (Ser) un abrigo azul muy bonito. Ella y su madre me

_____ (invitar) a almorzar. Nosotras _____ (ir) a

un restaurante en el centro comercial. Nosotras _____

(comer) hamburguesas y unos postres exquisitos. Yo _____

(despedirse) de ellas y _____ (tomar) el metro. Cuando yo

_____ (llegar) a mi casa, mi mamá _____ (estar)

esperándome. Ella _____ (querer) ir a visitar a unos parientes

que viven en un pueblo cerca de mi casa. Yo _____ (estar)

muy cansada pero _____ (decidir) ir con ella. Nosotras

_____ (regresar) a casa a las diez de la noche.

B. Anoche Raquel y yo _____ (ir) a un concierto en el parque.

Nosotros _____ (invitar) a varios de nuestros amigos pues

_____ (ser) una ocasión muy especial. _____

(Ser) el cumpleaños de Raquel. Por la tarde yo _____ (ir) a

la tienda y _____ (comprar) jamón, queso, pan, jugos y un

pastel. En mi casa yo _____ (hacer) bocadillos. Julio

_____ (traer) ensalada de papas y las mantas para sentarnos en el suelo. El tiempo _____ (contribuir) al éxito de la noche. Cuando llegamos _____ (hacer) fresco y en el cielo nosotros _____ (poder) ver muchas estrellas y hasta la luna. Nosotros _____ (llegar) muy temprano y _____ (conseguir) sentarnos muy cerca del escenario. Raquel _____ (estar) muy contenta. Mientras nosotros _____ (comer), _____ (escuchar) la fabulosa música de Manuel de Falla. Al final del concierto _____ (ver) los fuegos artificiales *(fireworks)*. Raquel _____ (emocionarse) y yo _____ (ver) que _____ (sonreír) y al mismo tiempo _____ (tener) lágrimas *(tears)* en los ojos.

PART G: Talking About What Has (or Has Not) Occurred

PRESENT PERFECT TENSE

When talking about past events, actions, or states that have been going on up to the present time, Spanish speakers use the present perfect tense.

Mi hermana no ha tocado el piano hoy.
My sister has not played the piano today.

Carlos ha viajado mucho este mes.
Carlos has traveled a lot this month.

In Spanish, the present perfect tense is formed with the present of the verb *haber* (to have) and the past participle.

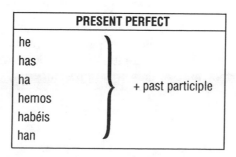

PRESENT PERFECT	
he	
has	
ha	
hemos	+ past participle
habéis	
han	

To form the past participle of regular verbs, make the following changes:

-ar → *-ado*   (i.e. *tocar-tocado*—played)

-er → *-ido*   (i.e. *vender-vendido*—sold)

-ir → *-ido*   (i.e. *recibir-recibido*—received)

¿Has visitado a tía Elena esta semana?
Have you visited aunt Elena this week?

¿Cuántos coches han vendido Uds. este año?
How many cars have you sold this year?

The verb *oír* (to hear) and verbs ending in *-aer* and *-eer* have written accents on the past participle ending (i.e. *oír-oído, traer-traído, leer-leído*).

The following verbs have irregular past participles:

abrir—abierto (opened)   poner—puesto (put)

decir—dicho (said)   romper—roto (broken)

cubrir—cubierto (covered)   ver—visto (seen)

escribir—escrito (written)   volver—vuelto (returned)

hacer—hecho (done)

Josefina no ha abierto los regalos.
Josefina has not opened the gifts.

Mis amigos y yo hemos visto cinco películas este mes.
My friends and I have seen five films this month.

The past participle of compounds of verbs with irregular past participles is also irregular. Some of these are:

descubrir—descubierto (discovered)   descomponer—descompuesto (broken, not working)

describir—descrito (described)

componer—compuesto (composed, repaired)   devolver—devuelto (returned)

Andrés no ha devuelto el libro.
Andrés has not returned the book.

EXERCISES

A. Practice. State what the following people have already done by ten o'clock in the morning by completing the following sentences. Write the present perfect tense of the verbs in parentheses.

1. Son las diez y yo ya _____. (bañarse, vestirse, desayunar)

144

2. Mi mamá _____. (hacer la cama, leer el periódico, terminar de preparar los bocadillos)

3. Mi hermana y yo _____. (limpiar nuestro cuarto, oír el pronóstico del tiempo, ir a comprar leche)

B. Help Inés complete her Spanish homework by writing the ideas in parentheses in Spanish.

1. ¿Dónde _____ (have put) tú el abrigo?

2. Roberto ya _____ (has seen) esa película.

3. Nosotros no _____ (have gone out) esta semana.

4. Yo _____ (have returned) todos los libros a la biblioteca.

5. Jacinta y Rosa _____ (have run) en el parque.

PART H: Talking About What Had Occurred at a Certain Moment in the Past

PLUPERFECT TENSE

When talking about past events, actions, or states that took place in the past prior to another event that is also situated in the past, Spanish speakers use the pluperfect tense.

The pluperfect tense is formed in Spanish with the imperfect of the verb *haber* (to have) and the past participle.

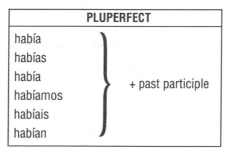

PLUPERFECT	
había	
habías	
había	+ past participle
habíamos	
habíais	
habían	

Cuando José llegó, la familia ya había cenado.
When José arrived, the family had dined already.

¿Te habías vestido cuando Alejandra llamó?
Had you gotten dressed when Alejandra called?

Note that when using the perfect tenses in Spanish:

145

- The past participle always ends in -o
- No word can be placed between the verb *haber* and the past participle

EXERCISES

A. Practice. Guillermo is talking to his friends about things that had happened at a certain time last week. Complete what they say by writing the verb in parentheses in the pluperfect tense.

1. Cuando nosotros llegamos de la escuela Ricardo _____.
   (estar en mi casa, traer los programas para mi computadora, arreglar el impresor)

2. Antes de salir de la escuela yo _____. (leer la enciclopedia, organizar mis apuntes *(notes),* escribir varios párrafos para el informe)

3. Juan, el viernes pasado tú _____. (no hacer nada, no escoger el tema para tu informe, no pensar en las consecuencias)

B. Graciela's parents are very busy and she and her brothers want to do everything possible to make them relax when they arrive home. Complete the following statement using the information given.

> **MODELO:** Ignacio/abrir las ventanas
> *Ignacio había abierto las ventanas.*

Cuando los padres de Graciela llegaron a su casa . . .

1. Ignacio y Roberto/limpiar la casa

   _____

2. Graciela/poner la mesa

   _____

3. Graciela/preparar la cena

   _____

4. Roberto/hacer todas sus tareas

   _____

5. Ignacio y yo/escribir nuestros informes para la clase

   _____

LESSON 5
Providing and Obtaining Information
About Needs and Opinions

PART A: Making Personal Statements of Necessity, Preference, and Opinion

VERBS AND EXPRESSIONS OF NECESSITY, PREFERENCE,
AND OPINION + INFINITIVE

There are several Spanish verbs and expressions that can be used to express one's needs, preferences, and opinions. Some important ones are:

desear—to want, to wish	preferir—to prefer
deber—ought to	necesitar—to need
esperar—to hope	tener ganas de—to feel like
pensar—to plan	tener que—to have to
querer—to want	

These verbs and expressions can be used in the construction subject + conjugated verb + infinitive

Alberto desea encontrar un buen trabajo.
Alberto wants to find a good job.

Bárbara y yo queremos ir a la playa.
Bárbara and I want to go to the beach.

Tengo que comprar un impresor.
I have to buy a printer.

To express what a person *would like to do* it is possible to use one of the following forms of *querer* or *gustar:*

QUERER		
quisiera	I would like to	
quisieras	You would like to	
quisiera	He (she, you) would like to	+ infinitive
quisiéramos	We would like to	
quisierais	You would like to	
quisieran	They (you) would like to	

Marcos quisiera vivir en el campo.
Marcos would like to live in the country.

GUSTAR	
me gustaría	I would like to
te gustaría	You would like to
le gustaría	He (she, you) would like to
nos gustaría	We would like to
os gustaría	You would like to
les gustaría	They (you) would like to

+ infinitive

¿Te gustaría comer en un restaurante chino?
Would you like to eat in a Chinese restaurant?

EXERCISES

A. You and your friends have different wishes and preferences for the future. Use the lists below to write sentences about their desires and yours. Write at least eight sentences. You may also add any expression you think is necessary.

yo	desear	ser arquitecto
mi mejor amiga	esperar	tener mucho dinero
tú	tener ganas de	viajar alrededor del mundo
mi mejor amigo y yo	querer	casarse a los cuarenta años
mis amigos	pensar	conseguir un buen trabajo
	preferir	trabajar en el extranjero
		vivir cerca de la playa
		tener una casa en las montañas
		comprar un coche alemán

MODELO: *Yo deseo comprar un coche alemán en diez años.*

1. _____

2. _____

3. _____

4. _____

5. _____

6. _____

7. _____

8. _____

B. Answer the following questions truthfully.

1. ¿Debes continuar tus estudios en el futuro? ¿Por qué?

_____

2. ¿Qué tienen que hacer tus amigos para tener éxito?

_____

3. ¿Necesitan tus padres trabajar mucho? ¿Por qué?

_____

4. ¿Te gustaría ser médico(a)?

_____

5. ¿Quisieras vivir en un país extranjero?

_____

C. There are certain things that you would like to do or would never like to do. Use *querer* or *gustar* and the list of topics below to express your ideas.

> ir a Madrid/asistir a una universidad lejos de mi casa/jugar en un equipo profesional/ser profesor(a)/estudiar fotografía/aprender muchos programas de computadora/cantar con un grupo popular/ser famoso/viajar al espacio

MODELO: *Un día quisiera ir a Madrid.* Or,
Un día me gustaría ir a Madrid.
No me gustaría ir a Madrid nunca. Or,
No quisiera ir a Madrid nunca.

1. _____

2. _____

3. _____

4. _____

5. _____

6. _____

7. _____

8. _____

PART B: Making Impersonal Statements of Necessity, Preference, and Opinion

IMPERSONAL EXPRESSIONS + INFINITIVE

If there is no definite subject (i.e. a person), it is possible to express necessity, preference, and opinion by using the construction: impersonal expression + infinitive. Some of the expressions that can be used in this construction are:

Es aconsejable	It is advisable
Es importante	It is important
Es mejor	It is better
Es necesario	It is necessary
Es preferible	It is preferable
Hay que	It is necessary (One must)

Es aconsejable practicar todos los días.
It is advisable to practice every day

Hay que estudiar mucho.
It is necessary to study a lot. (One must study a lot.)

EXERCISES

A. You and your friends are taking a long trip by car. Use the following expressions to write sentences that express what you must keep in mind for the trip. You may want to include some other ideas you consider important but which do not appear on the list. Use as many impersonal expressions as possible.

es preferible	dormir mucho antes de salir
es necesario	poner suficiente gasolina en el tanque
es aconsejable	llevar mucha comida
es importante	no conducir muy rápido
es mejor	conducir de noche

151

hay que   hacer reservaciones en un hotel
                                    llamar a nuestros padres frecuentemente
                                    conversar mientras conducimos
                                    no parar frecuentemente
                                    quedarse en hoteles muy caros

MODELO: *Es importante dormir mucho antes de salir.*
              Or,
              No es importante dormir mucho antes de salir.

1. _____

2. _____

3. _____

4. _____

5. _____

6. _____

7. _____

8. _____

9. _____

10. _____

B. One of your friends comes to you for advice because he/she is having problems with his/her girlfriend/boyfriend. Use the expressions below to give him/her some advice that you consider useful for anyone.

es importante/es necesario/hay que/es aconsejable/es mejor

MODELO: *Es aconsejable tener buena comunicación.*

1. _____

2. _____

3. _____

4. _____

5. _____

PART C: Expressing Physical and Emotional Needs

IDIOMS WITH *TENER*

In addition to using the construction *estar* + adjective to express physical and emotional states, in Spanish the verb *tener* can also be used with certain nouns to express many physical and emotional needs. It is often equivalent to the English construction: *to be* + adjective.

To express the idea of feeling:

- Hot or cold

  tener calor
  tener frío
  No tengo calor, tengo frío.
  I am not hot, I am cold.

- Hungry or thirsty

  tener hambre
  tener sed
  Juan tiene hambre pero Pedro tiene sed.
  Juan is hungry but Pedro is thirsty.

- Sleepy

  tener sueño
  No tenemos sueño.
  We are not sleepy.

- Afraid

  tener miedo
  Tengo miedo.
  I am afraid.

To express the idea of:

- Being in a hurry

  tener prisa
  Mis amigos corren cuando tienen prisa.
  My friends run when they are in a hurry.

- Being lucky

  tener suerte
  Josefina tiene suerte.
  Josefina is lucky.

To express the idea of feeling *very (cold, hungry, lucky, etc.),* use *mucho* (*mucha,* if the noun is feminine).

Los niños tienen mucho sueño.
The children are very sleepy.

Mateo tiene mucha sed.
Mateo is very thirsty.

EXERCISES

A. Read the following situations, then use *tener* + noun to write a sentence expressing how the people are feeling.

> **MODELO:** Hace mucho sol y llevo mucha ropa.
> Yo *tengo mucho calor.*

1. Mis padres ganaron diez millones de dólares en la lotería. Ellos

   _____.

2. ¡Rápido! ¡Rápido! Tenemos que llegar a tiempo. Nosotros

   _____.

3. Nevó mucho y no hay calefacción *(heat)* en mi apartamento. Yo

   _____.

4. Hace más de cinco horas que no comes nada. Tú

   _____.

5. Nos levantamos muy temprano. Queremos dormir. Nosotros

   _____.

6. Ellos corren mucho y después quieren beber mucha agua porque

   ellos _____.

7. ¡Qué horror! Esa película es muy violenta. Carlos

   _____.

8. La temperatura está muy alta. Josefina

   _____.

B. One of your friends is going to Peru for a few weeks. Help him with some phrases that will be very important for him to know. Express the following ideas in Spanish.

1. We are very thirsty.

   _____

2. Are they afraid to go out late?

   _____

3. I need to buy a coat. My sister is very cold.

   _____

4. You (formal) are in a hurry.

   _____

5. My friends are sleepy.

   _____

6. Is there a restaurant here? We are very hungry.

   _____

LESSON 6
Providing and Obtaining Information About Attitudes and Feelings

PART A: Expressing Likes and Dislikes

GUSTAR

To express your likes and dislikes, use the verb *gustar,* meaning "to please or give pleasure," in the construction:

indirect object pronoun + *gustar* + subject

Me gustan las canciones románticas.
I like romantic songs.

¿Les gusta ese cantante español?
Do they like that Spanish singer?

Note that:

- The indirect object of the verb *gustar* is the person who likes something. The indirect object pronouns *(me, te, le, nos, os, les)* represent the person
- The subject of the verb *gustar* is the person, thing, or activity that the person likes

Since the indirect object pronouns *le* and *les* each have several different meanings, these pronouns are often clarified. With the verb *gustar,* the structure *a* + person usually precedes the indirect object pronoun that it is clarifying.

A mis padres les gusta ver películas extranjeras.
My parents like to see foreign films.

A mi hermano no le gustan esas películas.
My brother does not like those films.

It is also possible:

- To clarify *le* or *les* by placing *(a él, a ella, a Ud., a ellos, a ellas, a Uds.)* before them

A él le gusta dormir pero a ella le gusta levantarse temprano.
He likes to sleep but she likes to get up early.

- To emphasize *me, te, nos,* or *os* by placing *a mí, a ti, a nosotros(as), a vosotros(as)* before them

A ti te gusta leer revistas pero a mí me gusta leer periódicos.
You like to read magazines but I like to read newspapers.

Notice that the subject of the verb *gustar* can be a person, an activity, or a thing. When the subject is an activity, the verb *gustar* is always in the third person singular *(gusta)* and is followed by an infinitive.

Nos gusta visitar los museos.
We like to visit the museums.

When the subject of the verb *gustar* is a person or thing, use:

• The third person singular *(gusta),* if the subject of *gustar* is singular

Me gusta la profesora de español pero no me gusta el libro.
I like the Spanish teacher but I do not like the book.

• The third person plural *(gustan),* if the subject of *gustar* is plural

Me gustan las clases de ciencia pero no me gustan los profesores.
I like science classes but I do not like the teachers.

Remember that the subject pronouns *it* and *they* (when referring to things) do not exist in Spanish. When the subject of the verb *gustar* is a thing, it cannot be replaced by a pronoun; it is understood.

¿Te gustan los sándwiches de queso? Sí, me gustan.
Do you like cheese sandwiches? Yes, I like them.

In the question above, the subject of the verb *gustar* is *los sándwiches de queso.* In the answer, the subject is understood.

VERBS LIKE *GUSTAR*

The following verbs are used in the same construction as *gustar:*

(indirect object pronoun + verb + subject)

doler—to hurt

Me duele la cabeza (el oído, la espalda, etc.)
I have a headache (earache, backache, etc.)

encantar—to be very fond of a person or thing

Nos encanta la comida francesa.
We love French food.

faltar—to need, lack

¿Qué te falta?
What do you need?
What are you lacking?

importar—to matter

A él no le importa el programa.
The program does not matter to him.

interesar—to interest

Me interesa el partido.
The match interests me.

preocupar—to worry

¿Te preocupa el problema?
Does the problem worry you?

quedar—to be left

A ellos les quedan dos dólares.
They have two dollars left.

EXERCISES

A. Preferences. Although Miguelina and her friend get along very well, they have different tastes. Use the list below to write sentences expressing what Miguelina says they like.

yo	mi amigo
1. los vegetales	la carne
2. la ciencia ficción	los libros históricos
3. la camisa roja	la camisa azul
4. las canciones populares	la música clásica
5. salir por las noches	salir por las mañanas

> **MODELO:** las revistas   los periódicos
> *A mí me gustan las revistas, a mi amigo le gustan los periódicos.*

1. _____

2. _____

3. _____

4. _____

5. _____

B. Your preferences. Use the following list to express your personal preferences regarding the following activities.

> **MODELO:** comer helado
> *A mí (no) me gusta comer helado.* Or,
> *A mí me encanta comer helado.*

1. correr en la lluvia

_____

2. saltar de un avión con paracaídas

_____

3. viajar en tren

_____

4. jugar al baloncesto con el equipo nacional

_____

5. nadar en el río

_____

6. patinar por las calles de Nueva York

_____

C. Felipe arrives at the gym and all his friends are complaining because the coach has made them work too hard. Write sentences with the information below expressing their complaints. Use the verb *doler.*

> **MODELO:** Uds./el pecho
> *A Uds. les duele el pecho.*
> Ud./los brazos
> *A Ud. le duelen los brazos.*

1. yo/la cabeza

_____

2. Teresa/las piernas

_____

3. Ignacio/el brazo

_____

4. nosotros/el estómago

_____

5. tú/los pies

_____

6. ellos/las rodillas

_____

D. The environment *(el medio ambiente)*. Help one of your friends who does not speak Spanish well to communicate with a newly arrived student from Caracas. Translate the ideas that he wants to express into Spanish.

1. I worry about pollution *(contaminación)*.

_____

2. We need more laws *(leyes)* to protect the environment.

_____

3. They are very interested in new ideas.

_____

4. He loves the national parks.

_____

5. How much money do they need (lack) for the project?

_____

6. The money problem does not matter to me.

_____

PART B: Expressing Attitudes, Feelings, and Emotions

EXCLAMATIONS

There are many exclamations that can be used to convey one's attitudes, feelings, and emotions. Some of these are:

¡Qué bueno!	How great!	¡Qué alegría!	What joy!
¡Qué estupendo!	How wonderful!	¡Qué felicidad!	What happiness!
¡Qué maravilloso!	How marvelous!	¡Qué lástima!	What a shame (a pity)!
¡Qué horrible!	How horrible!	¡Qué pena!	What a shame (a pity)!
¡Qué malo!	How bad!	¡Qué vergüenza!	What a shame (an embarrassment)!
¡Qué terrible!	How terrible!	¡Qué tristeza!	What sadness!
¡Qué triste!	How sad!	¡Qué desastre!	What a disaster!
¡Qué extraño!	How strange!	¡Qué sorpresa!	What a surprise!
¡Qué raro!	How strange!		

IMPERSONAL EXPRESSIONS + INFINITIVE

In addition to expressing one's attitudes and feelings with an exclamation, many impersonal expressions can be used with the infinitive to make a general statement about one's emotional reaction to something. Some of these expressions are:

es bueno—it's good

es estupendo—it's terrific, great

es malo—it's bad

es imposible—it's impossible

es maravilloso—it's wonderful, marvelous

> Es maravilloso viajar en primera clase.
> It is marvelous to travel in first class.

INDICATIVE AFTER IMPERSONAL EXPRESSIONS OF CERTAINTY

Impersonal expressions are often used in Spanish to express certainty about facts, events, needs, opinions, attitudes, and feelings. To express certainty, the following construction is used:

impersonal expression of certainty + *que* + subject + verb in the indicative

> Es cierto que Juan vive en New Mexico.
> It is true that Juan lives in New Mexico.

Some of the impersonal expressions that indicate certainty are:

Es cierto que—It is true that

Es seguro que—It is certain that

Es evidente que   It is evident that

Es verdad que—It is true that

Es obvio que—It is obvious that

> Es verdad que el programa empieza a las dos.
> It is true that the program begins at two
>
> Es obvio que a Gregorio le gusta bailar.
> It is obvious that Gregorio likes to dance.

VERBS AND EXPRESSIONS OF EMOTION + INFINITIVE

There are also many verbs that convey feelings and emotions. When these verbs are used to convey feelings and emotions regarding an action or state of *the subject himself (herself)* they are followed by the infinitive.

> María se alegra de estar aquí.
> María is happy to be here.
>
> Antonio tiene miedo de ir solo.
> Antonio is afraid to go alone.
>
> Felipe y Elena están orgullosos de recibir el premio.
> Felipe and Elena are proud of receiving the prize.

Some verbs that convey feelings and emotions are:

alegrarse de—to become (be made) happy

enorgullecerse de—to become (be made) proud

enojarse de—to get angry

sentir (ie)—to regret

molestarse de—to get upset, annoyed

enfadarse—to get angry

temer—to fear

tener miedo (de)—to be afraid

sorprenderse de—to be surprised

emocionarse—to become emotional

It is also possible to convey feelings and emotions regarding an action or state of *the subject himself (herself)* with the construction:

estar + adjective that conveys emotion + *de* + infinitive

Some adjectives that can be used in this construction are:

alegre—sad

contento—happy

encantado—delighted

desilusionado—disillusioned

enfadado—angry

enojado—angry

triste—sad

orgulloso—proud

Elena y José están orgullosos de ganar el primer premio.
Elena and José are proud to win the first prize.

Remember that adjectives must agree with the noun they are describing.

EXERCISES

A. Emotions. Read the following situations, then write an exclamation expressing your feelings about it.

> **MODELO:** Hace mucho viento. No podemos jugar en el patio.
> ¡Qué desastre!

1. Juan se rompió una pierna.

2. La profesora no vino a clase hoy.

3. Mi primo llegó del Brasil. No lo esperábamos hasta el lunes.

4. No sé las respuestas a las preguntas.

5. Llueve mucho y nuestro coche está descompuesto.

_____

6. Mañana salimos para Europa.

_____

7. Mis dos hermanos están enfermos.

_____

8. Laura siempre viene a visitarnos los fines de semana, pero hoy no vino.

_____

B. Opinions. Use an impersonal expression to give your personal opinion about the following topics. Use complete sentences in your answers.

> **MODELO:** acostarse tarde
> _Es malo acostarse tarde._

1. fumar

_____

2. hablar varias lenguas extranjeras

_____

3. tener mucho tiempo libre

_____

4. ser amable con los compañeros

_____

5. vivir en un país tropical

_____

6. sacar malas notas

_____

C. Reactions. Read the following situations and then complete the phrases with a logical ending.

> MODELO: Tu amigo tiene miedo de salir mal en el examen.
> Es cierto que él *no estudió mucho anoche.*

1. Tu amiga Lucinda acaba de ganar una competencia de ajedrez. Es obvio que ella . . .

2. El director de tu escuela prometió que la comida de la cafetería iba a mejorar. Es evidente que el director . . .

3. Tú y tus amigos salieron muy bien en el último examen de español. Es cierto que nosotros . . .

4. Las composiciones de tres de tus amigos fueron seleccionadas como las mejores de la escuela. Es seguro que ellos . . .

5. El profesor de español decidió que no iba a darles tarea durante el fin de semana. Es verdad que él/ella . . .

D. It is always a good idea to let your friends and acquaintances know your feelings so that they know you better. Use the list of verbs and the topics below to express your feelings about these topics.

> alegrarse de/temer/sorprenderse de/sentir/enojarse de/
> tener miedo de/enorgullecerse de

llegar tarde a una cita	tener novio(a)
recibir un regalo de un(a) amigo(a)	tener que esperar a un(a) amigo(a)
estar solo(a)	mucho tiempo
no conseguir un buen trabajo	sacar buenas notas en la escuela
no asistir a una buena universidad	

> MODELO: *Temo salir solo(a) por la noche.*

1. _____

2. _____

3. _____

4. _____

5. _____

6. _____

7. _____

8. _____

E. Answer the following questions truthfully so that your classmates know how these people feel about certain things.

1. ¿De qué te enorgulleces?

_____

2. ¿De qué se alegran tus amigos?

_____

3. ¿De qué se enojan tus padres?

_____

4. ¿Temen tú y tus amigos viajar en avión?

_____

5. ¿Siente tu profesor(a) no tener vacaciones más largas?

_____

F. Imagine that you and some of your clasmates have been invited to an exclusive party at Mr. Miranda's home in the country. He is a wealthy man who likes to help students financially with their studies. You want to be gracious and express how those involved feel about the invitation, being there, etc. Use the following cues to express what you might say.

> **MODELO:** Yo estoy alegre de . . .
>
> Yo estoy alegre de _recibir una invitación._

1. Mi compañero(a) está orgulloso(a) de . . .

2. Nosotros estamos contentos de . . .

3. El señor Miranda está encantado de . . .

4. Los estudiantes que no están aquí están desilusionados de . . .

5. Mis padres están tristes de . . .

Unit Three

EXPRESSING PERSONAL FEELINGS

LESSON 7
Expressing Attitudes, Feelings, and Emotions

PART A: Expressing Attitudes, Feelings, and Emotions About Present (and Future) Occurrences

SUBJUNCTIVE AFTER VERBS AND VERBAL EXPRESSIONS OF EMOTION

Up to this point, you have reviewed the constructions used to express the feelings and emotions of the subject regarding his or her own actions or states.

> Me alegro de estar aquí.
> I am happy to be (that I am) here.

Spanish speakers use the subjunctive after verbs that express their personal attitudes, feelings, and emotions when the subject of the verb to which they are reacting is different from the subject of the expression of emotion.

> Me alegro de que tú estés aquí.
> I am happy that you are here.

> Es mejor que el examen no sea hoy.
> It is better that the exam is not today.

Verbs and verbal expressions of attitude, feeling, and emotion are followed by a verb in the subjunctive if the subject of that verb is different. These expressions of feeling follow the construction:

> verbal expression of emotion + *que* + subject + verb in the subjunctive

es bueno que—it's good that

es malo que—it's bad that

es maravilloso que—it's wonderful (marvelous) that

es estupendo que—it's terrific (great) that

es imposible que—it's impossible that

es mejor que—it's better that

> Es maravilloso que Uds. hablen español.
> It's wonderful that you speak Spanish.

alegrarse de que—to become (be made) happy that

enorgullecerse de que—to become (be made) proud that

enojarse de que—to get angry that

sentir (ie) que—to regret that

molestarse de que—to get angry (annoyed) that

enfadarse de que—to get angry that

temer que—to fear that

tener miedo (de) que—to be afraid that

sorprenderse de que—to be surprised that

emocionarse de que—to become emotional that

> Me sorprendo de que tú tengas tanto trabajo.
> I am surprised that you have so much work.

estar alegre de que—to be happy that

estar contento de que—to be happy that

estar encantado de que—to be delighted that

estar desilusionado de que—to be disillusioned that

estar enfadado de que—to be upset that

estar enojado de que—to be angry that

estar triste de que—to be sad that

estar orgulloso de que—to be proud that

> Es triste que Elena no pueda ir con nosotros.
> It is sad that Elena cannot go with us.

SUBJUNCTIVE AFTER EXCLAMATIONS

Exclamations can also be used in the construction:

> exclamation + *que* + subject + verb in the subjunctive

¡Qué bueno que . . . !	How great that . . .	¡Qué alegría que . . . !	What happiness that . . . !
¡Qué estupendo que . . . !	How wonderful that . . . !	¡Qué felicidad que . . . !	What happiness that . . . !
¡Qué maravilloso que . . . !	How marvelous that . . . !	¡Qué lástima que . . . !	What a shame (pity) that . . . !
¡Qué horrible que . . . !	How horrible that . . . !	¡Qué pena que . . . !	What a shame (a pity) that . . . !
¡Qué malo que . . . !	How bad that . . . !	¡Qué vergüenza que . . . !	What a shame (an embarrassment) that . . . !
¡Qué terrible que . . . !	How terrible that . . . !	¡Qué tristeza que . . . !	What sadness that . . . !
¡Qué triste que . . . !	How sad that . . . !	¡Qué desastre que . . . !	What a disaster that . . . !
¡Qué extraño que . . . !	How strange that . . . !	¡Qué sorpresa que . . . !	What a surprise that . . . !
¡Qué raro que . . . !	How strange that . . . !		

¡Qué raro que Elena y Tomás no estén aquí!
How strange that Elena y Tomás are not here!

¡Qué lástima que ellos no viajen con nosotros!
What a shame that they are not travelling with us!

Remember, however, that impersonal expressions that indicate certainty are never followed by the subjunctive. They are followed by

que + a verb in the indicative

Es verdad que Angela conduce bien.
It is true that Angela drives well.

The present subjunctive follows an expression of personal feelings when:

- There is a different subject
- The emotions are felt at the moment expressed, and
- What is being reacted to occurs at the same time (or is expected to occur after) the feelings are expressed

Siento que estés enfermo hoy.
I regret (am sorry) that you are sick today.

Es bueno que tomes el autobús mañana.
It is good that you will take the bus tomorrow.

PRESENT SUBJUNCTIVE OF REGULAR VERBS

The present subjunctive of most Spanish verbs is formed by removing the
-*o* from the *yo* form of the present indicative, and adding the following
endings:

- For -*ar* verbs *(-e, -es, -e, -emos, -éis, -en)*

HABLAR (TO SPEAK)	
hable	hablemos
hables	habléis
hable	hablen

- For -*er* verbs *(-a, -as, -a, -amos, -áis, -an)*

COMER (TO EAT)	
coma	comamos
comas	comáis
coma	coman

- For -*ir* verbs *(-a, -as, -a, -amos, -áis, -an)*

ESCRIBIR (TO WRITE)	
escriba	escribamos
escribas	escribáis
escriba	escriban

EXERCISES

Practice. Sara is talking with the staff of the school newspaper. Complete
what she says with the correct form of the verb in parentheses in the present subjunctive. Then, substitute the underlined subject of the original sentence with the subjects in parentheses and make the necessary changes.

1. Es bueno que <u>Adela</u> _____ (escribir) el editorial para el
   periódico de esta semana. (yo, nosotros, Uds.)

2. Nos alegramos de que <u>tú</u> _____ (leer) los artículos
   regularmente. (ellas, Ud., él)

3. El director está orgulloso de que <u>nosotros</u> _____ (diseñar)
   las páginas del periódico tan profesionalmente. (tú, yo, los reporteros)

4. ¡Qué lástima que <u>tú</u> no _____ (entrevistar) a los actores de
   la obra de teatro! (nosotros, Uds., ella)

5. Al profesor le molesta que <u>nosotros</u> _____ (aburrirse) en las reuniones del periódico. (tú, yo, ellas)

6. Es mejor que <u>yo</u> _____ (prometer) terminar este número para la semana próxima. (Uds., nosotros, Ud.)

VERBS WITH SPELLING CHANGES IN THE PRESENT SUBJUNCTIVE

Verbs ending in *-car, -gar,* and *-zar* have spelling changes in all forms of the present subjunctive. These changes are:

- *-c* to *qu* for verbs ending in *-car*

TOCAR (TO TOUCH, TO PLAY AN INSTRUMENT)	
toque	toquemos
toques	toquéis
toque	toquen

Verbs like *tocar:*

acercarse—to come near, approach	dedicar—to dedicate, devote
buscar—to look for	educar—to educate
chocar—to crash	equivocarse—to make a mistake
colocar—to place, put	explicar—to explain
complicar—to complicate	pescar—to fish
comunicar—to communicate	practicar—to practice
criticar—to criticize, critique	secar—to dry

- *g* to *gu* for verbs ending in *-gar*

PAGAR (TO PAY)	
pague	paguemos
pagues	paguéis
pague	paguen

Verbs like *pagar:*

ahogarse—to drown	encargar—to put in charge, to order (goods)
apagar—to turn off	encargarse de—to be in charge
cargar—to carry, load	entregar—to hand over, deliver
castigar—to punish	llegar—to arrive
despegar—to take off	

- *z* to *ce* for verbs ending in *-zar*

CRUZAR (TO CROSS)	
cruce	crucemos
cruces	crucéis
cruce	crucen

Verbs like *cruzar:*

abrazar—to hug

alcanzar—to reach, catch up with

almorzar (ue)—to eat lunch

aterrizar—to land

comenzar (ie)—to begin

empezar (ie)—to begin

garantizar—to guarantee

gozar (de)—to enjoy

realizar—to carry out, attain, realize

rezar—to pray

tranquilizar(se)—to calm down

tropezar—to trip, stumble

utilizar—to use, make use of

EXERCISES

Practice. Adelaida is talking to a friend about her parents' feelings. Complete what she says with the correct form of the verb in parentheses in the present subjunctive. Then, substitute the underlined subject of the original sentence with the subjects in parentheses and make the necessary changes.

1. Mi mamá tiene miedo de que <u>nosotros</u> _____ (cruzar) la avenida. (tú, mi hermana, yo)

2. Mis padres están desilusionados de que <u>yo</u> no _____ (practicar) el piano regularmente. (Ud., tú, Uds.)

3. A mi padre le sorprende que <u>Uds.</u> no _____ (pagar) por los libros de texto. (ellos, tú, ella)

VERBS WITH STEM CHANGES IN THE PRESENT SUBJUNCTIVE

I. STEM-CHANGING VERBS *(E* TO *IE)*

- For *-ar* verbs: regular conjugation for *nosotros* and *vosotros,* and *e* to *ie* in all other forms

CERRAR (TO CLOSE, TO SHUT)	
cierre	cerremos
cierres	cerréis
cierre	cierren

Verbs like *cerrar:*

atravesar—to cross	negar—to deny
comenzar—to begin	nevar—to snow
confesar—to confess	pensar—to think, to plan
despertar—to awaken	recomendar—to recommend
despertarse—to wake up	sentar—to seat
empezar—to begin	sentarse—to sit down
encerrar—to enclose, to lock in	temblar—to tremble

- For *-er* verbs: regular conjugation for *nosotros* and *vosotros,* and *e* to *ie* in all other forms

PERDER (TO LOSE)	
pierda	perdamos
pierdas	perdáis
pierda	pierdan

Verbs like *perder:*

defender—to defend	entender—to understand
encender—to light, to ignite	querer—to want, to wish, to love (a person)

- For *-ir* verbs: change *e* to *i* for *nosotros* and *vosotros,* and *e* to *ie* in all other forms

MENTIR (TO LIE)	
mienta	mintamos
mientas	mintáis
mienta	mientan

Verbs like *mentir:*

divertir—to amuse	sentir—to regret, to feel (be) sorry
divertirse—to have a good time	sentirse—to feel (well, sick, etc.)
preferir—to prefer	

EXERCISES

Practice. Tomás is always talking about music. Complete what he says with the correct form of the verb in parentheses in the present subjunctive. Then, substitute the underlined subject of the original sentence with the subjects in parentheses and make the necessary changes.

1. Me sorprende que <u>mi vecino</u> _____ (empezar) a practicar el saxofón tan temprano. (Uds., nosotras, tú)

2. ¡Qué pena que <u>el pianista</u> no _____ (entender) al conductor! (nosotras, Ud., yo)

3. Ella está enojada de que <u>tú</u> _____ (preferir) tocar ese concierto. (nosotros, ellas, él)

II. STEM-CHANGING VERBS (O TO UE)

- For -ar verbs: regular conjugation for *nosotros* and *vosotros,* and o to *ue* in all other forms

CONTAR (TO COUNT, TO TELL)	
cuente	contemos
cuentes	contéis
cuente	cuenten

Verbs like *contar:*

acordarse (de)—to remember	mostrar—to show
acostar—to put to bed	probar—to try, to taste
acostarse—to go to bed	probarse—to try on
almorzar—to have lunch	recordar—to remember
costar—to cost	rogar—to beg, to ask, to request
demostrar—to demonstrate, to show	sonar—to ring, to sound
encontrar—to find	soñar—to dream
encontrarse (con)—to meet	volar—to fly
jugar (*u* to *ue*)—to play	

- For -er verbs: regular conjugation for *nosotros* and o to *ue* in all other forms

VOLVER (TO RETURN, TO GO BACK)	
vuelva	volvamos
vuelvas	volváis
vuelva	vuelvan

Verbs like *volver:*

devolver—to return, to give back	llover—to rain
doler—to pain, to ache	mover—to move
envolver—to wrap	poder—to be able

- For *-ir* verbs: change *o* to *u* for *nosotros and vosotros,* and *o* to *ue* in all other forms

DORMIR (TO SLEEP)	
duerma	durmamos
duermas	durmáis
duerma	duerman

Verbs like *dormir:*

dormirse—to fall asleep   morir—to die

EXERCISES

Practice. On her way home from the theater, Ana makes some comments to her friend. Complete what she says with the correct form of the verb in parentheses in the present subjunctive. Then, substitute the underlined subject of the original sentence with the subjects in parentheses and make the necessary changes.

1. Estoy desilusionada de que tú no _____ (acordarse) de ese actor. (nosotros, Ud., ellos)

2. Mi hermana siente que ellos no _____ (devolver) el dinero cuando la producción es mala. (Uds., él, nosotros)

3. ¡Qué vergüenza que Uds. _____ (dormirse) en el teatro! (yo, nosotros, tú)

III. STEM-CHANGING VERBS *(E TO I)*

- For *-ir* verbs: *e* changes to *i* in all the forms of the present subjunctive, including the *nosotros* and *vosotros* forms

PEDIR (TO ASK FOR, TO REQUEST)	
pida	pidamos
pidas	pidáis
pida	pidan

Verbs like *pedir:*

conseguir—to get, to obtain

despedir—to fire (let go)

despedirse (de)—to say goodbye to

medir—to measure

reír(se)—to laugh

seguir—to follow, to continue

repetir—to repeat

servir—to serve

sonreír(se)—to smile

vestir—to dress

vestirse—to get dressed

EXERCISES

Practice. Alejandro and his friends are celebrating in a restaurant. Complete what they say with the correct form of the verb in parentheses in the present subjunctive. Then, substitute the underlined subject of the original sentence with the subjects in parentheses and make the necessary changes.

1. Es maravilloso que <u>él</u> _____ (reírse) tanto. (nosotros, Uds., tú)

2. El está alegre de que <u>ellos</u> _____ (repetir) los chistes. (Ud., yo, nosotros)

3. Temo que ellos no _____ (servir) la comida a tiempo. (él, Uds., tú)

SUMMARY

In summary, note that:

Stem-changing *-ar* and *-er* verbs have the same stem changes in the present subjunctive as in the present indicative.

Stem-changing *-ir* verbs have the following stem changes:

- (*e* to *ie*)
  e to *ie* in *yo, tú, él, ella, Ud., ellos, ellas, Uds.*
  e to *i* in *nosotros* and *vosotros*
- (*o* to *ue*)
  o to *ue* in *yo, tú, él, ella, Ud., ellos, ellas, Uds.*
  o to *u* in *nosotros* and *vosotros*
- (*e* to *i*)
  e to *i* in all forms (including *nosotros* and *vosotros*)

PRESENT SUBJUNCTIVE OF IRREGULAR VERBS

The present subjunctive is irregular only when the *yo* form of the present indicative does not end in *-o.*

DAR (PRESENT INDICATIVE—*DOY*)	
dé	demos
des	deis
dé	den

ESTAR (PRESENT INDICATIVE—*ESTOY*)	
esté	estemos
estés	estéis
esté	estén

IR (PRESENT INDICATIVE—*VOY*)	
vaya	vayamos
vayas	vayáis
vaya	vayan

SER (PRESENT INDICATIVE—*SOY*)	
sea	seamos
seas	seáis
sea	sean

SABER (PRESENT INDICATIVE—*SÉ*)	
sepa	sepamos
sepas	sepáis
sepa	sepan

HABER (PRESENT INDICATIVE—*HE*)	
haya	hayamos
hayas	hayáis
haya	hayan

Remember that the verb *haber* is used impersonally (without a subject): *hay*—there is, there are. In the present subjunctive the form is *haya*.

Hay muchas nubes.
There are many clouds.

Temo que haya una tormenta hoy.
I am afraid that there may be a storm today.

EXERCISES

Practice. Cecilia is talking to her co-workers in the office where she has an internship. Complete what she says with the correct form of the verb in parentheses in the present subjunctive. Then, substitute the underlined subject of the original sentence with the subjects in parentheses and make the necessary changes.

1. Es maravilloso que tú les _____ (dar) dinero a los pobres. (ellos, nosotros, Ud.)

2. Nos enorgullecemos de que él _____ (estar) ayudando a las personas que no tienen casa. (ellos, Ud., nosotros)

3. ¡Qué extraño que ella no _____ (ir) a la oficina de servicios sociales! (Ud., tú, ellas)

4. Es estupendo que tú _____ (ser) tan compasivo. (nosotros, Uds., yo)

5. Ellos están tristes de que <u>los políticos</u> no _____ (saber) los problemas de la comunidad. (tú, ella, él)

6. ¡Qué desastre que <u>esas personas</u> _____ (haber) perdido su casa! (él, Uds., tú)

PART B: Expressing Attitudes, Feelings, and Emotions About Past Occurrences

PRESENT PERFECT SUBJUNCTIVE

Spanish speakers use the present perfect subjunctive to express attitudes, emotions, and feelings that are felt at the moment expressed when:

- There is a different subject, and
- What is being reacted to is expected to have occurred before the feelings expressed

    Siento que no hayas visto la película.
    I regret that you have not seen the film.

The present perfect subjunctive is formed by using the present subjunctive of the verb *haber* and the past participle.

PRESENT PERFECT SUBJUNCTIVE		
yo	haya	
tú	hayas	
él, ella, Ud.	haya	+ past participle
nosotros/as	hayamos	
vosotros/as	hayáis	
ellos, ellas, Uds.	hayan	

Es bueno que no hayas leído la carta.
It's good that you have not read the letter.

EXERCISES

A. Gregorio, one of Celia's friends, is sick in the hospital. She is talking about what has been happening. Complete the sentences with the correct form of the verb in parentheses in the perfect subjunctive.

1. Estoy contento de que mis compañeros _____ (visitar) a Gregorio.

2. Tenemos miedo de que Gregorio no _____ (seguir) las sugerencias del doctor.

3. Gregorio está triste de que el profesor de español no _____ (ir) a visitarlo.

4. Me sorprende que los padres de él no _____ (venir) frecuentemente.

5. ¡Qué alegría que nosotros le _____ (traer) tantas flores!

6. Es imposible que tú _____ (olvidarse) de traerle una tarjeta.

B. One of your classmates has gone to spend a year in a school in Costa Rica. Express some of the feelings and emotions you, your friends, and relatives have regarding his trip. Use the verbs and the list below to write your sentences.

> alegrarse de que/temer que/sentir que/estar encantado de que/ emocionarse de que/enfadarse de que

yo	él	estar orgulloso
sus padres	su hermano	no estar muy nervioso
su novia	nosotros	ir con él
sus profesores	sus parientes	venir a despedirse de él
tú	su novia	no viajar con él
nosotros	sus padres	echarle de menos (*to miss him*)
		tener una oportunidad tan especial
		poder practicar la lengua
		verlo por tanto tiempo

MODELO: *Yo estoy alegre de que sus padres hayan estado orgullosos.*

1. _____

2. _____

3. _____

4. _____

5. _____

6. _____

SEQUENCE OF TENSES (PRESENT VS. PRESENT PERFECT SUBJUNCTIVE)

MAIN VERB (INDICATIVE)	VERB IN THE SUBJUNCTIVE
present	present (same time or after main verb)
future	or
present perfect	present perfect (before main verb)
command	

Me alegro de que vayamos a clase juntos.
I am glad that we are going to class together. (either now or later)

Me alegro de que hayamos ido a clase juntos.
I am glad that we went (have gone) to class together. (in the past)

He sentido que no podamos ir a clase juntos.
I have regretted that we cannot go to class together.

He sentido que no hayamos podido ir a clase juntos.
I have regretted that we have not been able to go to class together.

Alégrate de que Rebeca no esté aquí.
Be glad that Rebeca is not (will not be) here.

Alégrate de que Rebeca no haya estado aquí.
Be glad that Rebeca was not here.

Ella va a sentir que tú no hayas ahorrado más dinero.
She is going to be sorry that you did not save more money.

EXERCISES

A. Julia has just received a letter from her best friend, Soledad. Soledad is planning to visit her with her daughter. Complete Julia's response to Soledad with the correct form of the verb in the present subjunctive. In three sentences you will need to use the present indicative.

Querida Soledad,

Ayer recibí tu carta. Es maravilloso que tú y tu hija _____

(poder) venir a visitarnos el mes próximo. Es cierto que la primavera

_____ (ser) la mejor estación para visitar Nueva York. Es

seguro que Carlos te _____ (poder) ir a buscar al aeropuerto.

179

El está encantado de que Uds. _____ (conocer) por fin a su

tía. ¡Qué alegre está él de que ella _____ (vivir) con nosotros

ahora!

Nos sorprende que Fernando no _____ (venir) contigo.

Sentimos que él no _____ (poder) tomar sus vacaciones

contigo. Es posible que nosotros _____ (tener) unos días

libres esa semana. Así podemos ir a Pennsylvania juntos. En los últimos

meses ha sido imposible que nosotros _____ (encontrar) un

hotel. Hoy llamé e hice las reservaciones. ¡Qué lástima que Fernando no

_____ (ir) a estar con nosotros! Nosotros estamos seguros de

que Uds. _____ (ir) a divertirse.

Bueno Soledad, todos estos años hemos estado contentos de que tú y

tu familia _____ (sentirse) cómodos en venir a visitarnos

cuando quieren. Te esperamos con mucha anticipación.

Un abrazo,

Julia

B. You have just heard a report of a terrible storm in the West. Your friend from Lima is with you and he wants to know what is happening. Express the following ideas in Spanish so that he knows.

1. What a shame that it snowed so much!

_____

2. It is true that everyone is helping.

_____

3. I am afraid that there will not be electricity tonight.

_____

4. It is evident that the wind caused many problems.

_____

5. How wonderful that nobody has died in the storm!

_____

6. The governor has been very proud that the people followed the instructions of the police.

_____

7. Mrs. Fontana is sad that her house is destroyed.

_____

8. They fear that the weather is going to worsen _(empeorar)._

_____

PART C: Expressing Skepticism, Doubt, Uncertainty, Disbelief, and Denial

PRESENT SUBJUNCTIVE AFTER VERBS AND VERBAL EXPRESSIONS OF SKEPTICISM, DOUBT, UNCERTAINTY, DISBELIEF, AND DENIAL

To express skepticism, doubt, uncertainty, disbelief, and denial Spanish speakers use the subjunctive.

Some useful verbs and verbal expressions that express skepticism, doubt, uncertainty, disbelief, and denial are:

dudar que—to doubt that	negar (ie) que—to deny that
no creer que—to not believe that	no es verdad que—it is not true that
no pensar (ie) que—to not think that	puede ser que—it may be that
no estar seguro de que—to not be sure that	

Es dudoso que—It is doubtful that	Es imposible que—It is impossible that
Es extraño que—It is strange that	
Es posible que—It is possible that	Es improbable que—It is improbable that
Es probable que—It is probable that	

Remember that when the speaker expresses no doubt (that is, he or she accepts something to be certain) the indicative is used. (See pages 75–93.)

No dudan que vamos a comprar el coche más caro.

They don't doubt that we are going to buy the most expensive car.

Creen (Piensan) que las carreteras son buenas.
They think that the highways are good.

Marcos está seguro de que María lo quiere mucho.
Marcos is certain that María loves him a lot.

   Remember also that if there is no change in subject, impersonal expressions are followed by the infinitive.

Es imposible manejar por esta carretera.
It is impossible to drive on this highway.

EXERCISES

A. After listening to your friends talk about their future plans, you express some skepticism about what they have said. Complete the following sentences with the correct form of the verb in parentheses.

1. Dudo que mi mejor amigo _____ (casarse) muy joven.

2. No creo que esa chica _____ (querer) ser cirujana *(surgeon)*.

3. Es posible que yo _____ (ir) a una universidad en un país de habla hispana.

4. Niego que ellos _____ (sacar) buenas notas si no estudian.

5. Es extraño que las clases no _____ (empezar) hasta octubre el año próximo.

6. Es dudoso que nosotros _____ (pagar) menos por los estudios universitarios.

7. No pienso que tú _____ (graduarse) el año que viene.

8. Es improbable que ellos _____ (conocer) a tantas personas famosas.

B. One of your favorite actors is making a musical. You have some doubts as to how good it may be. Use the following phrases to express your doubt, disbelief, etc. about his decision.

> **MODELO:**   no creer que . . . hacer un buen trabajo
> *No creo que él haga un buen trabajo.*

1. dudar que . . . saber cantar

_____

2. es extraño que . . . querer trabajar con esa actriz

_____

3. no creer que . . . ganar mucho dinero

_____

4. puede ser que . . . necesitar ensayar *(rehearse)* todos los días

_____

5. es probable que . . . conocer todas las canciones

_____

6. no estar seguro de que . . . tener mucho éxito

_____

C. The economic situation is unpredictable. Read the following statements, then complete the phrases using the verb in parentheses and the information from the statements.

> **MODELO:** Todos pueden ahorrar mucho dinero.
> Dudo que todos (poder) . . .
> *Dudo que todos puedan ahorrar mucho dinero.*

1. La economía va a mejorar *(improve)* pronto.
   Mis padres dudan que la economía (mejorar) . . .

2. La comida va a costar menos.
   Yo no creo que la comida (costar) . . .

3. Los políticos dicen que la situación no es problemática.
   Los políticos niegan que la situación (ser) . . .

4. Nadie va a perder su trabajo.
   Puede ser que muchas personas (perder) . . .

5. Las organizaciones comunitarias van a tener mucho dinero para ayudar a los necesitados.

No es verdad que las organizaciones comunitarias (tener) . . .

6. El presidente dice que nosotros vamos a pagar menos impuestos *(taxes)*.

No creo que nosotros (pagar) . . .

THE USE OF THE INDICATIVE OR THE SUBJUNCTIVE WITH *QUIZÁS* AND *TAL VEZ*

After *quizás* and *tal vez* (both meaning, *perhaps*):

- The indicative is used when certainty is implied

Tal vez (Quizás) va a comprar un disco compacto.
Perhaps he will buy a compact disk. (I think he will)

- The subjunctive is used when doubt or uncertainty is implied

Tal vez (Quizás) compre un disco compacto de Bob Dylan.
Perhaps he may buy a Bob Dylan CD. (I'm not certain that he will)

Note that *quizás* and *tal vez* do not require *que* before the subjunctive is used.

SUMMARY

In summary, remember that:

- The indicative is used when the speaker accepts something as certain

Creo (Pienso) que Miguel va a llegar tarde.
I think that Miguel will arrive late.

- The subjunctive is used when the speaker is uncertain or wants to express skepticism

No creo (No pienso) que Miguel llegue temprano.
I don't think that Miguel will arrive early.

- When there is a change in subject, impersonal expressions require the subjunctive (unless they indicate certainty on the part of the speaker)

Es dudoso que Miguel llegue temprano.
It is doubtful that Miguel will arrive early.

Es evidente que Miguel va a llegar tarde.
It is evident that Miguel is going to arrive late.

- The present subjunctive is used to refer to events that occur either at the same time or after the action of the main verb

No estoy seguro de que Miguel llegue temprano.
I am not sure Miguel (is arriving) will arrive on time.

- The present perfect subjunctive refers to actions or situations that may have occurred before the action of the main verb

Dudo que Miguel haya llegado temprano.
I doubt that Miguel arrived (has arrived) early.

Notice that when translating the present perfect into English, both the preterite and the present perfect can be used to convey the meanings that the present perfect subjunctive expresses in Spanish.

EXERCISES

Read the following situations, then use the phrases to express your opinion. You will not need to use the subjunctive in all the sentences. Think before you write and be creative!

> **MODELO:** Hay muchas personas bilingües en los Estados Unidos.
> Es importante *que todos aprendamos dos lenguas.*

1. Juan tiene muchos problemas en la escuela.
   Quizás él . . .

2. Dicen que va a llover mucho mañana.
   Es probable que . . .

3. Mañana es el primer día de verano.
   No dudo que . . .

4. Los trabajadores de los medios de transporte van a declararse en huelga *(on strike)* la semana próxima.
   No creo que . . .

5. Vamos a hacer un viaje a California este verano.
   Puede ser que . . .

6. Los profesores de mi escuela ganan mucho dinero.
   Es extraño que . . .

7. La semana próxima van a presentar el Ballet Folklórico de México.
   Es seguro que . . .

8. La comida de la cafetería es muy buena.
   No estamos seguros de que . . .

9. Mañana hay un examen de inglés.
   Es imposible que . . .

10. No hay mucho crimen en las ciudades grandes.

Dudo que . . .

PART D: Expressing Past Feelings, Emotions, Doubt, Denial, Disbelief, and Uncertainty

When the main verb in a sentence that requires the use of the subjunctive is in the imperfect, preterite, conditional, or pluperfect tense, Spanish speakers use either the imperfect or the pluperfect subjunctive.

Me alegré de que mis amigos fueran conmigo.
I was glad that my friends went with me.

Era dudoso que David hubiera ido sin Jonatán.
It was doubtful that David would have gone without Jonatan.

IMPERFECT SUBJUNCTIVE

The imperfect subjunctive tense has two forms, commonly known as the *-ra* and *-se* forms. In general the *-ra* form is used more often. For this reason, the *-ra* form will be used in the examples and in the exercises. However, be aware that you should be able to recognize the *-se* form since you may encounter it in your readings.

When forming the imperfect subjunctive:

- The stem is the *ellos* form of the preterite minus the *-ron* (i.e. *cantar:* preterite—*cantaron,* imperfect subjunctive stem: *canta-*)
- The imperfect endings are *(-ra, -ras, -ra, -ramos, -rais, -ran)* or *(-se, -ses, -se, -semos, -seis, -sen)*

For example:

PRETERITE	IMPERFECT SUBJUNCTIVE	
cantaron	yo cantara	nosotros/as cantáramos
	tú cantaras	vosotros/as cantarais
	él, ella, Ud. cantara	ellos, ellas, Uds. cantaran
vendieron	yo vendiera	nosotros/as vendiéramos
	tú vendieras	vosotros/as vendierais
	él, ella, Ud. vendiera	ellos, ellas, Uds. vendieran
tuvieron	yo tuviera	nosotros/as tuviéramos
	tú tuvieras	vosotros/as tuvierais
	él, ella, Ud. tuviera	ellos, ellas, Uds. tuvieran

Please note that the *nosotros* form has a written accent on the last vowel of the stem.

Many Spanish verbs have an irregular preterite. Some useful verbs are conjugated in the preterite on pages 112–130.

EXERCISES

A. Practice. After reviewing the verbs in the preterite, fill out the following chart as follows:
- The *ellos* form of the preterite on the first blank
- The *yo* form of the imperfect subjunctive on the second blank

	Preterite (ellos)	Imperfect Subjunctive (yo)
1. andar	_____	_____
2. dar	_____	_____
3. decir	_____	_____
4. dormir	_____	_____
5. estar	_____	_____
6. haber	_____	_____
7. hacer	_____	_____
8. ir	_____	_____
9. leer	_____	_____
10. oír	_____	_____
11. poder	_____	_____
12. poner	_____	_____
13. querer	_____	_____
14. reír	_____	_____
15. saber	_____	_____
16. ser	_____	_____
17. servir	_____	_____
18. traer	_____	_____

19. venir   _____   _____

20. ver   _____   _____

B. More practice. Teresa had a dinner party and some of her guests had problems arriving on time. Complete what she says with the correct form of the verb in parentheses in the imperfect subjunctive tense. Then, substitute the underlined subject of the original sentence with the subjects in parentheses and make the necessary changes.

1. Fue imposible que <u>ellos</u> _____ (llegar) a tiempo. (nosotros, tú, Uds.)

2. Nosotros no estábamos seguros de que <u>él</u> _____ (salir) temprano. (Ud., ellas, tú)

3. Se molestó de que <u>Uds.</u> _____ (perder) tanto tiempo en el centro comercial. (nosotros, yo, él)

4. Temía que <u>nosotros</u> no _____ (ver) a sus abuelos. (ellos, tú, Uds.)

5. No dudábamos que <u>su hermanita</u> _____ (despertarse) con tanto ruido. (Ud., tú, ellas)

6. Era posible que <u>ellos</u> les _____ (pedir) excusas a los invitados. (yo, nosotras, ellas)

USES OF THE IMPERFECT SUBJUNCTIVE

The imperfect subjunctive is used when the speaker is conveying emotions and uncertainties that were felt **in the past** about:

- Occurrences or situations that took place at the same time as that of the main verb

  En ese momento sentí que mi hermana no condujera el coche.
  At that moment I regretted (was sorry) that my sister was not driving the car.

- Occurrences or situations that took place after that of the main verb

  Ayer dudábamos que él hiciera los arreglos necesarios hoy.
  Yesterday we doubted that he would make the necessary repairs today.

EXERCISES

A. Last week was the opening of the school play. It was a major success. These are some of the comments that were heard. Complete the sentences with the correct form of the verb in the imperfect subjunctive.

1. Estuvimos alegres de que el público _____ (reaccionar) tan positivamente.

2. Juan fue la estrella de la presentación. Sus padres estaban orgullosos de que él _____ (actuar) tan bien.

3. Fue maravilloso que todos los profesores _____ (poder) venir.

4. Nos enorgullecimos de que el autor de la obra _____ (estar) en el público.

5. Era estupendo que la gente _____ (aplaudir) con tanta emoción.

6. Teníamos miedo de que no _____ (haber) suficientes asientos en el auditorio.

7. Sentí mucho que mis abuelos no _____ (venir) a ver la obra.

8. El director de la escuela estaba encantado de que los estudiantes _____ (hacer) tan buen trabajo.

B. Diego and his friends went on vacation last summer and now he is talking about some of his feelings. Use the information below to express what he said.

> **MODELO:** Yo dudaba que . . .
>
> Yo dudaba que *conociéramos a nadie.*

poder ir de vacaciones/haber tanta gente en la playa/
hacer buen tiempo/los precios ser muy altos/
el dinero ser suficiente/no divertirnos/
haber un guía en el museo/sentirse solo(a)/el hotel costar poco

1. No pensé que . . .

2. Era extraño que . . .

3. Fue imposible que . . .

4. No era verdad que . . .

5. Nos alegramos de que . . .

6. Temía que . . .

7. Fue maravilloso que . . .

PLUPERFECT SUBJUNCTIVE

The pluperfect subjunctive is formed with the imperfect subjunctive of the verb *haber* plus the past participle of the verb.

PLUPERFECT SUBJUNCTIVE		
yo	hubiera	
tú	hubieras	
él, ella, Ud.	hubiera	+ past participle
nosotros/as	hubiéramos	
vosotros/as	hubierais	
ellos, ellas, Uds.	hubieran	

For example:

INFINITIVE	PLUPERFECT SUBJUNCTIVE
bailar	yo hubiera bailado
comer	(tú) hubieras comido
hacer	(él, ella, Ud.) hubiera hecho
recibir	(nosotros/as) hubiéramos recibido
abrir	(vosotros/as) hubierais abierto
poner	(ellos, ellas, Uds.) hubieran puesto

USES OF THE PLUPERFECT SUBJUNCTIVE

The pluperfect subjunctive is used when the speaker is conveying emotions and uncertainties that were felt **in the past** about occurrences or situations that took place before the action of the main verb.

Anoche temí que Juan no hubiera entendido la clase de ayer.
Last night I feared that Juan had not understood yesterday's class.

No estaban seguros de que el vuelo hubiera salido la noche antes.
They were not sure that the flight had left the night before.

SEQUENCE OF TENSES (IMPERFECT VS. PLUPERFECT SUBJUNCTIVE)

The following chart summarizes the sequence of tenses when the main verb is in a past or conditional tense.

MAIN VERB	VERB IN THE SUBJUNCTIVE
preterite	imperfect subjunctive
imperfect	or
pluperfect	pluperfect subjunctive
conditional	

Remember that when the main verb is in the imperfect, preterite, conditional, or pluperfect tense:

- The imperfect subjunctive refers to events that occur either at the same time or after the action of the main verb

  Mi madre dudaba que mis hermanos estuvieran en casa.
  My mother doubted that my brothers were (would be) home.

- The pluperfect subjunctive refers to actions or situations that occurred before the action of the main verb

  Mi madre dudaba que mis hermanos hubieran estado en casa.
  My mother doubted that my brothers had been home.

EXERCISES

A. Practice. Felix's father is talking about his day in the office. Complete what he says with the correct form of the verb in parentheses in the pluperfect subjunctive tense. Then, substitute the underlined subject of the original sentence with the subjects in parentheses and make the necessary changes.

1. Era imposible que <u>ellos</u> _____ (terminar) el informe antes de las cinco. (nosotros, él, Uds.)

2. Estábamos contentos de que <u>él</u> _____ (reconocer) nuestro esfuerzo. (Ud., tú, ellas)

3. Nos sorprendió que <u>todos</u> _____ (hacer) tanto trabajo en poco tiempo. (yo, Uds. él)

B. Last summer Alfredo got into trouble. It was all a misunderstanding, and you and your friends doubted that he had done anything wrong. Complete the statements that were made regarding his situation. Use the pluperfect subjunctive in your answers.

1. No pensaba que él _____ (hacer) tal *(such)* cosa.

2. No era verdad que sus padres _____ (ser) indiferentes.

3. Era probable que nosotros no lo _____ (ayudar) bastante.

4. En aquel momento dudamos (pret.) que su hermana _____ (llamar) a la policía.

5. El no pensó que yo lo _____ (defender).

6. Yo no estaba seguro de que tú _____ (tener) confianza en él.

Unit Four

GETTING OTHERS TO ADOPT A COURSE OF ACTION

LESSON 8
Giving Direct Commands

PART A: Giving Formal Direct Commands

AFFIRMATIVE AND NEGATIVE COMMANDS *(UD., UDS., NOSOTROS)*

When addressing someone formally:

- To tell them to do something, use the *Ud.* or *Uds.* form of the present subjunctive

  ¡Compren Uds. esa computadora!
  Buy that computer!

- To tell them *not* to do something, use *no* in front of the *Ud.* or *Uds.* form of the present subjunctive

  ¡No escriban Uds. con lápiz!
  Don't write with a pencil!

When giving commands that include the speaker:

- In the affirmative, use the *nosotros* form of the present subjunctive

  ¡Bailemos!
  Let's dance!

- In the negative, put *no* before the *nosotros* form of the present subjunctive

  ¡No estudiemos esta noche!
  Let's not study tonight!

The following *nosotros* commands are irregular:

  ¡Vamos!   Let's go!

  ¡Vámonos! Let's go!/Let's leave!/Let's go away!

Remember that when forming the *Ud., Uds.,* and *nosotros* commands:
- The root is the *yo* form of the present indicative minus the *-o*
- The endings are:

For *-ar* verbs: *-e, -en, -emos*
i.e. *compre Ud., compren Uds., compremos*
For *-er* verbs: *-a, -an, -amos*
i.e. *beba Ud., beban Uds., bebamos*
For *-ir* verbs : *-a, -an, -amos*
i.e. *comparta Ud., compartan Uds., compartamos*

The following verbs are irregular:

INFINITIVE	*UD.* COMMAND	*UDS.* COMMAND	*NOSOTROS* COMMAND
dar	dé Ud.	den Uds.	demos
estar	esté Ud.	estén Uds.	estemos
ir	vaya Ud.	vayan Uds.	vamos
ser	sea Ud.	sean Uds.	seamos
saber	sepa Ud.	sepan Uds.	sepamos

To review spelling changes and stem-changing verbs in the present subjunctive, look at pages 169–177.

EXERCISES

A. One of Yolanda's neighbors is an elderly lady. Read the situations and then, using the information in parentheses, write a command. Remember that you must use the *Ud.* command.

> **MODELO:** Hace mucho viento hoy. (Cerrar las ventanas)
> *¡Cierre las ventanas!*

1. Esa esquina es peligrosa. (No cruzar la calle en esa esquina)

   _____

2. Los precios son muy altos en ese supermercado. (No hacer las compras allí)

   _____

3. Hace mucho frío. (Ponerse el abrigo antes de salir)

   _____

4. Hay mucho crimen en este barrio. (No salir muy tarde)

_____

5. En esa farmacia dan descuentos. (Comprar las medicinas allí)

_____

6. En ese hospital hay un buen médico. (Ir a verlo)

_____

7. Yo llego de la escuela muy temprano los viernes. (Venir a cenar en mi casa)

_____

8. Pienso ir al parque mañana. (Estar lista a las dos)

_____

B. Your friends are meeting with some representatives from a university. It is an important meeting and they want to give a good impression. Give them some advice by using the information in the phrases below.

> **MODELO:** Levantar la mano para hacer una pregunta
> _Levanten la mano para hacer una pregunta._

1. Saber todos los nombres

_____

2. Poner sillas y mesas en el escenario

_____

3. Estar en el auditorio temprano

_____

4. No masticar chicle

_____

5. Preparar algunas preguntas para ellos

_____

6. Servir refrescos durante la reunión

PART B: Giving Informal Direct Commands

AFFIRMATIVE AND NEGATIVE COMMANDS (TÚ, VOSOTROS)

When addressing someone informally in the singular *(tú)*, tell him/her to do something by using the *él/ella* form of the present indicative tense.

¡Compra leche!
Buy milk!

¡Bebe leche todos los días!
Drink milk every day!

The following verbs are irregular:

INFINITIVE	TÚ COMMAND
poner	pon
salir	sal
tener	ten
venir	ven
hacer	haz
decir	di
ser	sé
ir	ve

¡Pon los vasos en la mesa!
Put the glasses on the table!

¡Ve en seguida!
Go immediately!

When addressing someone informally in the plural *(vosotros, vosotras),* tell them to do something by dropping the final *-r* of the infinitive and adding *-d.*

¡Hablad en voz alta!
Talk loud.

¡Conducid con cuidado!
Drive carefully!

When addressing someone informally, tell them *not* to do something by putting *no* in front of the *tú* and *vosotros* form of the present subjunctive.

¡No cruces la calle aquí!
Don't cross the street here!

¡No hagáis tanto ruido!
Don't make so much noise!

Notice that the only forms of direct commands that do not use the present subjunctive are the affirmative informal commands (*tú*, *vosotros*, *vosotras*).

¡(No) practique ahora!	(Don't) practice now!
¡(No) practiquen ahora!	(Don't) practice now!
¡Practica (tú) ahora!	Practice now!
¡No practiques ahora!	Don't practice now!
¡Practicad ahora!	Practice now!
¡No practiquéis ahora!	Don't practice now!
¡(No) practiquemos ahora!	Let's (not) practice now!

EXERCISES

An exchange student is visiting you for a few weeks. You want to make sure that he/she has a good time and does interesting things. Use the phrases below to write the commands you would give him/her.

1. no ir a la escuela en metro

_____

2. ir en autobús

_____

3. comprar boletos para una obra de teatro

_____

4. almorzar en la cafetería porque es más barato

_____

5. asistir a todas las clases

_____

6. escribir a menudo

_____

7. tener paciencia si no entiendes inglés

_____

8. hacer amigos en tus clases

---

9. no salir de la escuela demasiado tarde

---

10. no cruzar el parque solo(a)

THE POSITION OF DIRECT OBJECT, INDIRECT OBJECT, AND REFLEXIVE PRONOUNS WITH DIRECT COMMANDS

When telling someone to do something, direct object, indirect object, and reflexive pronouns follow and are attached to the verb.

¿El piano? Sí, ¡practíquelo Ud.!
The piano? Yes, practice it!

¡Levántense Uds!
Get up!

¡Dame la maleta!
Give me the suitcase!

Before the reflexive pronoun *nos* is attached to the *nosotros* command, the final -*s* of the verb is dropped.

¡Cortémonos el pelo!
Let's cut our hair!

¡Vámonos ahora mismo!
Let's leave right now!

When a pronoun is attached to a verb that is normally stressed on the next to the last syllable, an accent mark is used to keep the stress on that syllable. One-syllable words do not need this accent.

¿Devuelvo el libro? Sí, ¡devuélvelo!
Do I return the book? Yes, return it!

¿Me acuesto? Sí, ¡Acuéstese Ud.!
Do I go to bed? Yes, go to bed!

Dale el dinero a mi hermano.
Give the money to my brother.

When telling someone *not* to do something, the object pronouns and the reflexive pronouns are placed between the negative word (usually *no*) and the verb. Remember that no other word may be placed between the negative and the verb.

¡No los devuelvas!
Do not return them (the books)!

¡No te vistas todavía!
Don't get dressed yet!

If a verb has a direct and an indirect object, the indirect object precedes the direct object in affirmative and negative commands.

¡No se lo des a Carlos! ¡Dáselo a Catalina!
Don't give it to Carlos! Give it to Catalina!

EXERCISES

A. Your friend stayed with you last night. You both have to be in school on time, but he is still in bed. Write the commands you would give him. If the direct object is underlined, replace it with a pronoun in your command.

> **MODELO:** tomar <u>el desayuno</u>
> *¡Tómalo!*

1. despertarse

   _____

2. levantarse pronto

   _____

3. afeitarse primero

   _____

4. bañarse ahora

   _____

5. vestirse rápidamente

   _____

6. poner <u>los libros</u> en la mochila

   _____

7. no ponerse <u>ese abrigo</u>

   _____

8. no olvidar <u>la calculadora</u>

_____

9. no poner <u>la ropa sucia</u> en la cama

_____

10. preguntarle a mi padre si nos puede llevar en coche

_____

B. You are helping a friend clean his room. He asks you what he should do with certain things and you tell him what to do with them.

> **MODELO:** ¿Los vasos? Lavar
> *¡Lávalos!*

1. ¿El libro? Devolver/a la biblioteca

_____

2. ¿Las camisas? Llevar/a la tintorería *(dry cleaners)*

_____

3. ¿La basura? Echar/en el cesto *(basket)*

_____

4. ¿Los juguetes? Poner/en el armario

_____

5. ¿El periódico? Darle/a tu padre

_____

6. ¿Los zapatos? Ponerse

_____

7. ¿La mochila? No dejar/en la cama

_____

8. ¿Los discos compactos? No poner/en el suelo

_____

LESSON 9
Expressing Wishes and Desires, and Making Requests and Suggestions

SUBJUNCTIVE AFTER VERBS OF WILLING, WISHING, AND SUGGESTING

You have reviewed how to tell others what to do (or not to do) by giving a direct command.

> ¡Vaya Ud. al cine durante el fin de semana!
> Go to the movies on weekends!

When the speaker is trying to influence the actions of others by expressing his or her wishes and desires and by making requests and suggestions, the present subjunctive can also be used. Such sentences follow the construction:

> Subject + verb of influencing + *que* + subject + verb in the subjunctive

> Los médicos sugieren que comamos muchos vegetales.
> Doctors suggest that we eat a lot of vegetables.

Some Spanish verbs that can be used to express the desire to influence the actions of others are:

aconsejar—to advise	querer—to want
desear—to want	recomendar—to recommend
decir—to tell	pedir—to request, ask for
esperar—to hope, to expect	permitir—to permit, allow
exigir—to demand	preferir—to prefer
mandar—to order, to command	prohibir—to forbid
necesitar—to need	rogar/suplicar—to beg
	sugerir—to suggest

> (Yo) quiero que Ud. vaya al cine conmigo.
> I want you to go to the movies with me.

Notice that in the English translation, the infinitive is sometimes used.

The verbs above are followed by the construction *que* + subject + verb in the subjunctive when their subject is different from the subject of the second verb.

> Mi madre ruega que nos levantemos temprano.
> My mother begs us to get up early.

La profesora exige que estudiemos.
The teacher demands that we study.

You have already reviewed the use of these verbs in the construction subject + verb + infinitive, which is used when the second verb does not have a different subject.

Quiero ir al cine esta noche.
I want to go to the movies tonight.

EXERCISES

A. Use the following verbs to express what your parents request or suggest to you, your friends, or your brothers and sisters.

querer/desear/aconsejar/prohibir/recomendar/sugerir/
exigir/permitir

MODELO: nosotros/estudiar mucho
Ellos quieren que nosotros estudiemos mucho.
no/nosotros/jugar demasiado
Ellos no quieren que nosotros juguemos demasiado.

1. nosotros/salir bien en los exámenes

_____

2. mi hermano/acostarse temprano

_____

3. yo/no llegar muy tarde a casa

_____

4. mis amigos/venir a visitarme todas las noches

_____

5. no/mis hermanos/mentir nunca

_____

6. tú/dar las gracias siempre

_____

7. nosotros/almorzar siempre en la cafetería

_____

8. yo/practicar el piano frecuentemente

_____

B. Jorge likes his chemistry class very much, but at times he thinks that the teacher is very demanding. Write complete sentences to express what Jorge says about the teacher.

> **MODELO:** esperar   nosotros   llegar a tiempo
> _El profesor espera que nosotros lleguemos a tiempo._

1. esperar   yo   limpiar los instrumentos

_____

2. prohibir   nosotros   jugar con fósforos _(matches)_

_____

3. sugerir   tú   hacer el experimento cuidadosamente

_____

4. recomendar   nosotros   medir bien los líquidos

_____

5. preferir   Uds.   terminar antes del fin de la clase

_____

6. no permitir   Alfredo   concluir su experimento más tarde

_____

7. pedir   ellas   leer toda la información antes de empezar

_____

8. suplicar   nosotros   acordarse de tener cuidado en el laboratorio

_____

C. Answer the following questions in complete sentences according to your personal experience.

1. ¿Qué te prohiben tus padres?

    _____

2. ¿Cuándo te exigen tus padres que llegues a tu casa?

    _____

3. ¿Te permiten hacer muchas cosas? ¿Qué te permiten hacer? (Name two things)

    _____

4. ¿Qué te aconsejan ellos?

    _____

5. ¿Prefieren que tú salgas los fines de semana? ¿Por qué?

    _____

6. ¿Te dicen que hagas muchas cosas en la casa? (Name two things)

    _____

SUBJUNCTIVE AFTER IMPERSONAL EXPRESSIONS OF WILLING

Impersonal expressions can be used to express a desire to influence the actions of others. When they imply an indirect command, impersonal expressions are followed by the construction *que* + subject + verb in the subjunctive.

> Es importante que tú digas la verdad.
> It is important that you tell the truth. (for you to tell the truth)

Some impersonal expressions that can be used give an indirect command are:

es aconsejable—it is advisable
es importante—it is important
es mejor—it is better

es necesario—it is necessary
es preferible—it is preferable

Remember that when there is no intention to influence the actions of others, that is, when the statement is totally impersonal, the construction impersonal expression + infinitive is used.

> Es preferible ir al cine los fines de semana.
> It is preferable to go to the movies on weekends.

Notice the difference between the following statements:

Es mejor depositar el dinero en el banco.
It is better to deposit the money in the bank. (totally impersonal)

Es mejor que tú deposites el dinero en el banco.
It is better for you to deposit the money in the bank. (the speaker is trying to influence another person's behavior)

EXERCISES

A. One of your friends has a very difficult test tomorrow. He or she wants to do well and asks for your advice. Use the following lists to write complete sentences.

> escribir los ejercicios/acostarse temprano/no beber café/
> no ponerse nervioso/hacer apuntes de la información

MODELO: repasar juntos
Es aconsejable que nosotros . . .
Es aconsejable que nosotros repasemos juntos.

1. Es importante que tú . . .

2. Es preferible que tú . . .

3. Es mejor que tú . . .

4. Es importante que nosotros . . .

5. Es necesario que tú . . .

B. Some of your friends are having some problems. You hear what they say and you offer some advice as to what they should do. Read their statements and then complete the phrases in a creative and logical manner.

MODELO: Carlota no puede dormir.
Es mejor que ella *lea un libro.*

1. Teresa perdió su cartera en el concierto.
Es aconsejable que ella . . .

2. Carlos no sabe usar el correo electrónico.
Es necesario que él . . .

3. Nosotros no tenemos dinero para ir al concierto.
   Es mejor que nosotros . . .

4. Sebastián y Julián quieren ir a tu casa a escuchar música pero tú tienes mucho trabajo.
   Es importante que ellos . . .

5. Yo no puedo terminar mi informe esta noche.
   Es preferible que tú . . .

PRESENT AND PRESENT PERFECT SUBJUNCTIVE AFTER VERBS AND EXPRESSIONS TO INFLUENCE OTHERS TO ADOPT A COURSE OF ACTION

When using the subjunctive in order to get others to adopt a course of action:

I. The **present subjunctive** is used when:

- The main verb is in the present, present perfect, future, or is a command, and either
- The action of the verb in the subjunctive occurs at the same time as that of the main verb

  Exigen que paguemos ahora mismo.
  They demand that we pay right now.

- Or the action of the verb in the subjunctive is expected to take place after that of the main verb

  Es importante que asistamos a la conferencia mañana.
  It is important that we attend the conference tomorrow.

II. The **present perfect subjunctive** is used when:

- The main verb is in the present, present perfect, future tense, or is a command, and
- The action of the verb in the subjunctive is expected to have taken place before that of the main verb

  Mis padres exigen que haya estudiado antes de salir.
  My parents demand that I study before going out.

EXERCISES

A. You and some of your family's friends are taking a trip abroad. People give you all kind of advice. Complete what they say with the correct form of the verb in the present subjunctive.

1. Te aconsejo que _____ (llevar) el pasaporte contigo siempre.

2. ¿Prohiben que los turistas _____ (entrar) al país con animales o plantas?

3. Si compras algo, pídele al dependiente que te _____ (dar) un recibo.

4. Siempre les han rogado a los viajeros que no _____ (comprar) regalos en las calles.

5. Es preferible que tú _____ (declarar) todo lo que compres.

6. Han sugerido que todos _____ (decir) si han estado en una finca *(farm)*.

7. Aconséjale a tus amigos que no _____ (perder-ellos) el pasaporte.

8. Va a ser necesario que Uds. _____ (hacer) una lista de todo lo que compran.

9. Desde el año pasado han exigido que los ciudadanos norteamericanos _____ (conseguir) una visa.

10. Ahorren algún dinero, es necesario que Uds. _____ (pagar) el impuesto *(tax)* de salida.

B. Daniel is working at an animal clinic. Complete the statements he makes by writing the correct form of the verb in parentheses in the present perfect subjunctive.

1. El veterinario desea que tú _____ (limpiar) las jaulas antes de salir de la oficina.

2. Es mejor que tú no _____ (sacar) a los perros hoy. Llueve mucho.

3. Va a ser necesario que Uds. les _____ (dar) la comida a los gatos antes de las dos.

4. El Departamento de Sanidad *(Health)* ha sugerido que los asistentes _____ (recibir) entrenamiento antes de empezar a trabajar en la oficina.

5. Espero que la secretaria _____ (enviar-ella) los formularios al hospital antes de cerrar la oficina.

6. Quieren que yo _____ (poner) todos los intrumentos en el armario antes de cerrar la oficina.

IMPERFECT AND PLUPERFECT SUBJUNCTIVE AFTER VERBS AND EXPRESSIONS TO INFLUENCE OTHERS TO ADOPT A COURSE OF ACTION

When using the subjunctive in order to get others to adopt a course of action:

I. The **imperfect subjunctive** is used when:
- The main verb is in the preterite, imperfect, conditional, or pluperfect tense, and either
- The action of the verb in the subjunctive is at the same time as that of the main verb

Dorotea quería que yo pagara la cuenta.
Dorotea wanted me to pay the bill.

- Or the action of the verb in the subjunctive is after that of the main verb

Alvaro recomendó que fuéramos al día siguiente.
Alvaro recommended that we go the next day.

II. The **pluperfect subjunctive** is used when:
- The main verb is in the preterite, imperfect, conditional, or pluperfect tense, and
- The action of the verb in the subjunctive is expected to have taken place before that of the main verb

Era necesario que hubiéramos dormido ocho horas.
It was necessary for us to have slept eight hours.

EXERCISES

A. Santiago spent a summer at a camp in the mountains. He was a little disappointed about all the rules. Complete what he says with the imperfect subjunctive of the verb in parentheses.

1. Deseaban que nosotros _____ (levantarse) a las siete.

2. Les habían mandado a los chicos más pequeños que no _____ (salir) de su cuarto después de las diez.

3. Exigieron a los padres que no _____ (venir) a vernos durante la semana.

4. Era importante que nosotros _____ (tener) cuidado en el bosque.

5. Fue necesario que yo _____ (recoger) leña *(firewood)* para las fogatas *(bonfires)*.

6. Siempre era preferible que los grupos _____ (ir) a pescar con el líder.

7. Nos habían rogado que nosotros no _____ (hacer) demasiado ruido después de las once.

8. Querían que yo _____ (lavar) la ropa cada dos días.

B. Carolina also had a similar experience. Complete what she says with the correct form of the verb in the pluperfect subjunctive.

1. Nos aconsejaban que antes de hacer ejercicios _____ (dormir) por lo menos siete horas.

2. Prohibieron que nuestros padres _____ (mandar) dulces.

3. Antes del desayuno esperaban que tú _____ (hacer) la cama.

4. Les recomendaron a las chicas que _____ (bañarse) antes de entrar a la piscina.

5. Había sido necesario que todos _____ (comprar) los materiales para las clases de arte.

6. Esperaban que cada chico les _____ (escribir) a sus padres todas las semanas.

7. Yo había deseado que nos _____ (quedar) en casa.

8. Antes de volver a casa, exigían que _____ (limpiar) todo el campamento.

LESSON 10
Expressing Personal Hopes and Expectations

PRESENT AND PERFECT SUBJUNCTIVE AFTER *OJALÁ (QUE)*

When Spanish speakers are expressing their own hopes and expectations they often use the expression *Ojalá (que)*. This expression can mean either "I hope" or "I expect," and is always followed by the subjunctive because with your hope you are trying to affect someone or something else.

Ojalá (que) Raúl vaya al concierto.
I hope that Raúl goes (is going) to the concert.

Ojalá (que) el concierto empiece a tiempo.
I hope the concert starts on time.

The tense of the subjunctive you use with *Ojalá (que)* changes the meaning of the sentence:

- When referring to something that may be happening in the present, the present subjunctive follows *Ojalá (que)*

  Ojalá (que) Gloria no esté en casa ahora.
  I hope Gloria is not at home now. (she may or may not be home now)

- When referring to something that may happen in the future, the present subjunctive follows *Ojalá (que)*

  Ojalá (que) no llueva este fin de semana.
  I hope it does not (will not) rain this weekend. (it may or may not rain)

- When referring to something that may have happened in the past, the present perfect subjunctive follows *(Ojalá que)*

  ¡Ojalá (que) haya hecho buen tiempo!
  I hope that the weather was good! (It may or may not have been good)

EXERCISES

A. In the last few weeks you have tried to organize a full day of activities in the park with your friends and it will finally take place next weekend. Use *Ojalá que* and the phrases below to write complete sentences expressing what you hope or expect to happen.

> **MODELO:** ellos/llegar a tiempo
> *¡Ojalá que ellos lleguen a tiempo!*

1. hacer buen tiempo

_____

2. todos mis amigos/venir

_____

3. ellos/traer las pelotas para jugar al fútbol

_____

4. nosotros/poder almorzar al aire libre

_____

5. no haber muchos insectos

_____

6. nosotros/divertirse mucho

_____

7. tú/convencer a tus padres para poder venir

_____

8. ellos/saber donde nos vamos a encontrar

_____

9. el sol/salir temprano

_____

10. ser un día inolvidable

_____

B. Now express your nopes and expectations with regard to your life in the future. Here are some ideas you may want to use. Write at least six sentences using *Ojalá que.*

> terminar los estudios/casarse/conseguir un trabajo/ganar mucho dinero/tener una familia/vivir en una casa, etc.

MODELO: *¡Ojalá que (yo) termine mis estudios pronto!*

1. _____

2. _____

3. _____

4. _____

5. _____

6. _____

IMPERFECT AND PLUPERFECT SUBJUNCTIVE AFTER *OJALÁ (QUE)*

The imperfect subjunctive and the pluperfect subjunctive can also follow *Ojalá (que)*. When followed by these tenses, *Ojalá (que)* is often translated as *I wish that* (or *Would that*).

When referring to something that is unlikely to happen in the present or future, the imperfect subjunctive follows *Ojalá (que)*.

¡Ojalá (que) pudiera ir al parque hoy (mañana)!
I wish (Would) that I could go to the park today (tomorrow)!
(but I am not able or I don't expect to be able to go)

When referring to something that did not happen in the past, the pluperfect subjunctive follows *Ojalá (que)*.

¡Ojalá (que) hubiera ido al parque!
I wish (Would) that I had gone to the park! (but I didn't)

Notice that:

* When the present subjunctive and the present perfect subjunctive are used with *Ojalá (que)*, your wishes may (or may not) come true
* When the imperfect subjunctive and the pluperfect subjunctive are used with *Ojalá (que)*, you already know that what you are wishing for is not true (or you don't expect it to come true)

EXERCISES

A. You had made some plans, but you are unlikely to carry them out today because the weather is horrible. Use *Ojalá que* and the imperfect subjunctive to express what you wish would happen.

> **MODELO:** yo/ir de compras
> *¡Ojalá que yo fuera de compras!*

1. mis amigos/visitarme

_____

2. haber mejores programas en la televisión

_____

3. el museo/estar abierto

_____

4. yo/tener un coche

_____

5. yo/tener ganas de leer

_____

6. mi amiga/venir a jugar conmigo

_____

7. mis amigos y yo/poder jugar al fútbol

_____

8. tú/traer un video de una buena película

_____

B. Orlando went to Puerto Rico for a week last year. He did not have time to do everything he wanted to do. Express what he wishes he would have done by using *Ojalá que* and the pluperfect subjunctive to express his ideas.

> **MODELO:** ir a Ponce
>
> *¡Ojalá que hubiera ido a Ponce!*

1. pasar más tiempo en El Yunque

_____

2. no quemarse tanto en el sol

_____

3. poder quedarse más tiempo en San Juan

_____

4. descubrir la playa de Luquillo cuando llegué

_____

5. hacer más amigos en Mayagüez

_____

6. ver los monumentos históricos

_____

7. leer la guía antes de salir de Nueva York

_____

8. aprender más español

_____

HYPOTHESIZING

Unit Five

LESSON 11
Speculating and Wondering (Part I)

PART A: Speculating and Wondering About the Present and Future

To wonder, speculate, or make conjectures about present and future actions, events, or situations, Spanish speakers use the future tense.

¿Estarán en casa Miguel y Guadalupe?
I wonder if Miguel and Guadalupe are at home.

Guadalupe estará en casa, pero Miguel estará en el gimnasio.
Guadalupe is probably home but Miguel is probably at the gym.

FUTURE TENSE OF REGULAR VERBS
The future of regular verbs of all three conjugations is formed by adding the endings -é, -ás, -á, -emos, -éis, -án to the infinitive.
For example:

TRABAJAR (TO WORK)		BEBER (TO DRINK)	
trabajaré	trabajaremos	beberé	beberemos
trabajarás	trabajaréis	beberás	beberéis
trabajará	trabajarán	beberá	beberán

ABRIR (TO OPEN)	
abriré	abriremos
abrirás	abriréis
abrirá	abrirán

Notice that:

- The future tense is always stressed on the ending;
- The *nosotros* form is the only form that does not carry an accent
- verbs that have an accent mark on the infinitive, lose that accent when the infinitive is used to form the future.

SONREÍR (TO SMILE)	
sonreiré	sonreiremos
sonreirás	sonreiréis
sonreirá	sonreirán

FUTURE TENSE OF IRREGULAR VERBS

The following verbs have irregular stems in the future:

INFINITIVE	STEM	ENDINGS FOR ALL CONJUGATIONS (-É, -ÁS, -Á, -EMOS, -ÉIS, -ÁN)
decir	dir-	diré, dirás, dirá, diremos, diréis, dirán
hacer	har-	haré, harás, hará, haremos, haréis, harán
poner	pondr-	pondré, pondrás, pondrá, pondremos, pondréis, pondrán
salir	saldr-	saldré, saldrás, saldrá, saldremos, saldréis, saldrán
valer	valdr-	valdré, valdrás, valdrá, valdremos, valdréis, valdrán
tener	tendr-	tendré, tendrás, tendrá, tendremos, tendréis, tendrán
venir	vendr-	vendré, vendrás, vendrá, vendremos, vendréis, vendrán
poder	podr-	podré, podrás, podrá, podremos, podréis, podrán
querer	querr-	querré, querrás, querrá, querremos, querréis, querrán
saber	sabr-	sabré, sabrás, sabrá, sabremos, sabréis, sabrán
caber	cabr-	cabré, cabrás, cabrá, cabremos, cabréis, cabrán

The future of *hay* (there is, there are) is also irregular: *habrá* (there will be).

Habrá mucha gente en el desfile.
There will (probably) be many people at the parade.

USING THE FUTURE TENSE TO EXPRESS FUTURE ACTIONS OR SITUATIONS

The future expresses future actions or situations and is translated as *will* or *shall*.

El almuerzo estará listo a la una. Almorzaremos en seguida.
Lunch will be ready at one. We will (shall) have lunch right away.

Remember, that in conversation it is common for Spanish speakers to use the construction *ir + a +* infinitive to talk about actions, events, or situations that are going to occur in the not too distant future. This construction is reviewed on page 108.

Vamos a ir a las montañas este verano.
We are going to go to the mountains this summer.

EXERCISES

A. Practice. A group of friends is moving to a new apartment. Complete the following sentences with the correct form of the verb in parentheses in the future tense. Then, substitute the underlined subject of the original sentence with the subjects in parentheses and make the necessary changes.

1. Los apartamentos en ese edificio _____ (valer) más de medio millón de dólares. (esos coches, el diamante)

2. Yo le _____ (decir) todo al dueño. (nosotros, ellas, tú)

3. ¿Dónde _____ (poner) nosotros la lámpara? (ella, Uds. yo)

4. Hugo _____ (venir) a ayudarme con la mudanza *(moving)*. (ellos, tú, Ud.)

5. Nosotros _____ (poder) tener plantas en todas las ventanas. (Ud., yo, ellos)

6. Todos mis amigos _____ (saber) la dirección pronto. (nosotros, tú, él)

7. Ellos _____ (querer) venir a mi primera cena. (ella, Uds., tú)

8. ¿_____ (Tener) tú una lavadora en el apartamento? (nosotros, él, ellos)

9. Yo _____ (hacer) todo lo posible por tener el apartamento siempre limpio. (ellas, tú, Ud.)

10. Tú _____ (salir) de compras todos los fines de semana en el nuevo vecindario. (yo, nosotros, Uds.)

11. Uds. _____ (decorar) este cuarto con antigüedades. (nosotros, Ud., yo)

12. Ella _____ (construir) algunos estantes en esta pared.
    (tú, Uds., yo)

B. Carolina is having a party. Read the following statements, then write a question or a statement to speculate or make a conjecture about what is probably happening or will happen. Use the information in parentheses in your statement or question.

> **MODELO:** Ya es hora del almuerzo. (ser las doce)
> *Serán las doce.*

1. Carolina cambió la hora de la fiesta. (Ignacio/no saberlo)

   _____

2. Ignacio no sabe a qué hora empieza la fiesta. (Carolina/decírselo mañana)

   _____

3. Carolina ha invitado a mucha gente. (haber muchas personas allí)

   _____

4. El tren no llega al pueblo de Tomás. (él/venir en autobús)

   _____

5. Julio no tiene coche. (él/caminar a la fiesta)

   _____

6. A Rosa no le gusta ir a las fiestas sola. (ella/llevar a un amigo)

   _____

7. El anillo *(ring)* que su novio le compró tiene muchos diamantes. (valer mucho)

   _____

8. El novio parece muy viejo. (él/tener . . . años)

   _____

C. Imagine that some of your friends invite you to a concert in the park. Answer the following questions truthfully.

1. ¿Irás con ellos?

_____

2. ¿Invitarás a alguien?

_____

3. ¿Te permitirán tus padres quedarte en casa de un(a) amigo(a)?

_____

4. ¿Harás tus quehaceres *(chores)* antes de salir de casa?

_____

5. ¿Qué ropa te pondrás?

_____

6. ¿Habrá varios grupos en el concierto?

_____

7. ¿Qué música tocarán?

_____

8. ¿Tendremos que llegar temprano?

_____

9. Tu novio(a), ¿podrá ir?

_____

10. ¿Manejarás al concierto?

_____

PART B: Talking About Actions, Events, or Situations, that Are Taking or Will Take Place if Certain Conditions Are Met

INDICATIVE IN *SI* CLAUSES

When stating that if certain conditions are met, the result will be that certain actions, events, or situations will also take place, Spanish speakers use one of the following constructions:

Si (If) + verb in the present tense + verb in the present
(or future) tense.
Or,
Verb in the present (or future) tense + *si* (if) + verb in the present tense.

In this type of condition the present indicative tense is used in both clauses to express the result of an assumption concerning the present.

Si Julia está en casa, lee el periódico.
If Julia is at home, she reads the newspaper.

The future tense is used in the main clause to express the result of an assumption concerning the future.

Comeremos mucho, si la comida está rica.
We will eat a lot, if the food is tasty.

Notice that:

- The order of the clauses does not matter; the following sentences mean the same thing:

Iremos a la playa, si no llueve.
We will go to the beach if it doesn't rain.

Si no llueve, iremos a la playa.
If it doesn't rain, we will go to the beach.

- If the main clause is in the present or future tense, the verb in the *si* clause is always in the present tense.

EXERCISES

A. What do you do when . . . ? Answer the following questions truthfully expressing what you usually do or what you will do if the following conditions are met.

MODELO: ¿Qué harás si tienes dinero?
Si tengo dinero, compraré un coche nuevo.

1. ¿A dónde irás si tienes tiempo?

_____

2. ¿Qué tipo *(kind)* de libros lees si no tienes mucho trabajo?

_____

3. Si tienes mucho trabajo el semestre próximo, ¿qué harás?

_____

4. ¿En qué actividades participas si quieres relajarte?

_____

5. Si hace mal tiempo durante las vacaciones, ¿cómo te sentirás?

_____

6. ¿Qué les dirás a tus amigos si no te llaman regularmente?

_____

7. Si tus maestros no son muy estrictos, ¿qué les pedirás?

_____

8. Si conoces a un(a) chico(a) que te gusta y quieres salir con él/ella, ¿qué haces?

_____

B. Nothing changes. Some people always do the same thing in certain situations. Read the following statements and then write a sentence expressing what they do under those conditions.

> **MODELO:** Tu hermano está cansado.
> *Si mi hermano está cansado, él duerme.*

1. Tu profesor(a) de inglés tiene hambre.

_____

2. Uno de tus amigos se siente muy triste.

_____

3. Tu mejor amigo no puede salir de su casa hoy.

_____

4. Hace mucho frío y nieva. (tu madre)

_____

5. Tus padres no quieren cocinar hoy.

_____

6. Tú y tus amigos reciben buenas notas.

_____

7. Van a servir comida hispana en la cafetería. (tus compañeros)

_____

8. Los estudiantes que salen mal van a tener que ir a la escuela durante el verano.

_____

LESSON 12
Expressing Restrictions About the Time, Purpose, or Other Aspects of an Action

PART A: Restricting the Time of an Action

INDICATIVE IN TIME CLAUSES

Spanish speakers use a number of conjunctions to express restrictions about the time an action, event, or situation takes place. Some common conjunctions that introduce time clauses are:

cuando—when	hasta que—until
después (de) que—after	mientras—while
en cuanto—as soon as	tan pronto como—as soon as

Cuando Gloria se cayó, se rompió la pierna.
When Gloria fell, she broke her leg.

The indicative is used in time clauses if the actions, events, or situations:

- Are stated as habitual

  En cuanto Guillermo entra a casa, él enciende el televisor.
  As soon as Guillermo enters the house, he turns on the TV.

- Have already taken place

  Te llamé, después de que Juan llegó.
  I called you, after Juan arrived.

Remember that when there is no change in the subject, *después de* and *hasta* are always followed by the infinitive.

Josefina corrió hasta llegar a casa.
Josefina ran until she got home.

Después de llegar a casa, me llamó.
After getting home, she called me.

EXERCISES

A. Ramón and his family missed their flight. They had to wait for the next flight and something unexpected happened. Complete his description with the correct form of the verb in parentheses in the preterite. Note that for the second sentence you will need the imperfect.

1. Cuando _____ (llegar) al aeropuerto el avión ya había salido.

2. Mientras nosotros _____ (esperar) el próximo vuelo, fuimos a almorzar.

3. Salimos corriendo tan pronto como _____ (anunciar—ellos) el vuelo.

4. En cuanto nosotros _____ (llegar) a la puerta de salida mi papá entregó las tarjetas de embarque.

5. Después de que nosotros _____ (entrar) en el avión mi mamá se dio cuenta de que no teníamos la cámara.

6. Tuvimos suerte. Pudimos decírselo al asistente de vuelo tan pronto como él _____ (venir).

7. El avión no pudo salir hasta que el asistente de vuelo _____ (volver) con la cámara.

8. Cuando él nos _____ (devolver) la cámara, nos pusimos muy contentos.

B. Complete the following phrases creatively with what normally occurs in the following situations.

1. Generalmente yo me divierto cuando . . .

2. Durante la semana yo me quedo en la escuela hasta que mis amigos . . .

3. Tan pronto como llega el fin de semana, mis amigos y yo . . .

4. Mis padres se enojan cuando yo . . .

5. Los sábados, yo llamo a mi mejor amigo(a) en cuanto yo . . .

6. Todas las mañanas yo leo el periódico mientras yo . . .

7. Cuando llegamos a la escuela nos quedamos en el patio hasta que los profesores . . .

8. A las doce y media mis amigos corren a la cafetería después de que la profesora . . .

SUBJUNCTIVE IN TIME CLAUSES

The following conjunctions can also be followed by the subjunctive:

cuando—when

después (de) que—after

en cuanto—as soon as

hasta que—until

mientras—while

tan pronto como—as soon as

> Te llamaré, después de que Juan llegue.
> I will call you, after Juan arrives.

> Tan pronto como terminemos la tarea, saldremos.
> As soon as we finish the homework, we will go out.

Notice that in the examples above none of the actions has taken place. In the first example the speaker intends to call you sometime in the future (when? after John arrives). However, John may or may not arrive. In the second example you intend to go out sometime in the future (when? as soon as you finish the homework). However, you may or may not finish the homework.

When the action of the main clause is to take place at a future time, the completion of the actions, events, or situations in the time clause is uncertain. Because of this uncertainty, the subjunctive is used in the time clause.

SUBJUNCTIVE AFTER *ANTES (DE) QUE*

Antes (de) que (before) always requires the subjunctive because the action it introduces is always future in relation to the action of the main verb.

> La cena estará lista antes de que Teresa regrese.
> Dinner will be ready before Teresa returns.

Remember that when there is no change in subject, *antes de* is always followed by the infinitive.

> Julio empezó a trabajar antes de graduarse.
> Julio began to work before graduating (before he graduated).

EXERCISES

A. One of Alfonso's friends is going away for a few weeks and has asked him to take care of her apartment. Complete the following sentences with the present subjunctive of the verb in parentheses to find out what Alfonso promises to do.

1. Iré al apartamento regularmente mientras tú _____ (estar) de vacaciones.

2. No voy a dar una fiesta en tu apartamento cuando tú _____ (irse).

3. Les echaré agua a las plantas antes de que _____ (morirse).

4. Tan pronto como alguien te _____ (escribir), te enviaré la carta.

5. En cuanto yo _____ (recibir) la cuenta del alquiler *(rent),* la pagaré.

6. Me quedaré con el perro hasta que _____ (comerse) toda la comida.

7. Llámame después de que tú _____ (saber) la fecha de tu regreso.

8. Limpiaré el apartamento antes de que tú _____ (regresar).

B. Libertad is going to get her driver's license. She makes statements as to what she will do. Complete the following sentences with the correct form of the verb in parentheses.

1. Mi padre seguirá dándome clases hasta que yo _____ (recibir) la licencia.

2. Mis amigos se alegrarán mucho cuando yo la _____ (obtener).

3. Yo llevaré a mis amigos a la escuela en cuanto yo _____ (empezar) a ir a la escuela en coche.

4. Yo te podré ir a buscar tan pronto como yo _____ (acostumbrarse) a conducir de noche.

5. Mis hermanos y yo podremos dormir más tarde, después de que yo _____ (aprender) el camino más rápido para llegar a la escuela.

6. Mi madre irá de compras conmigo cuando yo la _____ (poder) llevar.

7. Yo conduciré con cuidado mientras _____ (conducir) de noche.

8. Tendremos que tomar el metro hasta que mis padres me _____ (permitir) conducir.

PART B: Expressing Proviso or Restrictions of an Action

SUBJUNCTIVE AFTER CONJUNCTIONS THAT ESTABLISH A PROVISO OR RESTRICTION

Certain conjunctions introduce clauses that establish a proviso or restriction of an action. Since the actions, events, or situations that these conjunctions introduce may not take place, they are always followed by the subjunctive. Some common conjunctions of this type are:

a menos que—unless   sin que—without

con tal (de) que—provided that   en caso de que—in case

Julia no nadará a menos que tú nades también.
Julia won't swim unless you swim also.

El profesor siempre entra en la clase sin que nosotros lo veamos.
The teacher always enters the class without our seeing him.

Remember that the infinitive is used after the preposition *sin* when there is no change in subject.

Nunca salgo sin cerrar la puerta con llave.
I never go out without locking the door.

EXERCISES

A. José Antonio's friends talk about him and the activities of his football team. Complete the statements with the present subjunctive of the verb in parentheses.

1. José Antonio no jugará en el partido a menos que el otro equipo _____ (perder).

2. El equipo jugará bien con tal de que ellos _____ (estar) listos.

3. No podremos ganar a menos que nosotros _____ (tener) un plan.

4. Debes descansar hoy en caso de que tú _____ (tener) que jugar mañana.

5. El equipo no empieza a jugar sin que todos los jugadores _____ (ponerse) el casco *(helmet)*.

6. Iremos al partido con tal de que las entradas no _____ (costar) mucho.

B. At times you may not do the work you should for school. In those cases, what happens? Complete the sentences logically using the correct form of one of the following verbs or expressions.

enojarse/planear/tener una buena excusa/darnos una extensión

1. Si no tengo la tarea, hablo con el/la profesor(a) en caso de que él/ella . . .

2. Mis padres no le escriben una carta al/a la profesor(a) a menos que yo . . .

3. Todos los profesores nos dan consejos *(advice)* con tal de que nosotros . . .

4. De vez en cuando nosotros podemos entregar *(hand in)* el trabajo sin que los profesores . . .

C. You and your friend are going to the movies, but, before you go, you tell him that there are certain things that he must keep in mind. Complete the phrases using your imagination.

1. Iré contigo con tal de que tú . . .

2. No debes salir de tu casa sin que tus padres . . .

3. Por favor, llega temprano en caso de que la película . . .

4. Me encontraré contigo a las dos a menos que . . .

PART C: Expressing the Purpose or Intention of an Action

SUBJUNCTIVE AFTER CONJUNCTIONS THAT EXPRESS THE PURPOSE OR INTENTION OF AN ACTION

Common conjuctions that introduce clauses that express the purpose or intention of an action are:

a fin de que—in order that	de manera que—so as, so that
para que—in order that	de modo que—so as, so that

A fin de que and *para que* are always followed by the subjunctive. Regardless of its purpose or intention, the outcome of an action is always uncertain.

Mi madre cocina para que (a fin de que) yo coma.
My mother cooks so that I will eat. (in spite of her efforts, I may or may not eat)

Remember that when there is no change in subject, the preposition *para* is always followed by the infinitive.

Nosotros escuchamos la radio para saber las noticias.
We listen to the radio (in order) to know the news.

De modo que (so that) and *de manera que* (so that) are followed by:

• The subjunctive when they express a purpose or intention

Escribe con cuidado de modo (de manera) que entendamos.
Write carefully so that we will understand. (in spite of your efforts we may not understand)

• The indicative when they express the result of an action

Rita escribió con cuidado de modo (de manera) que entendimos.
Rita wrote carefully so we understood. (the result of their efforts was that we understood)

EXERCISES

A. The students in Marco's school seem to be unhappy about the social life they have. Choose a logical ending to the sentences from the following list. Remember to use the correct form of the verb.

> conocer a otra gente/sentirse más unidos/venir más personas/
> divertirse juntos/entusiasmarse a venir/
> apoyar a nuestros compañeros

> **MODELO:** haber más variedad de personas
> Debemos asistir a las funciones teatrales de modo que . . .
> *Debemos asistir a las funciones teatrales de modo que*
> *haya más variedad de personas.*

1. Nosotros debemos tener más fiestas a fin de que todos los alumnos . . .

2. Vamos a invitar a los chicos de otras escuelas de manera que . . .

3. Yo le voy a pedir a los profesores que apoyen *(support)* nuestro club para que . . .

4. Todos tenemos que ir a los partidos de fútbol de modo que . . .

5. La entrada a los bailes tiene que ser barata a fin de que . . .

6. Cada estudiante traerá a un amigo o amiga de manera que . . .

B. It pays to be organized. Eduardo is very organized because he always likes to be prepared. Complete the statements he makes with a phrase from the list below.

> no mojarme/no tener que hacerlo durante la semana/
> salir temprano de mi casa/no olvidarse de nada/
> estar preparado para la lluvia/tener el fin de semana libre/
> tener que apresurarme/tener que hacerlo por la mañana

1. Antes de acostarme mi padre pone el despertador *(alarm clock)* para que por la mañana yo . . .

2. En la escuela, yo escribo todas mis tareas en el calendario de modo que mis amigos y yo . . .

3. Si parece que va a llover mi hermano pone el paraguas en mi mochila a fin de que yo . . .

4. Durante los fines de semana mis amigos me ayudan a limpiar mi cuarto de manera que yo . . .

5. Los viernes yo termino todas mis tareas para . . .

6. Anoche mi madre dejó toda mi ropa lista de modo que hoy yo . . .

PART D: Expressing Certainty or Uncertainty

SUBJUNCTIVE VS. INDICATIVE WITH *AUNQUE*

When *aunque* is followed by the subjunctive, it means *even if* and expresses doubt or uncertainty about whether an action, event, or situation is going to happen.

> Aunque consiga el apartamento, no me mudaré este mes.
> Even if I get the apartment (but I doubt it), I will not move this month.

When *aunque* is followed by the indicative, it means *even though* or *although* and presents an action, event, or situation as an established fact.

> Aunque conseguí el apartamento, no voy a mudarme este mes.
> Even though I got the apartment, I am not going to move this month.

EXERCISES

A. Diana has very strong convinctions and there are certain things she will never do. Choose the correct verb in parentheses to complete the statements Diana makes.

1. Nunca viviré en una ciudad grande aunque (me regalan/me regalen) un apartamento.

2. Aunque me (gano/gane) la lotería no contribuiré a las campañas políticas.

3. Me gustaría ahorrar dinero, pero nunca iré a esa tienda aunque (venden/vendan) las cosas muy baratas.

4. Aunque (hablo/hable) español, no me siento cómoda al hablar con hispanohablantes.

5. No le permito a Juan hablar mal de otra gente aunque él (sea/es) mi amigo.

B. Complete the following sentences according to your personal experience.

1. El año próximo iré a México aunque yo . . .

2. Mis padres comprarán un coche aunque ellos . . .

3. El/La profesor(a) de español se enfadará aunque nosotros . . .

4. Tú vas a tener mucho éxito en la vida aunque tú . . .

5. Yo voy al supermercado aunque mi madre . . .

6. Aunque Uds . . . , siempre van a tener muchos amigos.

LESSON 13
Speculating and Wondering (Part II)

PART A: Speculating and Wondering About the Past

CONDITIONAL TENSE

On page 215 you reviewed the use of the future tense to speculate and wonder about the present and the future. To speculate or wonder about past actions, events, or situations, Spanish speakers use the conditional tense.

> Llevaría su vestido rojo ayer.
> She probably wore her red dress yesterday.

> ¿Iría Elena a la fiesta anoche?
> I wonder if Elena went to the party last night.

Notice that in both of the examples above, the point of reference is in the past.

The conditional tense of regular verbs of all three conjugations is formed by adding the endings *-ía, -ías, -ía, -íamos, -íais, -ían* to the infinitive.

For example:

TRABAJAR (TO WORK)	
trabajaría	trabajaríamos
trabajarías	trabajaríais
trabajaría	trabajarían

BEBER (TO DRINK)	
bebería	beberíamos
beberías	beberíais
bebería	beberían

ABRIR (TO OPEN)	
abriría	abriríamos
abrirías	abriríais
abriría	abrirían

Notice that:

- The endings of the conditional tense always have an accent

- The stem of the conditional tense is the same as the stem of the future tense

INFINITIVE	FUTURE	CONDITIONAL
ir	yo iré	yo iría
saber	tú sabrás	tú sabrías
poner	ellos pondrán	ellos pondrían
haber	habrá	habría

- Verbs that have an accent mark on the infinitive, lose that accent when the infinitive is used to form the conditional

SONREÍR (TO SMILE)	
sonreiría	sonreiríamos
sonreirías	sonreiríais
sonreiría	sonreirían

OTHER USES OF THE CONDITIONAL TENSE

The conditional is:

- Often translated by *would*

  Sería una locura salir tan tarde.
  It would be crazy to go out so late.

  Tomás dijo que me escribiría.
  Tomás said that he would write to me.

- Used with verbs such as *gustar, poder, deber* to soften statements or to make polite requests

  Me gustaría ir con Uds.
  I would like to go with you.

  ¿Podrías hacerlo esta tarde?
  Could (Would) you do it this afternoon?

  Uds. deberían llamar por teléfono.
  You should call.

EXERCISES

A. Do you remember the stem of verbs that are irregular in the future tense? Complete the following list of irregular stems. Check your answers by looking at p. 216 (irregular roots of the future tense). Then, using those stems write the conditional tense for the person given in the right column.

INFINITIVE	STEM	CONDITIONAL ENDINGS FOR ALL CONJUGATIONS (ÍA, -ÍAS, -ÍA, -ÍAMOS, -ÍAIS, -ÍAN)	
1. decir	_____	ellas	_____
2. hacer	_____	Uds.	_____
3. poder	_____	tú	_____
4. poner	_____	nosotros	_____
5. querer	_____	él	_____
6. saber	_____	ella	_____
7. salir	_____	nosotras	_____
8. tener	_____	yo	_____
9. valer	_____	ellos	_____
10. venir	_____	Uds.	_____
11. caber	_____	tú	_____

B. Practice. Antonio's teacher asked for some help in arranging the classroom. Complete what Antonio and his classmates say with the correct form of the verb in parentheses in the conditional tense. Then, substitute the underlined subject of the original sentence with the subjects in parentheses and make the necessary changes.

1. Le prometí que <u>nosotros</u> _____ (hacer) todo el trabajo. (él, Uds., yo)

2. Me dijo que <u>él</u> _____ (poner) todos los libros en orden. (nosotros, ellas, tú)

3. El expresó satisfacción porque <u>nosotros</u> _____ (poder) ayudarlo. (yo, Ud., tú)

4. Le dijimos que <u>él</u> _____ (estar) muy contento con nuestro trabajo. (yo, tú, ellos)

5. ¿Qué le _____ (decir) <u>tú</u> a los otros estudiantes? (Uds., yo, él)

C. One of your friends is very sad because he is going away for the summer and is afraid he is going to miss his friends. Complete the sentences with the conditional of the verb in parentheses stating what you and other friends would do to cheer him up.

1. Nosotros le _____ (escribir) regularmente.

2. Yo lo _____ (llamar) de vez en cuando.

3. Tú lo _____ (visitar) por lo menos una vez.

4. Paco y Graciela le _____ (enviar) sus pasteles favoritos.

5. Su novia le _____ (dar) una foto de ella.

6. Nosotros le _____ (decir) todas las noticias.

D. Some of your friends are expressing their wishes, but they sound very demanding. Soften their requests by using *gustar, poder,* or *querer* in the conditional to express their wishes in a more polite way.

> **MODELO:**   ¡Dame una taza de café!
>
>   *¿Podrías darme una taza de café?* Or,
>
>   *Me gustaría beber una taza de café.* Or,
>
>   *Quisiera una taza de café, por favor.*

1. Antonio quiere ir a la heladería.

2. Yo quiero comprar un disco compacto.

3. Nosotros queremos dar un paseo.

4. Tú quieres correr en el parque.

5. Uds. quieren patinar en el hielo.

6. ¡Dame tu radio!

PART B: Talking About Actions, Events, or Situations that Would Take Place if Certain Conditions Were Met

CONTRARY-TO-FACT SENTENCES

One of the most important uses of the conditional tense is to express what would (or would not) happen, if something else were to (or not to) happen. For example:

What would happen in the following hypothetical situations?

- If it were to snow in Puerto Rico? All traffic would be paralyzed.

- If you were to grow three inches overnight? Your clothes would not fit.

This type of sentence is called a contrary-to-fact condition because the *if* clause states something that is not a fact and is not likely to become a fact in the future. In contrary-to-fact conditions, Spanish speakers use:

- The imperfect subjunctive in the *if* clause, i.e.,

  Si nevara en Puerto Rico, . . .
  If it were to snow in Puerto Rico, . . .

  Si yo creciera tres pulgadas esta noche, . . .
  If I were to grow three inches tonight, . . .

- The conditional in the *result* clause, i.e.,

  . . . , el tránsito se paralizaría.
  . . . , the traffic would be paralyzed.

  . . . , la ropa no me quedaría bien.
  . . . , my clothes would not fit me.

Note that the order of the clauses is not important; the following sentences mean the same thing:

Si fuera verano, nadaría en el mar. = Nadaría en el mar si fuera verano.
If it were summer, I would swim in the ocean. = I would swim in the ocean, if it were summer.

EXERCISES

A. What would you or the following people do? Use the phrases below to write contrary to fact statements.

  MODELO: estar enfermo/quedarse en casa
  Si estuviera enfermo, me quedaría en casa.

  1. ella/ser el presidente/destruir las armas nucleares

  _____

2. tú/querer ser médico(a)/ir a la universidad

   _____

3. mi amigo/poder comprar un disco compacto/comprar el de Janet Jackson

   _____

4. mi madre/tener la oportunidad de conocer a alguien famoso/conocer a Mel Gibson

   _____

5. ellos/ser profesores/nunca dar tarea

   _____

6. Uds./no tener una computadora/volverse locos(as)

   _____

7. nosotros/no mirar tanto la televisión/salir mejor en las clases

   _____

8. ellos/ganar más dinero/poder enviar a su hijo a una universidad mejor

   _____

9. Ud./conducir en las calles de Nueva York/ponerse muy nervioso

   _____

10. tú/ir al gimnasio regularmente/sentirse mejor

   _____

B. Now it is your turn to express what you would do if certain conditions were met. Be creative and use your imagination!

> **MODELO:** ser alcalde *(mayor)*
> *Si yo fuera alcalde, construiría más casas.*

1. ser profesor

_____

2. poder conocer a alguien famoso

_____

3. saber hablar ruso

_____

4. tener un(a) hijo(a)

_____

5. vivir en Alaska

_____

6. ser abogado(a)

_____

7. ser un actor o actriz famoso(a)

_____

8. poder vivir por doscientos años

_____

C. Think of your best friend and read the statements above. Would he or she do anything differently? Give a response for each of the situations.

> **MODELO:** *Si mi amigo(a) fuera alcalde/alcaldesa, él/ella pondría más policías en las calles.*

1. _____

2. _____

3. _____

4. _____

5. _____

6. _____

7. _____

8. _____

PART C: Talking About Hypothetical Actions, Events, or Situations

SUBJUNCTIVE WITH *COMO SI*

The expression *como si* (meaning, *as if*) always refers to actions, events, or situations that are not part of reality. This expression must always be followed by the imperfect subjunctive or the pluperfect subjunctive.

This is an example of the imperfect subjunctive:

Fernando toca el piano como si practicara mucho.
Fernando plays the piano as if he practiced a lot. (but he doesn't)

This is an example of the pluperfect subjunctive:

Fernando toca el piano como si hubiera practicado mucho.
Fernando plays the piano as if he had practiced a lot. (but he didn't)

EXERCISES

A. How do the following people act? Use the expression *como si* and the words and expressions below to express how these people act. Use the imperfect subjunctive.

> **MODELO:** Ella/gastar/ganar mucho dinero
>
> *Ella gasta como si ganara mucho dinero.*

1. Eduardo/ayudar a los pobres/ser rico

_____

2. tú/cantar opera/tener entrenamiento *(training)*

_____

3. Yolanda y Benito/caminar por la calle/conocer a todo el mundo

_____

4. esos chicos/comer/estar a dieta

_____

5. Adelaida/correr/huir de alguien

_____

6. Gilberto/hablar/saber lo que dice

_____

7. Nosotros/actuar/llegar a la clase a tiempo siempre

_____

8. yo/esperar al cartero/recibir cartas todos los días

_____

B. Things are not always what they seem. The following people act as if something had happened that didn't really happen.

> **MODELO:** hablar español/vivir en España
> _Julio habla español como si hubiera vivido en España._

1. Carlos/comer/no comer en meses

_____

2. La Sra. Franco/gastar/ganar la lotería

_____

3. Los niños/gritar/ver un fantasma

_____

4. yo/estar cansado/correr cuarenta millas

_____

5. Uds./recomendar remedios _(remedies)_/estudiar medicina

_____

6. nosotros/saber lo que pasa en la novela/leerla

_____

7. tú/caminar/romperse una pierna

_____

8. Salvador/reírse/oír un chiste muy cómico

_____

LESSON 14
Describing People, Places, and Things

SUBJUNCTIVE VS. INDICATIVE IN ADJECTIVE CLAUSES

On page 33 you reviewed the use of adjectives to describe nouns and pronouns.

Buscan una computadora **rápida.**
They are looking for a **fast** computer.

It is also possible to describe a noun or a pronoun by using a group of words that includes a conjugated verb.

Ellos buscan una computadora **que funcione rápidamente.**
They are looking for a computer **that works fast.**

A group of words that describes a noun or a pronoun is called an adjective clause. Adjective clauses are usually introduced by *que* (meaning *that, which, who,* or *whom*).

La profesora necesita a alguien **que la ayude.**
The teacher needs someone **who will help her.**

Necesito un libro **que no sea muy difícil.**
I need a book **that is not too difficult.**

Spanish speakers use the subjunctive in an adjective clause when the clause describes a person or thing that:

* The speaker is not sure exists (such as in the examples above)
* The speaker does not believe exists (considers nonexistent)

No conozco a nadie que pueda ir.
I do not know anyone who can go.

No tienen ningún libro que me interese.
They do not have any book that interests me.

Keep in mind that when the adjective clause is describing a person or thing whose existence is known to the speaker, the verb in the adjective clause is in the indicative. Notice the use of the indicative or the subjunctive in the following sentences.

Buscamos un hotel que no sea muy caro.
We are looking for a hotel that is not very expensive. (we are not sure it exists)

Buscamos el hotel que no es muy caro.
We are looking for the hotel that is not very expensive. (we know it exists)

Note that:

- The personal *a* is used in adjective clauses to refer to a specific person [and with *alguien, nadie, alguno (-a, -os, -as), ninguno (-a)*], but it is not used to refer to a person whose existence is uncertain

  ¿Buscas a alguien?
  Are you looking for someone?

  Busco a la chica que escribió el ensayo.
  I am looking for the girl who wrote the essay.

  Busco una chica que escriba el ensayo.
  I am looking for a girl to write the essay.

  ¿Hay un alumno que pueda escribir el ensayo?
  Is there someone who can write the essay?

- After prepositions (especially *a, con, de,* and *en*), Spanish speakers use *quien (quienes)* instead of *que* to refer to people

  ¿Conoces a la chica con quien llegó Marcos?
  Do you know the girl with whom Marcos arrived?

EXERCISES

A. The Sánchez family is looking for a school for their son Enrique. It is very frustrating and they need help. Complete their description with the present subjunctive of the verb in parentheses.

1. Buscamos una escuela que _____ (estar) cerca de la casa y que _____ (tener) buenos profesores.

2. Su madre prefiere una escuela donde Enrique _____ (practicar) varios deportes y _____ (aprender) francés.

3. Enrique necesita un lugar que no _____ (ser) demasiado estricto.

4. Quieren hablar con algunos padres que _____ (enviar) a sus hijos a una escuela buena.

5. Ellos necesitan enviar a Enrique a un lugar donde él _____ (sentirse) cómodo.

6. ¿Hay alguien que _____ (conocer) una buena escuela?

7. No conozco a nadie que _____ (saber) cuánto cuesta esa escuela.

8. No hay nadie que _____ (querer) ayudarnos.

B. While in the employment agency you hear several people talking. Tell your friend what they are saying by expressing the following sentences in Spanish.

1. I need a job that pays well.

_____

2. He is looking for somebody in the company who is called Mr. Miró.

_____

3. We need to work in an office that has many windows.

_____

4. They are looking for someone who can use the computer.

_____

5. We are looking for a boss who is not too demanding *(exigente)*.

_____

Unit Six

SITUATIONS FOR WRITING

The following situations are designed to give you further practice in writing after certain lessons. They have been divided into four sections, so that you can do them at any time after having studied and reviewed the material that appears in those lessons.

SITUATIONS I
(After Lesson 2)

When doing the following exercises, you may want to go to the Appendix section of the book and review the thematic vocabulary that pertains to a given situation.

1. Imagine that you want to write an ad for a youth magazine asking for pen pals who may want to correspond with you. In your ad include your age, nationality, address, some of your physical characteristics, personality, likes and dislikes, and interests. Don't forget to mention the type of person with whom you would like to correspond.

2. Write a paragraph in which you describe the physical characteristics of your favorite actor or actress. Explain why you like him or her. Then, compare him/her to an actor or actress you do not like as much.

3. Write a paragraph in which you describe the characteristics you look for in a friend. Describe his/her character, personality, likes, dislikes, and interests.

4. Write a note to your friend in Mexico and describe your house/apartment. In your description give your address and include the number of rooms, some of the furnishings, your favorite room, etc.

5. Your pen pal wants to know more about your family. Write him/her a note and describe your family. Include all the members and tell their age, relationship to you, height, weight, color of hair, color of eyes, facial features, etc.

6. Describe your favorite family member. Include his/her relationship to you, occupation, character, personality, likes, dislikes, and interests. Compare him/her to another member of your family.

7. Imagine that you can decide what your neighborhood should look like. Describe what it is going to look like. Include a description of the stores, living facilities, recreational facilities, etc. Then compare this "ideal" neighborhood to the one in which you live.

8. You have been asked by the school newspaper to express your opinion about living in the city vs. living in the country. Write a paragraph explaining which of the two you like better and explain why. Make sure that you compare the two places.

9. Describe your last visit to a restaurant. State what type of restaurant it is and describe it, including the food, the service, etc. Also explain whether you would like to go back and why. Compare this restaurant to another one you know well.

10. Your friend asks you what you would like to be when you finish school. Choose the occupation or profession you think is the best, then compare it with the profession that you consider to be the worst, and tell why you would like to have the best profession.

SITUATIONS II
(After Lesson 4)

When doing the following exercises, you may want to go to the Appendix section of the book and review the thematic vocabulary that pertains to a given situation.

1. Choose a hero or heroine you admire. Write a paragraph telling everything you know about him or her. In your description include his/her nationality, occupation, personality, his or her interests, and why you consider him/her a person to be admired.

2. You broke your friend's radio. You are very upset because he/she liked the radio very much. Write him/her a note explaining what happened and apologizing to him/her.

3. Write a note to your teacher explaining why you did not do the homework last night. Explain to him/her that you did not have time to do it because of your responsibilities at home. Be specific.

4. One of your pen pals has asked you about the recreational activities in your community. Write him/her a note describing the activities that are available and tell him/her in which activities you participate.

5. A newspaper in Mexico is doing a survey about the eating habits of American teenagers. Write a paragraph describing what you ate yesterday in as much detail as possible.

6. Write a letter to your Mexican friend in San Antonio explaining what you like to do to relax and have fun in school and at home. You may want to include the people with whom you do these activities.

7. One of your friends wants to know about the things you fear. Imagine that the last time you were really frightened was during a storm. Describe the stormy weather you experienced and tell why you were afraid.

8. Write a paragraph describing the meals in your house, include who prepares them, why that person is the one who prepares them, and if you like them.

9. You are in school and you are supposed to meet a friend later in the day. You become sick and have to go home. Leave a note for your friend explaining what is wrong with you and why you had to leave. Apologize to him/her.

10. Describe your last visit to your doctor. Include a description of your doctor and the reason why you visited him/her in as much detail as possible.

11. Write a list of the things that could go wrong if you are not careful when practicing sports.

12. While in the park one of your friends has an accident. Describe the events surrounding the accident and tell what you would do to make him/her feel better.

13. Many people enjoy going shopping; others do not. Write a note to a friend explaining whether or not you like to go shopping. To emphasize your point of view, include a description of your last shopping trip.

14. Last night you heard a very interesting news item. Write a note to your friend in Chile telling him/her what you heard.

15. Your school has a sister school in Los Angeles. You and your friends write to the students there about things that interest you. The discussion lately has been about changes taking place in the world. Write a note to your pen pal about an important event that took place in the last year and why you consider it to be an important world event.

SITUATIONS III
(After Lesson 10)

When doing the following exercises, you may want to go to the Appendix section of the book and review the thematic vocabulary that pertains to a given situation.

1. You are organizing a student election. Write a list of recommendations to your classmates telling them what you want them to do. Use the list of verbs to express your ideas.

aconsejar que	exigir que	preferir que
sugerir que	recomendar que	esperar que

2. You have ordered an article of clothing from a catalogue and you want to return it. Write a note to the company explaining why. Here are some verbs and expressions you may want to use in your note.

dudar que	no pensar que	puede ser que
es probable que	es extraño que	no creer que

3. A friend has lost his/her wallet. Write him/her a note expressing your regrets. Tell him/her what to do. You may want to use some of the following expressions in your note.

es obvio que	es bueno que	es malo que
estar triste de que	sentir que	estar enojado(a) de que
es importante que	recomendar que	

4. Imagine that you have to write a paragraph about the future of the world, but you are a bit pessimistic about it. Use at least three of the following expressions to express your doubts, skepticism, etc.

no creer que	es imposible que	dudar que
no estar seguro de que	es posible que	negar que

5. Your younger friend is beginning ninth grade and asks your advice about high school. Write him/her a note telling him/her some of the things he/she must do and some of the things he/she must not do. Use the familiar command in your note.

6. One of your friends writes to you because he is not getting along with a friend. Write him a note giving him some advice. You may want to use some of the following expressions in your note.

es aconsejable que   es necesario que   es importante que

es mejor que   es preferible que

7. Your friend has very little time for fun activities. Obviously he/she is having problems with time management. Use the following expressions to write a note telling him/her some of your feelings and giving him/her some advice.

querer que . . .   es necesario que . . .   es aconsejable que . . .

no creer que . . .   es cierto que . . .   tener miedo de que . . .

es dudoso que . . .

8. Write a letter to the mayor of your town or city explaining why, in your opinion, it is necessary to have more police on the streets. You may want to use some of the following expressions in your letter.

es importante que   dudar que   es cierto que

rogar que   esperar que   recomendar que

9. A friend is staying with you and you need to go out. Leave him/her a note stating all the things you would like him/her to do. Use familiar commands. For example: Haz la cama, etc.

10. A friend writes to you saying that he is going to visit Mexico. Use *Ojalá que* + the present subjunctive to express your wishes and desires for the success of his trip.

11. You invited some friends to the movies but the film you saw was not very good. Write a note apologizing. Use the expression *Ojalá que* + the pluperfect subjunctive at least four times in your note.

12. One of your friends had planned to go to a party but did not make it because he/she had problems at the last minute. Write him/her a note expressing your feelings about his/her absence from the party.

13. Write a note to your friend telling him/her that you regret not being able to attend an event he/she is organizing because you have other commitments. You may want to use some of the following expressions in your note.

Siento que . . . , Dudo que . . . , Es posible que . . .

SITUATIONS IV
(After Lesson 14)

When doing the following exercises, you may want to go to the Appendix section of the book and review the thematic vocabulary that pertains to a given situation.

1. Unfortunately, you have had a bad experience with a friend. Write a paragraph explaining how you would do things differently the next time you have problems with a friend. Use at least five contrary-to-fact statements in your paragraph. You may want to go to p. 237 to review the grammar point you will need to write your paragraph.

2. One of your friends has written you because he/she has heard that the weather has been very bad in your area and the winter promises to be very harsh this year. Write him/her a note telling him/her what you and your parents are planning to do to prepare yourselves. Use at least three of the following expressions in your note.

   de modo que/de manera que/para que/
   en caso de que/con tal de que

3. Imagine that you have graduated from high school. Write a paragraph explaining how your life will be different. Use the future tense in your response.

4. Next weekend your family is planning a big celebration that will be attended by many of your relatives. You know them very well and can tell how they will behave at the party. Write a note to a friend telling him/her what you are sure will happen.

5. One of your friends has a cold. Write him/her a note of advice, using some of your personal experiences. Use at least three of the following expressions in your note.

   cuando/después de que/en cuanto/hasta que/
   mientras/tan pronto como

6. You are very busy all the time, and yearn for the time when you will be able to do all the things you want to do. Write a note to a friend telling him/her what you would do if you had the time.

7. One of your friends is planning to stay in your apartment/house while you and your family are on vacation. Write him/her a note telling what he/she should or should not do while you are away. Use at least four of the following expressions and the subjunctive in your note.

   antes de que/cuando/después de que/en cuanto/hasta que/ mientras/tan pronto como

8. Before you agree to tutor one of your classmates, you need to tell him/her certain things that you expect. Use the following expressions to write him/her a note about your expectations.

   a menos que/con tal de que/sin que/en caso de que

9. What would you do? Write a note expressing what you would do if you were to win a scholarship *(una beca)* to attend your favorite university. Use the conditional tense to express your ideas.

10. As part of Career Day at your school you have been asked to write a paragraph about your ideal job. Write a paragraph explaining what you are looking for in an ideal job.

PREPARING FOR THE NEW YORK STATE REGENTS EXAMINATION

INTRODUCTION

Description of the Regents Examination

The Regents Comprehensive Examination in Spanish is designed to measure what you are able to do using Spanish in a real-world context. The exam tests your proficiency in all four skills:

- Speaking—through face to face social interactions
- Listening comprehension—through audio texts of social interactions
- Reading comprehension—through short narratives, ads, brochures, and other printed media
- Writing—through short guided compositions, notes, and letters, and short stories based on a drawing

In the speaking and writing section of the Regents you will be expected to use Spanish to:

- Socialize
- Provide and obtain information
- Express personal feelings
- Give advice and commands

LEARNING FOR THE REGENTS

Regardless of whether you are listening, speaking, reading, or writing, you will be able to do it better if you build your vocabulary and improve your accuracy in Spanish.

The vocabulary and structures that you need to perform one function will overlap with those needed to perform another function (i.e. when you are socializing you often ask and answer questions). However, since your goal is to use Spanish creatively and spontaneously to communicate, both the grammar and the vocabulary in this book are grouped in a way that will help you to express your ideas as accurately as possible.

VOCABULARY

A large vocabulary will help you to understand and express ideas. It is much easier to learn words when they are used in context and practiced often. You should try to read in Spanish as much as possible. Pick up a newspaper or magazine from your local store. Lists of words that are organized in a logical way are easier to remember. To help you increase your vocabulary, you will find vocabulary lists of many types throughout this book:

- Lists of idioms formed with certain verbs
- Words and idioms for a specific situation
- Lists of words with a specific function (i.e. connecting words)
- Lists of problem words (i.e. jugar/tocar)
- Lists of deceptive cognates (i.e. *lectura* means *reading,* not *lecture*)

Start building your vocabulary today. But remember that the maxim "Use it or lose it" applies to vocabulary as much as to anything else. Whenever you encounter a word that you think will be useful to express your ideas, incorporate it into your expression.

GRAMMAR

In this book you will review most of the grammar you have been exposed to in the first two levels and study some new structures. We will concentrate only on those grammar points that are particularly useful in making your speaking and writing comprehensible and appropriate for your level. You have probably mastered some of the points we will be reviewing. Nevertheless, it will be helpful to test yourself by completing the practice exercises.

PART 1
Speaking

The speaking part of the Regents Comprehensive Examination in Spanish consists of two communication tasks that you will perform with your teacher. Each task prescribes a simulated conversation in which you will always be yourself and your teacher will play whatever role is indicated in the task. In each task you may be asked to perform one or more of the following:

- Socialize
- Provide and obtain information
- Express personal feelings or opinions
- Get others to adopt a course of action

Each task consists of a brief statement in English that indicates:

- The situation
- The role the teacher will play
- Which of you is to initiate the conversation

Sample task:

(Student initiates) We are making plans to go to the movies this weekend. You start the conversation.

Hints for Speaking Tasks

Make sure you understand the situation before the conversation begins (you can ask questions in English to clarify any doubts). Once the conversation begins, you will not be able to do so.

It is the responsibility of your teacher to:

- Keep you on task
- Ensure the continuity of the conversation
- Bring the conversation to a natural conclusion

It is your responsibility to:

- Provide evidence of your ability to initiate and sustain a conversation
- Respond in a comprehensible and appropriate manner

You should find a way to accomplish the task in whichever way you find appropriate. You are not expected to know how to express everything, but rather to "get around" what you do not know in a way that can be understood by someone who does not speak English. It is appropriate to say more than one sentence at a time and it is often appropriate to include a question. However, certain things that appear in natural conversation will be disregarded in the evaluation. Some of these are:

- Yes/no responses
- Restatements of all or essential parts of what the teacher has said
- Proper names used in isolation
- Socializing devices (i.e. "Hola," "¿Cómo está Ud.?"). These may serve to initiate a conversation but do not receive credit.

It is also important to listen to your teacher carefully. By doing so you may pick up words and verb tenses that you will be able to use in your responses and questions without repeating directly what the teacher has said.

Practice

As with any other type of skill, practice improves oral proficiency.

The practice section that follows is divided into four categories according to the purpose for the communication (socializing, providing and receiving information, expressing personal feelings and opinions, getting others to adopt a course of action).

Use the situations to practice with a friend. You should take turns playing each role, but remember that on the exam you will only "play" yourself.

Socializing

- I am a patient in the waiting room of the dentist's office. While we are waiting for our turn you start to talk to me. You start the conversation
- I am your friend. You have just moved into a new house and have to arrange your room. We talk about what you are planning to do. You start the conversation
- I am a new student at the school. You see me sitting by myself and come over to talk to me. You start the conversation
- I am an airline flight attendant and you are on your first flight abroad. You call me over to talk to me. I will start the conversation
- I am your friend. We meet after school to discuss our weekend plans. I will start the conversation
- I am your friend. It is the first day after a long vacation and we have not spoken since school ended. You start the conversation
- I am your parent. You come home after school and talk to me about your day. You start the conversation

Providing and Obtaining Information

- I am your friend. I am planning to spend next summer in *(Spanish-speaking country)*. You spent the last summer there. Tell me about it. I will start the conversation

- I am a student. This is your first day in a new school and you want to have lunch. Ask me about it. You start the conversation

- I am a clerk in a rollerblade store. You want to buy new skates. Tell me what you are looking for. I will start the conversation

- I am the security guard in a department store. You were shopping with your younger sister and she has disappeared. Ask for my help. You start the conversation

- I am your parent. You are going to a friend's house. Tell me what you are planning to do and any other information that I may need to know about the trip. You start the conversation

- I am your teacher. You will be leaving school three days before the spring vacation starts. You come to tell me and we discuss your options. You start the conversation

- I am a police officer. While on an exchange trip in *(Spanish-speaking country)* you are separated from the rest of the group. You approach me for directions

Expressing Personal Feelings or Opinions

- I am your parent. Your favorite teacher has been sick for two weeks. Tell me how you feel about the substitute. I will start the conversation

- I am your friend. Your ten-year-old brother has broken your favorite music tape. Tell me about it including how you feel. I will start the conversation

- I am your friend. Your sister is leaving for college. Tell me how you feel about it. I will start the conversation.

- I am your friend. Your pet is sick. Tell me how you feel. You start the conversation

- I am your teacher. You have just been accepted into an excellent summer program. Tell me how you feel. You start the conversation

- I am your teacher. We have just seen a Spanish movie in class. Tell me how you feel about it. I will start the conversation

- I am your friend. I just got a new outfit for the school dance. Tell me how you feel about it

Getting Others to Adopt a Course of Action

- I am your parent. You have a four-page paper to write and it is two days before it is due. I think it is time to get to work. You try to convince me that it is not necessary. I will start the conversation
- I am your parent. You want to dye your hair purple and I am opposed to it. You try to convince me to allow it. You start the conversation
- I am your parent. You want to have a party for 20 friends in our house. I am opposed to it. Convince me to allow it. You start the conversation
- I am your friend. There is a school trip after school. You want to go but I do not. Convince me to go. You start the conversation
- I am your parent. You want a separate phone line in your room. We are having a meeting to discuss it. You start the conversation
- I am your parent. You want to buy something. Convince me to give you the money to buy it. I will start the conversation
- I am your friend. You belong to the Spanish club and want me to join. Persuade me. You start the conversation
- I am your parent. You want to go to a rock concert on a school night. Convince me to let you go. I will start the conversation
- I am your friend. You want to be the Activities Leader of the student government. Convince me to vote for you. I will start the conversation

PART 2
Listening Comprehension

The listening comprehension section of the Regents Comprehensive Examination in Spanish consists of:

- Nine selections in Spanish, each of which is followed by a question and multiple-choice answers in English. For each selection you will hear some background information in English *once*. Then you will hear the selection in Spanish *twice* and the question in English *once*. The question and the answers are written in English in your answer booklet

- Six selections in Spanish, each of which is followed by a question and multiple-choice answers in Spanish. For each question you will hear some background information in English *once*. Then you will hear the passage in Spanish *twice* and the question in Spanish *once*. The question and the answers are written in Spanish in your answer booklet

For both types of questions you are to select the best suggested answer from among the answers given, based only on the content of the passage.

Suggestions for Listening

- Listen carefully to the background information, as it can give you important clues to meaning by limiting possibilities.
- Read the question and possible answers before you listen to the passage. Knowing what you are trying to hear makes it much easier to hear it.
- Remember that you are listening with the specific purpose of answering the question. Do not waste time trying to understand or translate each word.
- Keep focused on the relevant information. If you find yourself losing attention, refocus.
- Use what you know (i.e. cognates, words of the same family, and so on) to decipher what you don't know.
- Don't be afraid to guess.
- Use the process of elimination. If you do not see the correct answer right away, eliminate those you know to be wrong. This increases your chances of choosing the correct answer.

Practice

In order to make this part of the examination as authentic as possible, we have left the instructions intact, as they appear in the actual Regents Examination. The only difference is, that since you will not be using an actual Regents Examinations Answer Sheet, we have provided a space after each question for your response. The passages that you will hear appear on the compact disk that accompanies this book. In the CD, as in the actual Regents Examination, the passages are read twice. Stop the player after you hear the question, take about a minute to read the question and the four choices printed in the book, and then choose the best answer.

Practice

Directions (1–13): For each question, you will hear some background information in English *once*. Then you will hear a passage in Spanish *twice* and a question in English *once*. After you have heard the question, the teacher [speaker] will pause while you read the question and the four suggested answers in your test booklet. Choose the best suggested answer and write its *number* in the space provided. Base your answer *on the content of the passage, only*. The correct answers appear in Appendix 10 (page 359).

1 Why is Dolores' friend concerned?
  1 Someone seems to be allergic to flowers
  2 The weather may affect the plants
  3 Someone seems to be stealing the flowers
  4 The vegetables have rotted on the plants   1 ____

2 What problem do Alberto and Milagros have?
  1 Their friend is not at home
  2 They have had an accident
  3 Their car is broken
  4 They appear to be lost   2 ____

3 What is the clerk explaining?
  1 checkout time
  2 laundry service
  3 time change
  4 wake up service   3 ____

4 What problem does this person have?
  1 The post office has lost the mail
  2 The service the person wants is no longer available
  3 The person has not been able to get help
  4 The person does not have enough money for the transaction   4 ____

5 What service does this business offer?
  1 To sell the cheapest traveler's checks available
  2 To deliver foreign money any place in the world
  3 To replace any traveler's checks you lose
  4 To buy back foreign money that you do not use   5 ____

6 What happened in this football game?
  1 A mistake was made on the score
  2 Both teams tied the game
  3 One of the teams was suspended
  4 The fans protested a decision   6 ____

7 What service is offered at this airport?
  1 A new baggage check-in system
  2 A new lounge that is open all the time
  3 Trained baggage-handling personnel
  4 Easy connection between flights   7 ____

8 What problem does this person have?
  1 He could not sleep last night
  2 He has no electricity in his house
  3 His socks do not match
  4 His biology experiment did not work   8 ____

9 Why is this person worried?
  1 His friend is wasting too much money
  2 His friend lost all the money he saved
  3 His friend's mother doesn't give him enough money
  4 He can't get enough channels on his television   9 ____

10 What makes this newscast unique?
  1 It's always live
  2 It offers more news in less time
  3 It's the only one at that hour
  4 It's the only one in that city   10 ____

11 What is this student complaining about?
  1 The questions in the exam were not very clear
  2 The exam had too many questions he did not know
  3 He did not have enough time to finish the exam
  4 He had to write a lot on the exam   11 ____

12 What problem does Diana have?
  1 She is worried about her studies to be a lawyer
  2 She has been unable to make plans for a trip
  3 She has not been able to finish her studies
  4 She is disappointed about the trip she took to Los Angeles   12 ____

13 What does the speaker find interesting about the Mayas?
  1 Their use of the horse for transportation
  2 Their advanced transportation system
  3 Their knowledge of the area's vegetation
  4 Their ability to construct excellent roads   13 ____

Directions (14–26): For each question, you will hear some background information in English *once*. Then you will hear a passage in Spanish *twice* and a question in Spanish *once*. After you have heard the question, the teacher [speaker] will pause while you read the question and the four suggested answers in your test booklet. Choose the best suggested answer and write its *number* in the space provided. Base your answer *on the content of the passage, only*. The correct answers appear in Appendix 10.

14 ¿Por qué está preocupada Marta?
  1 No ha llegado el autobús
  2 Su amigo no ha traído lo que necesita
  3 Su amigo va a tener dificultad en caminar
  4 Ella va a tener que armar la tienda de campaña   14 ____

15 ¿Qué ofrece esta compañía de aviación?
  1 excelentes conexiones
  2 un viaje gratis
  3 vuelos directos a Latinoamérica
  4 un vuelo adicional a Caracas   15 ____

16 ¿Qué problema existe en las cataratas de Iguazú?
  1 No van muchos turistas
  2 No permiten helicópteros
  3 Hay demasiado ruido
  4 Han muerto muchos animales   16 ____

17 ¿Cuál es una de las atracciones de la playa del Carmen?
1 Hay muchos mayas
2 Está lejos de Cancún
3 Es muy tranquila
4 Está llena de tiendas turísticas   17 ____

18 ¿Qué dice la persona sobre los cafés?
1 que han cambiado mucho
2 que no permiten escuchar música
3 que muy pocas personas van a ellos
4 que siempre van a existir   18 ____

19 ¿Qué ofrece Mundo de Música?
1 poder comprar discos sin ir a una tienda
2 recibir discos gratis todos los meses
3 el catálogo de música popular más completo
4 la oportunidad de comprar discos de segunda mano   19 ____

20 ¿Qué no le gusta a esta persona?
1 La calidad de los periódicos ha disminuido
2 El uso del inglés le molesta mucho
3 Los periódicos tienen demasiados anuncios
4 El contenido de los artículos es insultante   20 ____

21 Según el guía, ¿quiénes están interesados en las regiones de los
   Andes?
1 las personas que hacen excavaciones arqueológicas
2 los médicos que investigan las causas de ciertas
  enfermedades
3 las personas que usan plantas para curar enfermedades
4 los estudiantes interesados en la agricultura de antiguas
  culturas   21 ____

22 ¿Cuál es el propósito de la campaña que el gobierno ha
   empezado?
1 dar a conocer la riqueza cultural de la región
2 establecer un intercambio con una ciudad japonesa
3 cambiar el día de la celebración del santo patrón
4 conmemorar el día internacional del libro a través del mundo 22 ____

23 ¿Qué se describe en este reporte?
   1 un anuncio de televisión
   2 un programa de radio
   3 una serie de conferencias
   4 un concierto folklórico   23 ____

24 ¿Qué servicio ofrece esta compañía que otras no ofrecen?
   1 Le da a Ud. la oportunidad de hacer recomendaciones
   2 Lo visita en su casa si Ud. lo necesita
   3 Le busca los libros que Ud. no encuentra
   4 Le recomienda otras librerías cerca de su casa   24 ____

25 ¿Qué beneficios tiene este producto?
   1 Recordar lo que Ud. tiene que hacer
   2 Escuchar mensajes telefónicos
   3 Organizar cuidadosamente los papeles
   4 Encontrar artículos que Ud. pierde   25 ____

26 ¿Qué producto se ofrece aquí?
   1 Un nuevo sistema de operación
   2 Unos juegos electrónicos para computadoras
   3 Nuevos programas para computadoras
   4 Cursos para usar las computadoras   26 ____

PART 3
Reading

The reading comprehension section of the Regents Comprehensive Examination in Spanish consists of three multiple-choice sections:

- The first section consists of a long passage followed by five questions or incomplete statements in Spanish
- The second section consists of five selections followed by either a question or an incomplete statement in English
- The third section consists of a long passage with five blank spaces. Each blank represents a missing word or expression. Four possible completions are provided. The answer is the one that makes sense in the context of the passage

In this part of the book you will be reviewing some strategies for reading comprehension and putting these strategies into practice on a variety of reading selections.

In reading these selections, you will, no doubt, encounter Spanish words you do not know. Since you will be reading these texts with the specific purpose of answering the comprehension questions, you do not need to (nor should you) spend time trying to understand each word.

Your purpose in reading these selections is to extract the information you need in order to answer the question. In doing so, you will be able to use some skills and strategies for guessing meaning in context that you have developed in reading English.

To read a text efficiently, you should pose and answer certain questions:

- What type of passage is it (conversation, radio broadcast, newspaper article, advertisement, announcement, and so on)?
- What do I know about the type of language used in this context?
- Can I predict or anticipate the type of message it is likely to be?
- Are there any key words that help me to find the main point of the text?
- Do I seem to need an unfamiliar word in order to answer the question(s)? If so,
  - Do the circumstances or situation point to certain meanings?
  - Does the context contain any clues about its meaning?
  - Do the words around it, endings, or other cues indicate that it is likely to belong to a particular part of speech (i.e. noun, verb, etc.)?

- Is it a cognate?
- Does it contain a prefix or suffix?
- Does it resemble another Spanish word I know?
- Are there any other grammar cues (i.e. words that connect ideas and might indicate a change in events or topic)?

HINTS FOR READING A LONGER PASSAGE FOLLOWED BY SEVERAL QUESTIONS

The first time you read the passage you should not be trying to decipher the words you do not know or reading any part over. You should simply determine what type of passage it is. The answer will give you an idea of the topic and structure of the overall passage.

This first reading will give you a sense of where things are in the passage. If there is a question about the main idea of the passage, this reading will probably enable you to answer it.

Then, to better understand the details and thus, to answer more specific questions, you will probably have to read the passage again. Remember that the order of specific questions is usually the same as the order in which the information appears in the passage. That is not to say, however, that something you read earlier may not help you to answer a question later on. In answering specific questions, it is useful to use the following approach.

First, find out what you need to search for, by reading the question. Then, read the section of the passage where you think the answer may be. Finally, find the answer that paraphrases what you just read. In answering a specific question, limit yourself to the information given in the passage. These questions are about what the author says in the passage. They do not require you to make assumptions, but rather to find the answer that uses a different way of saying what is said in the passage.

Eliminating the answers that do not make sense within the context of the passage will help you determine the best answer among those that are left.

Practice

Directions (1–5): Below each of the following passages, there are five questions or incomplete statements. For *each,* choose the word or expression that best answers the question or completes the statement *according to the meaning of the passage,* and write its *number* in the space provided. The correct answers appear in Appendix 10 (page 359).

El Libertador, Simón Bolívar

América vivió bajo la monarquía española desde el siglo XVI hasta el siglo XIX. Durante estos tres siglos las colonias españolas en las Américas sufrieron una serie de injusticias sociales, económicas y políticas a manos de la madre patria, España. Al mismo tiempo la pérdida del poderío español en Europa y el éxito de las revoluciones norteamericana y francesa daban esperanza a los que querían independizarse. En 1808, Napoleón invadió España y el descontento en las colonias españolas se convirtió en un movimiento revolucionario general.

Simón Bolívar, llamado el George Washington de la América del Sur, fue uno de los grandes libertadores del continente. Bolívar, quien era miembro de una distinguida familia venezolana, se educó en España pero pasó gran parte de su vida luchando por la libertad del norte del continente. Luchó desde 1810 hasta 1824, año en que su ejército ganó la batalla de Ayacucho. Con esta victoria consiguió la independencia del Perú.

El sueño de Bolívar era crear una América española unida, similar a la que se estableció en la América del Norte. Propuso la formación de la Gran Confederación de los Andes en la que se unirían los países del norte del continente sudamericano bajo su autoridad. No pudo conseguir que las naciones aceptaran su plan, pero sí pudo establecer las repúblicas de Venezuela, Colombia, Ecuador, Perú y Bolivia. A causa de esto se le da el título de "El Libertador".

1 ¿Cómo fueron para las Américas los tres siglos bajo la monarquía española?
  1 llenos de prosperidad
  2 llenos de explotación
  3 muy difíciles para España
  4 muy tranquilos para muchos países   1 _____

2 ¿Qué efecto tuvieron las revoluciones norteamericana y francesa?
  1 Hicieron que creciera la economía americana
  2 Hicieron que los españoles regresaran a España
  3 Le ayudaron a Napoleón a invadir España
  4 Les dieron ilusión a los que querían independencia   2 _____

3   ¿Por qué se llama a Simón Bolívar, el George Washington de la
    América del Sur?
    1 El conocía muy bien a George Washington
    2 El había nacido en los Estados Unidos
    3 El luchó por la libertad del continente
    4 La familia de él se mudó al norte del continente   3 ____

4   ¿Cuál era el sueño de Bolívar?
    1 unir a varios países hispanos
    2 conquistar su país natal
    3 poder vivir en la América del Norte
    4 luchar junto a George Washington   4 ____

5   ¿Por qué se le da el título de "El Libertador" a Bolívar?
    1 porque unió a los países del continente bajo su autoridad
    2 porque creó una América española unida
    3 porque estableció cinco repúblicas
    4 porque creó la Gran Confederación de los Andes   5 ____

2

Quiénes somos

La población hispana de los Estados Unidos es la quinta más numerosa del mundo. Los únicos países que tienen más habitantes hispanos son México, España, Colombia y la Argentina. A diferencia de estos países, sin embargo, la mayor parte de los hispanos en los Estados Unidos no nació aquí.

En los últimos 50 años, millones de inmigrantes hispanos han llegado de algunos de los 21 países que conforman el mundo hispanohablante. Más de la mitad del crecimiento de la población hispana de la última década se debe a la inmigración. Se estima que, de cada tres adultos hispanos en los Estados Unidos, dos nacieron fuera del país. De éstos, cuatro de cada cinco llegaron a este país cuando tenían más de 16 años de edad. Esto hace que los hispanos en los Estados Unidos sean una nación de inmigrantes relativamente recientes.

En 1970, por primera vez, la categoría de "Hispano" apareció en los formularios del censo. A diferencia de los grupos definidos racialmente, los hispanos se distinguen por provenir de países de habla española donde las razas blanca, negra e india llevan cinco siglos mezclándose en diferentes proporciones. Esto significa que los hispanos como minoría son definidos por lo que tienen en común, su herencia y su cultura. Sin embargo, no hay duda de que hay muchas diferencias.

Los grupos más grandes de hispanos en los Estados Unidos son los de origen mexicano, puertorriqueño y cubano.

Por razones históricas y geográficas, seis de cada diez hispanos en los Estados Unidos son de origen mexicano. Estos conforman el 80% de los hispanoamericanos que han nacido en los Estados Unidos. La mayoría de los mexicoamericanos se encuentra en el sudoeste del país.

Uno de cada diez hispanos es de origen puertorriqueño. Los habitantes de Puerto Rico empezaron a llegar en grandes cantidades después de la Segunda Guerra Mundial. A diferencia de los demás inmigrantes, los puertorriqueños son ciudadanos de los Estados Unidos desde 1917. A causa de esto no necesitan visa para entrar en los Estados Unidos y hoy en día hay casi tantos puertorriqueños en los Estados Unidos como en Puerto Rico. La mayoría está concentrada en el noreste del país, especialmente en Nueva York y Chicago.

Uno de cada veinte hispanos en Estados Unidos es de origen cubano. A pesar de que antes de 1960 ya había muchos de ellos establecidos en los Estados Unidos, a partir de ese año comenzaron a llegar cientos de miles de refugiados que huían de la revolución comunista. En 1980 una ola de más de 100.000 refugiados llegó al país como resultado del éxodo del Mariel. Hoy día los cubanos forman un núcleo minoritario muy importante en la Florida y también hay importantes concentraciones en Nueva York, Nueva Jersey y Chicago.

1 Según el artículo, el aumento reciente de la población hispanohablante en los Estados Unidos se debe principalmente:
1 a las oportunidades que existen para las personas bilingües
2 a la cantidad de hispanos que llegan de otros países
3 al gran número de niños hispanos que nace cada año
4 a la libertad con que los hispanos pueden entrar a los Estados Unidos ___ 1

2 Según el artículo, ¿qué caracteriza al hispano?
1 la mezcla de diferentes razas
2 la uniformidad de su herencia
3 su situación económica
4 su deseo de regresar a su país ___ 2

3 El grupo más grande de hispanos en los Estados Unidos es de
origen
1 colombiano
2 mexicano
3 puertorriqueño
4 cubano 3 ___

4 Los puertorriqueños se diferencian de otros hispanos en que
1 tienen nacionalidad estadounidense
2 llegaron a los Estados Unidos antes de la Segunda Guerra
Mundial
3 hay más puertorriqueños en los Estados Unidos que en
Puerto Rico
4 son refugiados políticos a causa de la guerra 4 ___

5 ¿Por qué vinieron los cubanos a los Estados Unidos?
1 No había mucho trabajo en Cuba
2 La economía cubana había sufrido mucho
3 Querían importar la revolución
4 A causa de la situación política en Cuba 5 ___

3

Tish Hinojosa o el arte de unir dos culturas

Tish Hinojosa, nacida en San Antonio de padres mexicanos,
canta a las dos culturas a las que pertenece por nacimiento y por
herencia; su arte es una forma de llegar al mayor número posible
de personas y de integrar sus diferencias culturales.

Desde muy temprano Tish empezó a moldear estas impre-
siones en forma de música utilizando las canciones mexicanas
que oía en casa y algo de la música *pop* y *folk* norteamericanas
de su alrededor. Después de grabar localmente, Tish Hinojosa ac-
cedió a la prominencia nacional de la música *country* con *Homeland,* un álbum en inglés. Ella se reveló como una artista
profundamente unida a su realidad multicultural a través de canciones que reflejaban la vida diaria de su gente.

Aquella noche, su segundo álbum grabado en vivo en español
confirmó su obligación con sus raíces. En la voz y la inter-
pretación de estas canciones sencillas Tish muestra la profunda
influencia de la música latinoamericana en su carrera.

Tish Hinojosa se identifica con múltiples causas, en especial
las relacionadas con los hispanos, a través de anuncios de servicio público, presentaciones y apariciones benéficas. Estas causas

incluyen a los trabajadores migrantes, la educación bilingüe, los derechos civiles, las mujeres, los niños y la salud.

Sus logros artísticos han sido ampliamente reconocidos en programas de PBS *(Public Broadcasting System)* y NPR *(National Public Radio),* entre otros. Entre sus videos está *Something in the Rain,* hecho en conjunción con el *National Migrant Resource Program,* sobre los trabajadores migratorios. Tish también ha hecho giras en el extranjero. Su música es especialmente apreciada en Corea, donde se vendieron más de 80.000 copias de *Homeland.*

Tarde o temprano la gente oirá hablar de Tish Hinojosa: un talento como el suyo rara vez pasa desapercibido. Su voz y sus canciones van más allá de lo comercial, se comprometen con la realidad de la gente y salen del corazón.

1 ¿Qué es el arte para Tish Hinojosa?
 1 el tratar de olvidar su herencia mexicana
 2 una manera de celebrar varias culturas
 3 una forma de enseñar español a muchos
 4 el medio por el cual critica la música pop y folk 1 ____

2 ¿Qué podemos apreciar en la música de Tish Hinojosa?
 1 la identificación con varias culturas
 2 la dificultad de su carrera artística
 3 la profundidad de sus problemas diarios
 4 la cualidad de su voz 2 ____

3 Según la lectura, por sus actividades Tish Hinojosa muestra
 1 un gran interés por regresar a México
 2 una gran identificación con la cultura norteamericana
 3 un deseo de escribir artículos para los inmigrantes
 4 una gran preocupación por los problemas sociales 3 ____

4 ¿Dónde se puede escuchar la música de Tish Hinojosa?
 1 solamente en México
 2 solamente en San Antonio
 3 en los programas de servicio público
 4 en muchos países del mundo 4 ____

5 ¿Qué impresión nos da el artículo sobre Hinojosa?
 1 que pronto dejará de cantar
 2 que se mudará a otro país
 3 que todavía no es muy conocida
 4 que su música es demasiado comercial 5 ____

4

Marzo y abril, dos meses para festejar

Fiestas, carnavales y festivales siempre han gozado de merecida popularidad entre nosotros los hispanos. Y los meses de marzo y abril, quizás por el buen tiempo y el ambiente primaveral, parecen ser la época del año preferida para realizar estos eventos.

El Carnaval Miami se lleva a cabo todos los años en la calle Ocho de la Pequeña Habana en la Florida. Cerca de un millón de personas asisten coda año a celebrar la cultura latina en esta fiesta llena de música, comida típica, bailes y actividades para toda la familia. Cientos de artistas se presentan en los numerosos escenarios colocados estratégicamente a lo largo de las 24 cuadras en las que se realiza el evento que este año se llevará a cabo en marzo a partir de las doce del día, entre las avenidas 4 y 27. Se grabará un especial de televisión que se transmitirá por la cadena Univisión. Antes del evento se darán otras actividades como la elección de la reina del carnaval, la Noche de Carnaval en el Orange Bowl, el Paseo (un desfile de carrozas, bandas y comparsas), la Carrera del Carnaval Miami, y, como culminación, el Carnaval Miami en Bayfront, un evento de 12 horas de entretenimiento continuo.

En Los Angeles, California, la Fiesta Broadway es en abril. Este año los organizadores, la estación KMEX de Univisión, prevén que cerca de un millón de personas asistirán al evento de siete horas. Un total de 36 cuadras en el centro de Los Angeles, en las calles Broadway, Hill y Spring, se utilizarán para la celebración. Más de 100 actos artísticos se presentarán en ocho escenarios gigantes. Parte de las ganancias del evento se dirigen a *Miracle on Broadway,* un programa para revitalizar el centro de Los Angeles, un área tradicionalmente utilizada por los hispanos para realizar sus compras.

La Fiesta de San Antonio, Texas, dura diez días y atrae a unos tres millones de personas anualmente. Este año, la fiesta, que tiene lugar en abril, incluye tres desfiles, fuegos artificiales, innumerables presentaciones musicales, fiestas étnicas, exhibiciones de arte, bailes, carrozas flotantes en el río y calles rebosantes de celebraciones. En total, habrá más de 150 eventos para satisfacer todos los gustos, organizados por más de 100 asociaciones afiliadas con la Fiesta San Antonio Commission, coordinadora del evento. Para la fiesta se eligen 16 reinas y varios reyes, entre ellos el Rey Feo. Este año, el Rey Feo es el ejecutivo publicitario Lionel Sosa, quien ganó el honor al haber colectado la mayor cantidad de dinero para beneficio de la organización benéfica LULAC.

El 7-Eleven Hispanic Arts Festival, una serie de presentaciones que se llevarán a cabo durante siete fines de semana en el sur de California, ha sido diseñado para ilustrar al público, especialmente a los estudiantes, sobre la historia y cualidades de la música del mariachi. Las presentaciones estarán a cargo del Mariachi Uclatlán, una agrupación de 12 personas con 30 años de experiencia. Los músicos presentarán sus instrumentos y luego procederán a interpretar canciones famosas como *Las Mañanitas, La Malagueña* y *La Bamba,* ilustradas con bailes típicos como el jarabe tapatío y la polka, a cargo de Mary Louise Díaz y José Vélez. Las presentaciones están complementadas por un libro de recuerdo y una guía escolar para ayudar a los profesores a enseñar a sus alumnos las características de esta música.

1 ¿Cuándo se celebran muchas de las fiestas hispanas en los Estados Unidos?
   1 al final del año
   2 en la primavera
   3 depende del clima de la ciudad
   4 en un mes diferente cada año   1 _____

2 Las personas que NO pueden ir al Carnaval Miami podrán . . .
   1 escuchar la celebración en la radio
   2 comprar un video de la celebración
   3 verlo en la televisión
   4 ver las fotos en un libro   2 _____

3 ¿Qué van a hacer con el dinero que se gane en Los Angeles?
   1 Van a usarlo para mejores artistas el año próximo
   2 Van a donarlo a una estación de televisión
   3 Van a dárselo a los hispanos para sus compras
   4 Van a usarlo para mejorar un barrio   3 _____

4 ¿Qué hizo el Rey Feo en San Antonio?
   1 Recogió mucho dinero
   2 Regaló dinero para la publicidad
   3 Bailó con la reina de la fiesta
   4 Organizó toda la fiesta este año   4 _____

‿ ¿Qué piensan hacer en las presentaciones en el sur de California?

1 darles experiencia a los músicos jóvenes
2 enseñar al público un poco de historia musical
3 celebrar los bailes europeos
4 dar clases de baile

5 ___

5

Vikki Carr encuentra el éxito en sus raíces

El éxito ha sido generoso con Vikki Carr, quien empezó a cantar en español en 1972. Este es el merecido premio a una mujer con voluntad de hierro, voz de oro y un corazón enorme.

En el caso de su último álbum, *Cosas del amor*, el esfuerzo y las largas horas de grabación no han sido en vano. Aunque ella sigue cantando en una vena romántica, el ritmo tras las canciones es decididamente moderno. "Al principio tenía un poco de temor de cambiar mi estilo", dice refiriéndose a la necesidad de adaptar sus canciones al gusto más movido del público. En este sentido, Vikki reconoce que grabar el álbum, producido por Roberto Livi, le costó un poco más de trabajo que los anteriores.

El álbum ha sido bien recibido por el público, especialmente la canción a dúo del mismo nombre que Vikki canta con Ana Gabriel. En esta canción la voz cristalina y delicada de Vikki establece un diálogo con la voz fuerte y casi ronca de Ana Gabriel: la primera aconseja a su amiga precisamente sobre cosas del amor. Es un diálogo intenso y apasionado que proyecta un gran sentimiento de urgencia. El resultado de este trabajo de colaboración ha sido un número uno en las listas de popularidad en el país y un auspicioso comienzo para el álbum.

Las inquietudes de la cantante de origen mexicano, nacida en El Paso y con residencia en Los Angeles, no se limitan al canto. Vikki ha formado una compañía de producción de películas y actualmente trabaja en una idea para una serie de televisión en inglés. Mientras tanto, se las arregla para promover su disco incansablemente y para hacer presentaciones a lo largo y ancho del país y en el extranjero, especialmente en América Latina.

Todavía hay quienes se preguntan por qué esta extraordinaria cantante, quien en los años sesenta y principios de los setenta tuvo tanto éxito cantando en inglés, quien ha cantado para cuatro presidentes en la Casa Blanca y para la reina de Inglaterra, quien ha recibido discos de oro y toda clase de honores, insiste en seguir cantando en español. El primer gran éxito de Vikki se produjo en Australia con una canción titulada *He Is a Rebel*. Más tarde, su canción *It Must Be Him* la llevó a la cima de la fama en Inglaterra y Estados Unidos. En 1967 fue invitada a cantar ante la reina Isabel II de Inglaterra. Su gira mundial fue un éxito total, donde consiguió teatros llenos en España, Holanda, Francia, Inglaterra, Australia y el Japón.

"La verdad es que quiero tener éxito tanto en inglés como en español". Esta inquietud la ha llevado a jugar con la idea de hacer series de tres conciertos, uno en inglés, otro en español y otro bilingüe para probar la lealtad de su público y mantener vivo el contacto con todos sus admiradores en los dos idiomas.

Su contacto artístico con México empezó relativamente tarde. La primera actuación en la capital federal se llevó a cabo en 1972. A partir de entonces, sin embargo, los lazos se fortalecieron de tal modo que Vikki Carr pasó a ser, además de una favorita del público norteamericano, una de las más reconocidas voces del panorama musical latino con su repertorio de canciones en español.

1 Vikki Carr tuvo que trabajar más en su último disco porque
  1 nunca había trabajado con el señor Livi
  2 no había cantado por mucho tiempo
  3 la música del álbum era muy diferente
  4 no era en su lengua natal   1 _____

2 ¿Qué distingue la canción con Ana Gabriel?
  1 Es una conversación entre dos personas
  2 Es la primera vez que canta con otra persona
  3 Es la única que no habla del amor
  4 Es una carta dedicada a un amigo   2 _____

3 ¿En qué está interesada también la cantante Vikki Carr?
  1 en otros artistas hispanos
  2 en actuar en una película
  3 en cantar en la televisión
  4 en el cine y la televisión   3 _____

4 ¿Qué se pregunta mucha gente sobre Vikki Carr?
  1 por qué no quiso cantar en la Casa Blanca
  2 por qué no le gusta recibir honores
  3 por qué no da más viajes al extranjero
  4 por qué no canta solamente en inglés   4 _____

5 ¿Cuándo empezó a cantar en español Vikki Carr?
1 cuando sus discos en inglés no se vendían
2 cuando dio un concierto en México
3 cuando la descubrieron los sudamericanos
4 cuando el panorama musical latino cambió   5 _____

Directions (6–25): Below each of the following selections, there is either a question or an incomplete statement. For each, choose the word or expression that best answers the question or completes the statement *according to the meaning of the selection,* and write its *number* in the space provided.

6

> En 1969, el gobierno mexicano decidió dar fuerte impulso al turismo. Le interesaba especialmente aquel turista cuyo destino eran las playas. En la zona del Pacífico se descubrieron las maravillosas bahías de Huatulco. Las carácteristas del área resultaron ideales para formar parte del proyecto. Huatulco consta de encantadoras playas de arena fina y blanca. En 1983 se terminó la construcción de la carretera Puerto Escondido-Salina Cruz y la de Oaxaca-Pochutla, pues antes las playas no estaban accesibles. Esto facilitó el desarrollo de las nueve bahías naturales de la región. Actualmente, el área ha alcanzado gran fama no sólo a nivel nacional, sino también internacional. Consta de hotelería, restaurantes, centros nocturnos, discotecas y campos de golf. Muy importante es el moderno aeropuerto internacional, ubicado a 19 kilómetros de la zona hotelera.

What prompted the development of Huatulco Bay?
1 an interest in Mexican cuisine and music
2 an international airport that was not being used
3 the interest in developing tourism at Mexican beaches
4 the discovery of old roads in the area   _____

What did the government have to do?
1 build new roads
2 advertise internationally
3 hold a golf tournament
4 destroy the old hotels   _____

7

CELEBRANDO NUESTRA CULTURA . . .

El Ballet Folklórico de Texas nació de la necesidad de su fundador, Roy Lozano, de expresar sus raíces a través del arte. Su padre era beisbolista profesional y Roy viajaba con él a pueblos de México donde asistía a fiestas típicas con música folklórica y trajes tradicionales. Ya en la escuela secundaria, Roy se integró a un grupo de danza mexicana. En 1976 Roy se presentó a las audiciones del Ballet Folkórico de México y fue invitado a Ciudad de México. Pronto se encontró recorriendo el mundo con la compañía. Después de unos tres años, regresó a Texas y fundó su propia compañía. Según Roy, su compañía busca "dar expresión visual" a su historia y cultura.

What is the goal of the Texas Folkloric Ballet?
1 to use dance to express their Mexican roots
2 to expose students in Mexico to traditional dances
3 to bring dance and sports to the same stage
4 to dispell myths about Mexican history

Roy Lozano's interest in dance seems to have started
1 when he was a baseball player
2 through his travels
3 after he left Texas
4 on his first visit to Mexico City

8

RECORDANDO A CLEMENTE

Por 18 años Roberto Clemente jugó con
los Piratas de Pittsburgh, quienes todas las
temporadas dedican una noche en su honor.
Clemente fue el primer hispano en sumar
3.000 *hits* e ingresar en el Salón de la Fama
de Béisbol. Hace más de 25 años el mundo
sufrió un duro golpe al perecer Roberto
Clemente en un accidente aéreo. El beisbolista puertorriqueño iba camino a
Nicaragua en un viaje que él mismo organizó para socorrer a las víctimas de un terre-
moto devastador. Además, para asegurar
que su espíritu no morirá nunca, las grandes
ligas otorgan anualmente un premio cívico
que lleva su nombre para conmemorar su
interés y compasión por los desafortunados.

Why was Roberto Clemente going to Nicaragua?
1 to play baseball
2 to help others
3 to receive a prize
4 to honor a baseball player   ____

What do the major leagues do to remember Roberto Clemente?
1 They contribute money to different causes
2 They play in Puerto Rico every year
3 They organize games on a regular basis
4 They give a prize in his name   ____

9

¿QUÉ ES ESA CAJA?

Un medidor de audiencia es una pequeña computadora que se instala sobre el televisor y que posee unos botones que la gente oprime cada vez que enciende o apaga el televisor. Contar el número de personas que ven la televisión todos los días y saber los programas que ven y dónde y cuándo los ven es muy importante para las cadenas de televisión. Estos informes les permiten ajustar su programación y establecer las tarifas que se pagan por publicidad.

Una de las compañías más importantes de medición de audiencia en los Estados Unidos, ha instalado miles de estos aparatos en hogares hispanos.

Para Univisión y Telemundo, cadenas de televisión hispanas, una medición adecuada significa poder demostrarles a los anunciantes el tamaño y la configuración de la audiencia en español. Así podrán convencer a las grandes compañías que se les considere de la misma manera que a las cadenas angloparlantes en cuanto a la publicidad.

Además de confirmar la creciente importancia de la audiencia hispana, se espera que los resultados permitan satisfacer mejor las preferencias del público hispano.

The product being described is used
1 to watch television in several languages
2 to count the Hispanic television viewers
3 to turn on or off the television in your home
4 to increase the number of television channels

According to the passage, Hispanic television companies expect
1 to increase the number of people who watch television
2 to give the public better information about their programs
3 to serve the public better
4 to sell more programs

10

La historia del cantante Jon Secada empieza en La Habana, Cuba, ciudad donde nació hace unos 38 años y donde, según su madre, escribió su primera canción a los tres años. Se crió y estudió en Miami donde recibió un diploma de maestría en música de la Universidad de Miami. Durante sus años de universidad trabajaba por la noche cantando con una banda llamada The Company. Finalmente, la banda se unió a Miami Sound Machine.

Durante casi seis años Jon fue músico, compositor y arreglista de Miami Sound Machine. Entre las canciones que escribió junto con Gloria Estefan se encuentran muchos éxitos. Finalmente llegó a ser cantante de coro del grupo. Luego, en su primer año como solista recibió dos nominaciones para el Grammy: como mejor artista popular nuevo del año y como mejor artista latino. Su canción *Just Another Day* estuvo en las primeras 10 durante doce semanas. Desde entonces se ha mantenido en la cima, conquistando el mercado inglés y el español con canciones como *Otro día más sin verte*. Hoy día es músico de éxito internacional.

What did Jon Secada do during his years at the university?
1 He sang at night
2 He worked as a teacher
3 He managed a band
4 He sold records ____

Jon Secada's relationship with Gloria Estefan can be described as
1 manager
2 interpreter
3 bodyguard
4 collaborator ____

11

ORGULLOSOS DE OCHOA

Ellen Ochoa, mexicanoamericana nacida en Los Angeles, se distingue por su inteligencia y su determinación y por lo variado de sus intereses. No sólo es doctora en ingeniería eléctrica sino también notable flautista clásica. Además, en 1993, tuvo la misión de dirigir un grupo de investigación de NASA, y así se convirtió en la primera mujer hispana astronauta al orbitar la Tierra. A Ellen le gusta reunirse con grupos de estudiantes. Le interesa especialmente, comunicarle a los estudiantes hispanos lo que considera el secreto de todo éxito: estudiar y trabajar mucho.

Why is Ellen Ochoa famous?
1 She discovered several stars
2 She conducted several orchestras
3 She formed students' groups
4 She travelled in space ____

According to the passage, Ellen Ochoa shows
1 a certain mystery about her investigations
2 little interest for engineering
3 great interest in Hispanic youth
4 compassion for Hispanic women ____

12

Who would be most interested in this ad?
1 someone who is going on a long trip
2 someone who is sunburned
3 someone who likes to draw
4 someone who wants to buy makeup ____

13

Deportivo y espacioso.

Transmisión manual de cinco velocidades.

(automática opcional)

Radio cassette estéreo. Asientos reclinables.

Asistencia en el camino.

¡Volar '98!

Visite hoy mismo a su concesionario local

y vea cómo vuela al conducir.

What does this ad invite readers to do?
1 register for a new driving school
2 visit a local car dealer to see a new model car
3 purchase a new stereo cassette player
4 visit a new furniture and electronics store _____

14

MODELO 823

¿Está lejos de su familia? Una contestadora telefónica

le permitirá recibir mensajes claros y a tiempo. Tener

una Secretaria Modelo 823 es como estar en casa.

Llame ahora mismo al 1-800-MENSAJE.

¡No se pierda una llamada más!

Esta oferta termina el 25 de agosto.

What does this ad offer?
1 a secretary to answer the telephone
2 a telephone answering machine
3 an easier way to call your family
4 a new business possibility from your home

15

Sugerencias de seguridad

• evite tomar taxis que no estén autorizados por el gobierno municipal

• no trate con vendedores ambulantes

• no le dé el número de su habitación a extraños

• no muestre demasiado dinero al pagar por sus compras

What is this flyer about?
1 safety measures for tourists
2 rules for employees of a large company
3 guidelines for campers
4 suggestions for savings while travelling

16

Las portátiles más vendidas del mundo.

Ultima tecnología, multimedia avanzada, la pantalla más grande y el peso más ligero. Estupenda mezcla de poder y funcionalidad al mejor precio. El procesador más rápido del mercado. Incluimos sistema de navegación y curso de informática.

Calle H, número 311
Tel: (7) 22-37-46
Fax: (7) 23-45-84

This ad is of interest to anyone interested in
1 portable radios
2 a new stereo system
3 laptop computers
4 high-resolution television

17

> Todas las recetas que hemos publicado en la sección de hoy se pueden obtener enviando un sobre con su nombre y dirección. Además, si Ud. es una persona creativa a quien le gusta cocinar, nos gustaría recibir cualquier receta que haya inventado. Envíenos sus ideas y recetas a la dirección que aparece en la primera página de nuestro periódico.

Who might be interested in contacting this newspaper?
1 someone who likes going to restaurants
2 someone who wants to become a chef
3 someone who is on a diet
4 someone who enjoys cooking _____

18

> No me gusta mucho el mes de septiembre. No, no es que no me guste regresar a la escuela. Siempre espero ver a mis amigos de nuevo con anticipación. Lo que me pasa es que en septiembre ya me doy cuenta de que el verano ha pasado y que pronto empezará el frío invierno. Me encantan las actividades al aire libre y cuando ya empieza a bajar la temperatura, sé que la nieve aparecerá y nos tendremos que quedar en casa.

What type of activities does this person like?
1 activities in the snow
2 activities he can do at home
3 activities he can do outdoors
4 activities related to school _____

19

> *¿Tiene Ud. problemas en encontrar un médico bueno? ¿Quiere Ud. que su familia reciba la mejor atención médica posible? Si Ud. se preocupa por la salud de sus familiares, llame a nuestra línea "Días Saludables". Nuestras operadoras le harán varias preguntas y le recomendarán el mejor médico en su área. Díganos algo sobre su familia y le encontraremos el servicio que Ud. y su familia merecen. Cerca de su casa. Siempre dispuestos a servir nuestra comunidad.*

Who might be interested in this announcement?
1 someone with excellent health
2 someone who wants to stay in good heath
3 someone wanting to work in the health field
4 someone worried about the problems of the community

20 __ CONDUCCIÓN Y JUVENTUD

La mayoría de los jóvenes que conducen lo hacen con mucho cuidado y responsabilidad. Son los pocos que no tienen cuidado, los que han creado una situación que ha obligado a muchas comunidades a tomar medidas para reducir el número de accidentes. En muchas comunidades la edad para recibir un permiso de conducir ha aumentado y en otras comunidades los padres se han visto obligados a firmar contratos con los hijos para que se hagan responsables cuando conducen.

What seems to be happening in some communities?
1 Young people are not driving carefully
2 Young people are breaking school rules
3 The number of accidents has decreased
4 More young people are getting their licenses

21

> Uno de los fenómenos que se puede apreciar en la televisión hispana es el aumento de programas de entrevistas. Antes sólo se veía *Cristina,* un programa donde podíamos ver artistas conocidos y de vez en cuando alguna familia que tenía algún problema. Hoy día el número de estos programas ha aumentado y esto ha contribuido a que la lucha por obtener el mayor número de televidentes haya forzado a muchos de los productores a usar el sensacionalismo para atraer al público. Esto preocupa mucho, pues temas que podrían instruir a la comunidad se convierten en conversaciones llenas de gritos y revelaciones que no son apropiadas para todo el público, principalmente cuando los muestran por las tardes.

How has the situation described here changed?
1 There seem to be more programs to help the community
2 The quality of interview programs has deteriorated
3 The number of television viewers continues to decrease
4 Sensationalism has been avoided so far in Spanish programs   ____

22 PARA CHUPARSE LOS DEDOS

Todos los pescados que llegan a nuestro restaurante vienen directamente del mar. Así, nuestros clientes pueden saborear la comida de mar más fresca de la región. Si es salmón lo que le apetece, o si disfruta más de unos camarones al ajillo, una visita a nuestro restaurante convencerá a todos de la calidad y la frescura de nuestros platos. Y ahora, el nuevo cocinero Pepín sorprende a los clientes con creaciones culinarias originales para todo paladar.

Who might be interested in this ad?
1 someone who likes seafood
2 someone who lives near the sea
3 someone who enjoys home-cooked meals
4 someone who wants to open a restaurant   ____

23

Como agua para chocolate, *una de las películas de más éxito en la historia del cine mexicano, ha salido ya en video. La cinta se basa en la exitosa novela de Laura Esquivel, quien también escribió el guión de la película. La trama es sencilla—a causa de la tiranía de su madre, la protagonista, Tita, tiene que renunciar a Pedro, el amor de su vida. Para estar cerca de su querida Tita, Pedro se casa con su hermana mayor. La vida de Tita se desarrolla con un fondo gastronómico, entre sabrosos chiles en nogada, exquisitos caldos de res, deliciosas torrejas de nata y otros platos mexicanos en los que se libera de su pasión frustrada. Todo tiene lugar en la época de la revolución mexicana.*

What does this passage describe?
1 a cooking program
2 the theme of some songs
3 a romantic film
4 the publication of a book

24

WILFREDO LAM

Wilfredo Lam nació en Cuba de madre de raza negra y padre chino. Vivió en el Caribe, España, Francia y Estados Unidos y por esto su obra muestra la diversidad cultural de sus raíces y sus experiencias.

En España entró en contacto con la obra de Picasso y de Matisse. A fines de los años treinta, encuentra en Francia a un grupo de pintores surrealistas con los que siente afinidad. Pero la presencia de palmeras y detalles de la cultura africana le dan a sus cuadros un sello distintivo.

Hoy día su obra se interpreta desde la perspectiva multicultural y ésta se ve como el lazo de unión entre el arte latinoamericano, norteamericano y europeo.

According to the passage, what can we appreciate in the works of
Wilfredo Lam?
1 the great cultural variety
2 the great sadness of his childhood
3 his Chinese background
4 his reaction against multiculturalism ____

25

> Una tradición inolvidable de la época de la
> Navidad es el día de los Reyes Magos. Los
> tres reyes salieron del Oriente camino a
> Belén para llevar sus ofrendas al Niño que
> acababa de nacer. Una estrella guió su
> camino. Cruzaron el desierto en sus cara-
> vanas de camellos con sus regalos de in-
> cienso, mirra y oro. El incienso y la mirra
> eran las esencias más deseables de sus
> países. El oro tanto hoy como entonces
> simboliza la seguridad material. Con estos
> regalos comenzó la tradición que todavía
> conservamos de intercambiar regalos en
> esta época del año.

What custom began with the *Reyes Magos?*
1 using gold as a symbol of security
2 following the stars
3 giving perfume as a present
4 exchanging gifts ____

CLOZE PASSAGES

HINTS FOR CLOZE PASSAGES

In cloze passages there are blanks that represent a missing word or expression. You are given four possible answers from which you are to choose
one that makes sense within the context of the passage.

A helpful strategy is to look at the answers and do the following:

- Find a word that would make sense in the passage

- Eliminate any word that does not fit in

- Think of a word that might fit in and see if the words left over could
  have that meaning

Practice

Directions (26–30): In the following passages there are several blank spaces. Each blank space represents a missing word or expression. For each blank space, four possible answers are provided. Only one of them makes sense *in the context of the passage*.

First read the passage in its entirety to determine its general meaning. Then read it a second time. For each blank space choose the completion that makes the best sense and write its *number* in the space provided. The correct answers appear in Appendix 10 (page 359).

26   **Juan Luis Guerra, poeta y músico del pueblo**

Según Juan Luis Guerra, famoso cantautor dominicano, la inspiración "surge de la vida, del espacio, de los libros y de la pintura". Añade que el mejor tipo de inspiración es la que se convierte en una necesidad de expresión.

Esa necesidad de __(1)__ fue la que le impulsó a componer por primera vez cuando era sólo un adolescente. A los dieciséis años cantaba en el coro estudiantil del colegio La Salle, en Santo Domingo. Pero en sus ratos libres ya empezaba a hacer los primeros experimentos de mezcla de voces con su grabadora y su guitarra inseparables.

En esa época entabló una amistad con Herbert Stern que se iría fortaleciendo a través de los años. En plena ebullición de los Beatles, Herbert y Juan Luis se dedicaron a colgarse la guitarra y tocar en los clubes sociales de la ciudad. Siguen siendo amigos, algo que lo hace sentirse __(2)__ .

Pero la inclinación de Juan Luis por la música no empezó

entonces sino que viene de __(3)__ . Cuando vivían en Gazcue, en una casa cerca del teatro Independencia, con sólo seis años, Juan Luis salía al patio para ver llegar a sus ídolos que iban a actuar en el teatro: Joselito y Marisol, que entonces hacían furor en España. Dice que vivía enamorado de ella y que iba a ver a todos los artistas que podía. Además, dice que su casa era una casa tan __(4)__ que "hasta los aguacates cantaban". Su padre oía boleros y a su mamá le encantaba la ópera italiana. A él le encantaban los Beatles aunque, como no hablaba inglés, no __(5)__ nada de las letras de sus canciones.

1 1 inspirarse
   2 expresarse
   3 hacerse famoso
   4 actuar
                    1 _____

2 1 triste
   2 avergonzado
   3 orgulloso
   4 libre
                    2 _____

3 1 más atrás
   2 más tarde
   3 después
   4 entonces
                    3 _____

4 1 ruidosa
   2 callada
   3 trabajadora
   4 musical
                    4 _____

5 1 entendía
   2 oía
   3 le gustaba
   4 encontraba
                    5 _____

El 1992 abrió sus puertas una exposición permanente en el Museo Nacional de Historia Americana, en Washington, D.C. La exposición llamada Encuentros Americanos examina una de las __(1)__ de la llegada de Colón en 1492: los encuentros entre gente de culturas distintas y la manera en que estas culturas han conservado sus leyendas tradiciones y costumbres. Además es un tributo a los pueblos que, como resultado de su convivencia y sus luchas, construyeron "el nuevo mundo".

La exposición muestra cómo, durante unos __(2)__ años, las culturas de los hispanos y de los nativos americanos se han relacionado entre sí. Muestra también cómo esos pueblos han sobrevivido frente a intentos de parte de la cultura dominante de quitarles su tierra, su idioma y su religión y han __(3)__ formar una sociedad dinámica en la que coexisten con anglos y afroamericanos.

Los visitantes llegarán a conocer a la gente que vive en el poblado indio de Santa Clara y en la villa hispana de Chimayó a través de 400 piezas de artesanía, por entrevistas en video y por grabaciones de sus cuentos, música, bailes y tradiciones.

Se aspira a que los visitantes se lleven tres __(4)__ : la presencia hispana en Norteamérica precede la creación de los Estados

Unidos, los indios americanos forman parte de la sociedad moderna y la lección más importante de todas: la sociedad pluralista es ___(5)___ si cada uno respeta la cultura y el idioma de los demás.

1 1 causas
    2 ideas
    3 consecuencias
    4 alternativas

1 ___

2 1 quinientos
    2 quince
    3 cinco
    4 cincuenta

2 ___

3 1 olvidado
    2 podido
    3 prohibido
    4 impedido

3 ___

4 1 problemas
    2 reglas
    3 tradiciones
    4 ideas

4 ___

5 1 necesaria
    2 importante
    3 posible
    4 cierta

5 ___

28 A pesar de que los seguros médicos no suelen cubrir los gastos de la terapia alternativa, hoy día millones de personas ___(1)___ tratamientos como la acupuntura, la homeopatía y las medicinas a base de hierbas. Lo que tienen en común todos los tratamientos llamados "holísticos" es que, ante cualquier enfermedad, siempre consideran a la persona no sólo desde el punto de vista físico sino también desde el mental. Los que la practican creen que

  (2)   y el cuerpo no sólo están relacionados sino que son inseparables. Por lo tanto, para curar al paciente hay que atender
ambas partes. Esta creencia rige todo el tratamiento.

  Frecuentemente los resultados de esta medicina son tan efec-
tivos como los de las más complejas tecnologías de la medicina
  (3) . Sin embargo, como frecuentemente se desconocen los
beneficios de cada una de las técnicas y no hay requisitos claros
para todos los que la practican, es posible caer en manos de un
charlatán sin escrúpulos a quien sólo le interesa   (4) . No se le
debe cerrar la puerta a la indudable eficacia de antiguas técnicas
médicas, pero hay que mantenerse alerta a los que aseguran tener
un remedio milagroso. Vale la pena pedirle al practicante que le
muestre estudios o artículos donde se explican los efectos del
método. Además, en algunos casos, como por ejémplo el de los
quiroprácticos, deben tener licencia del estado en que trabajan.
Como mínimo, un profesional debe poder decirle donde recibió
su entrenamiento.

  La medicina convencional reconoce que algunos tratamientos
como la acupuntura y la hipnosis tienen cierta eficacia, pero
  (5)   otros, menos comprobados, como el llamado "imágenes
guiadas" (en el que el paciente controla su enfermedad visual-
izándola hasta que ésta desaparece). Sea lo que sea, no se puede

negar que, hoy día, millones de personas creen en la eficacia de

las antiguas técnicas médicas.

1 1 huyen de
    2 se benefician de
    3 se alejan de
    4 tienen miedo de   1 ____

2 1 la persona
    2 el tratamiento
    3 la enfermedad
    4 la mente   2 ____

3 1 convencional
    2 alternativa
    3 holística
    4 antigua   3 ____

4 1 la técnica
    2 el cuerpo
    3 la enfermedad
    4 el dinero   4 ____

5 1 rechaza
    2 acepta
    3 recomienda
    4 requiere   5 ____

29   Los hispanos tienen su galería de arte

Después de invertir tiempo y esfuerzo en encontrar una galería

interesada en vender y promover su obra, la artista Linda Vallejo

se dio cuenta de la falta de apoyo que tenían los grupos minori-

tarios de Los Angeles por parte de las galerías de arte. Por eso

decidió   (1)   el oficio de vendedora de arte y convertirse ella

misma en artista empresaria.

Hace unos años que estableció la Galería las Américas, en el centro de Los Angeles, como un espacio alternativo que expone los nuevos valores del arte latinoamericano del sur de California. También ella __(2)__ su propio arte, constituido por obras en todos los medios.

Vallejo quiere desarrollar el interés de coleccionistas hispanos, de los cuales hay muy pocos. Por eso, se siente muy orgullosa de que la __(3)__ de los coleccionistas de su galería sean hispanos y que coleccionen arte por primera vez.

La filosofía de Galería las Américas se resume en dos ideas. Primero, Vallejo cree que los hispanos tienen derecho a coleccionar arte. Para eso, ha desarrollado planes especiales que facilitan el __(4)__ de las obras a los que no tienen el dinero. Segundo, dice que existen muchas voces distintas en la comunidad latina y que hay que respetarlas todas para apoyar el arte latino en su totalidad, sin importar cuál sea el mensaje. Según Linda Vallejo, ella es la única artista chicana propietaria de una galería comercial. El año pasado fue premiada por la Comisión Femenil de Los Angeles por su obra y su iniciativa empresarial.

En los años setenta Vallejo se dedicó a estudiar seriamente el __(5)__ del chicanismo y mexicanismo, así como su impacto dentro del arte oficial, y descubrió su identidad cultural como mexicana. Después de un ciclo de diez años de experimentar en el campo de las artes, encontró la manera de expresarse a través de la escultura y, recientemente, de la pintura. Este fin de año exhibe sus obras en óleo. Todo su arte siempre tiene el mismo motivo: los valores indigenistas.

1 1 enseñar
  2 aprender
  3 ocultar
  4 comprar   1 ___

2 1 regala
  2 encuentra
  3 muestra
  4 cambia   2 ___

3 1 mayoría
  2 cantidad
  3 parte
  4 agrupación   3 ___

4 1 costo
  2 pago
  3 dinero
  4 precio   4 ___

5 1 talento
  2 cuento
  3 significado
  4 ensayo   5 ___

30   Un maestro apasionado al piano

Santiago Rodríguez no llegó a tener éxito de la noche a la mañana. Aunque recibió en 1981, a los 29 años, la Medalla de Plata en la Competencia Internacional Van Cliburn, en Texas, y es considerado uno de los mejores intérpretes del compositor ruso Sergio Rachmaninov, el pianista cubanoamericano ha logrado el reconocimiento internacional estudiando y practicando mucho.

Hace unos años se cumplieron 50 años de la muerte de Rachmaninov, y Rodríguez, quien emigró a los Estados Unidos en 1960, recibió numerosas invitaciones para dar homenaje al ilustre compositor. Por eso, ofreció más de 80 recitales en el país y   (1)   del mundo. Rodríguez se destaca por la conjunción de pasión y maestría técnica con que interpreta al compositor ruso.

El pianista reside en Maryland con su esposa Natalia y sus dos hijos. Afirma que la música es su vida, pero dice también que para él es esencial balancear su   (2)   con su familia. El hecho de que Natalia sea la productora de sus discos, lo hace más fácil. Ambos, señala Rodríguez, preparan "una obra muy importante en mi vida": la grabación de tres   (3)   con la música del autor ruso en el próximo año.

Pero su repertorio no se limita al compositor ruso, sino que comprende más de 60 conciertos que van desde las famosas obras de Mozart hasta obras menos   (4)   como el concierto de Busoni. Su *Spanish Album,* con obras del compositor español Manuel de Falla y el padre Antonio Soler confirman   (5)   su talento.

1 1 alrededor
   2 esquina
   3 cuadra
   4 lado   1 ____

2 1 viaje
   2 pariente
   3 dinero
   4 carrera   2 ____

3 1 cuadernos
   2 libros
   3 discos
   4 canciones   3 ____

4 1 cantadas
   2 conocidas
   3 escritas
   4 descubiertas   4 ____

5 1 de nuevo
   2 de pronto
   3 de momento
   4 de importancia   5 ____

PART 4
Writing

The writing section of the Regents Comprehensive Examination consists of two parts. You are expected to write:

I. One well-organized note in Spanish that contains at least six clauses and follows specific instructions. You are given two topics from which to choose. The following example is from the June 18, 1996 Regents Comprehensive Examination in Spanish:

You attended a performance in which your friend Juan took part. Write a note in Spanish to Juan expressing your opinion about the performance.

In the note, you may wish to mention where and when you saw the performance, who went with you, and what your reaction to the performance was. You may also wish to mention what the other people thought about the performance.

II. One well-organized composition in Spanish that contains at least ten clauses. You may choose to write.

- A letter that follows specific instructions, or
- A narrative relating to a drawing provided

The following example is from the June 18, 1996 Regents Comprehensive Examination in Spanish:

In Spanish, write a story about the situation shown in the picture below. It must be a story relating to the picture, not a description of the picture. Do *not* write a dialogue.

You received a letter from your Spanish pen pal, who has told you about his or her plans for a future career. Your pen pal has asked you to respond by telling him or her about your plans for a future career. In Spanish, write a letter to your pen pal telling him or her about your career plans.

You <u>must</u> accomplish the purpose of the letter, which is *to tell your pen pal about your career plans*.

In your letter, you may wish to express your appreciation for your pen pal's last letter and explain why you are writing. In addition to telling your pen pal what plans you have in mind, you may wish to mention why you chose this career, who influenced you, and where you would like to work. You may also wish to discuss your feelings about this type of work and mention people you know who are already working in this field.

You may use any or all the ideas suggested above *or* you may use your own ideas. **Either way, you must tell your pen pal about your career plans.**

Use the following:

Dateline:	18 de junio de 1996
Salutation:	Querido (Querida) _____,
Closing:	Abrazos,

The dateline, salutation, and closing will *not* be counted as part of the ten required clauses.

Guidelines for Writing on the Regents

When you are writing for the Regents, there are several things you must do:

I. Focus on the purpose, that is, be sure to communicate what you have been asked to communicate. You may need to write more than the required number of clauses to accomplish your purpose. If you write more than what is prescribed, however, only the first six or ten clauses will be rated.

II. Pay attention to length:

- The short note must consist of at least six well-organized clauses
- The letter/narrative must consist of at least ten well-organized clauses

III. Always write a first draft on your scrap paper to check for length, purpose, and accuracy before copying to the exam paper.

How Your Writing Is Evaluated on the Regents

Your writing on the Regents Examination will be evaluated in the following manner:

Step 1. Your note and narrative/letter will be read in its entirety to determine whether you have accomplished the purpose of the task. If you have not done so, you will receive no credit.

Step 2. Each sentence will be divided into clauses. For the purpose of rating on the Regents, "a clause must contain a verb, a stated or implied subject, and additional words necessary to convey meaning." This means that the sentence *Tus padres me dijeron/*(1) *que llegas el sábado.*(2) can be divided into two clauses.

In order to ensure that your writing samples have the prescribed number of clauses, write at least six sentences for the note and ten sentences for the letter/narrative.

Step 3. The first six (or ten) clauses will be read to determine if each one is comprehensible and appropriate. *Comprehensibility* is determined by the rater based on his/her judgement "as to whether the clause would be understood by a literate native reader of Spanish who knows no English . . . *Appropriateness* is determined on the basis of the clause's contribution to the development of the note and narrative/letter." If a clause does not meet the criteria for either one of these, you will receive no credit for that clause.

Step 4. The errors in the first six (or ten) clauses will be underlined based on the rules of grammar and orthography. If a clause contains no more than one error, you will receive full credit.

Writing for the Regents

Good writing communicates exactly what you want to say. This is true even when you are writing a short message. Furthermore, because the reader is not there to give you feedback about the clarity of your message, writing usually requires more detailed information, better organization, and more accuracy in form (i.e grammar, usage) than speaking. Unnecessary or misused words and inaccurate spelling or punctuation impede communication.

The compositions you will be writing in this book will be:

- Short notes (usually a short message to friends or relatives)
- Friendly letters (usually telling friends or relatives about something that has happened recently in your life)
- Business letters (usually requesting information, ordering products, etc.)
- Narratives in which you tell about something that happened either to you or to someone else (sometimes based on a picture)

Compositions usually consist of a generalization that is illustrated (supported, explained) by specific facts, examples, and/or personal experiences.

Suggestions for Writing Compositions Beyond the Regents Requirements

I. Any compositions you write should consist of at least three paragraphs in the following pattern:

First paragraph—state what it is you are planning to say. Start out with a good "topic sentence" that states the main idea of the composition.

Second (and perhaps third) paragraph—in this or these paragraphs, say what you planned to say. Each should contain supporting ideas or arguments that explain, justify, or prove the main idea.

Last paragraph—in this paragraph summarize what you have said.

II. Each paragraph usually follows a pattern similar to that of the entire composition. Each one contains:

- An introductory sentence that states the main idea of the paragraph
- One or more supporting ideas or arguments that explain, justify, and support the idea
- Examples that illustrate the main idea
- A concluding sentence that restates the main idea in different terms

Once you have a topic, writing is a process that consists of several stages:

I. Planning stage
Outline what you want to say in the following manner:

- Make a list of any ideas (phrases or words you know in Spanish) that are related to your topic without worrying about their order
- Arrange your list in a logical order
- Discard any phrase that seems to stray from the topic
- Group the remaining phrases in such a way that all the phrases in a group support a main idea
- For each main idea add any examples you may want to use

II. Writing stage
Write your first draft using your outline. Remember to:

- Write in complete sentences
- Separate main ideas into paragraphs
- Have a concluding paragraph where you summarize what you have said

Read your first draft (from the reader's point of view), and:

- Revise organization, making sure the sequence of events and ideas is logical
- Revise content to make sure you are saying what you want to say:

    —elaborate or explain what seems unclear

    —expand by giving more details or examples

    —eliminate what seems unnecessary

    —revise:

    rewrite, reformulating ideas

    combine sentences for variation and interest

    use synonyms for variety

    use pronouns to avoid repetition

    correct grammar errors you find

    look up words you do not know

    check spelling

- Read the second draft going through same process as with first draft (a topic may require several drafts)

III. Final editing stage
Before writing your final draft of the composition, make sure you have checked for:

- Correct punctuation (accents, capitalization, punctuation)
- Appropriate use of words
- Correct spelling, tildes, diaeresis
- Agreement:
  —subject/verb agreement
  —pronoun agreement
  —adjective/noun (pronoun) agreement
  —article/noun agreement
- Accurate use of verbs:
  —correct ending
  —correct tense
  —correct mood (indicative, subjunctive, imperative)
  —correct sequence of tenses
- Accurate use of:
  —negative expressions
  —ser/estar
  —personal *a*
  —pronouns

In a letter, make sure you use proper:

Dateline: (i.e. el dos de septiembre)

Salutation: (i.e. Querido José,)

Closing: (i.e. Tu amigo,)

Practice

For each of the exercises below you may use any or all of the ideas in the description of the task or your own ideas, but you must accomplish the purpose of the note or letter. Remember that if you do not accomplish the purpose you will not receive any credit for what you write.

1 A student from Uruguay sends you an e-mail message requesting your help to find pen pals in the United States. Write him/her a note telling him/her that you are an American student who also likes to correspond with Spanish speakers.

   In your note you may wish to include some information about yourself, your interests, and your hope for being able to speak Spanish and travel to a Spanish-speaking country one day.

Use the following:

Salutation: Estimado (Estimada) _____,
Closing: Recibe un saludo afectuoso, [your name]

2 Several Hispanic restaurants have opened in your area. You visit one and want to tell a pen pal in Puerto Rico about your experience. Write him/her a note describing your visit to one of the restaurants.

   In your note you may wish to include where the restaurant is located, what kind of restaurant it is, the food you had, what you liked or disliked, and whether or not you plan to visit it again.

   Use the following:

Salutation: Muy querido (Muy querida) _____,
Closing: Recibe un abrazo muy fuerte de tu amigo(a),
              [your name]

3 One of your friends lent you a copy of a magazine published in Barcelona, Spain. You liked it very much and would like to receive a subscription. Write a note to the magazine requesting subscription information. After you have identified yourself and stated the purpose of your letter, you may want to inquire about cost, frequency of publication, and form of payment.

   You may also want to include the reason why you like the magazine so much.

   Use the following:

Salutation: Muy estimados señores,
Closing: Un atento saludo, [your name]

4 Your pen pal is coming to visit you and has asked you to tell him/her what is the best season to come. Write him/her a letter telling him/her which is the best season for him/her to come and why. Give him/her some advice as to what type of clothing to bring.

   Use the following:

Salutation: Querido (Querida) _____,
Closing: Cariños, [your name]

5 You are an exchange student in Santiago de Chile. Write a letter to the family where you are staying excusing yourself for not being able to eat dinner with them this evening.

Use the following:

Salutation: Estimados señores,
Closing: Les saluda, [your name]

6 One of your Hispanic friends cannot go on a trip to Costa Rica that your school has arranged because his/her grandmother is sick. Write a note in Spanish to your friend expressing your disappointment.

In your note you may want to include your concern for his/her grandmother and promise him/her that you will bring something back from the trip. You may also wish to mention how sorry your other classmates are about him/her not being able to come with you.

Use the following:

Salutation: Querido (Querida) _____,
Closing: Cariños, [your name]

7 You have been studying Spanish for a while and have decided to attend a school in Cuernavaca, Mexico to refine your knowledge of the language. Write a letter to a school in Cuernavaca requesting information about their summer program in Spanish language and Mexican culture.

In your note you may want to include information about your experience with Spanish, what you wish to accomplish while you are there, and also request information about the price, courses, etc.

Use the following:

Salutation: Estimado Sr. (Estimada Sra.) _____,
Closing: Sinceramente, [your name]

8 Your pen pal has received a note from you in which you tell him/her about your desire to get a computer. He/she does not quite understand why you need one. Write him/her a note explaining the reason why you want a computer.

In your note, you may wish to mention that your friends all have a computer, that you wish to use the Internet, and that you need it for your classes.

Use the following:

Salutation: Querido (Querida) _____,
Closing: Saludos, [your name]

9 Your friend from the Dominican Republic writes to you telling you how much he/she enjoys watching television and all the programs he/she watches. Write him/her a note expressing your concern about this.

In your note you may wish to mention some of the good programs he/she should be watching as well as the bad influence that television could have on him/her.

Use the following:

Salutation: Querido (Querida) _____ ,
Closing: Un abrazo [your name]

10 The host family with whom you stayed in Peru just sent you a present to congratulate you for your grades in Spanish. Write them a note thanking them for the present.

In your note you may want to include how much you liked it, how important their help was while you were in Peru, and some of your plans for the future in regard to your study of Spanish.

Use the following:

Salutation: Queridos _____ ,
Closing: Un abrazo [your name]

11 Last week it was your friend's birthday and you forgot to send him/her a card. Write him/her a note apologizing.

In your note you may want to include the reason why you did not send him/her a card, and what you will do in order to remember in the future. You may also want to extend an invitation to him/her to make up for your forgetfulness.

Use the following:

Salutation: Queridísimo (Queridísima) _____ ,
Closing: Un fuerte abrazo, [your name]

12 You plan to take courses during the summer this year. Write a letter convincing a friend to take classes with you. Talk about the advantages, i.e. learning new things, meeting new people, making new friends, spending time together, etc.

Use the following:

Salutation: Querido (Querida) _____ ,
Closing: Un abrazo, [your name]

13 Your friend is planning to wear a particular outfit for the biggest party of the year. Convince him/her to wear a different outfit than he/she is planning to wear, and mention why it would be more appropriate.

> *Use the following:*
>
> Salutation: Querido (Querida) _____,
> Closing: Cariños, [your name]

14 On your way to school you buy a local Spanish newspaper. One of the articles deals with the issue of American students not wanting to learn a foreign language. Write a note to the newspaper disclaiming the fact that American students do not want to learn a foreign language.
    In your note you may wish to mention how much you enjoy learning Spanish, what you hope it will do for you in the future, and how important you believe learning a foreign language is.

> *Use the following:*
>
> Salutation: Estimados señores,
> Closing: Les saluda atentamente, [your name]

15 One of the newspapers written in Spanish that you like to read has changed lately. Write a note to the editors suggesting that you would like to see more articles of interest to you and youth in general.
    In your note you may wish to include the type of articles you enjoy, and give some specific suggestions as to some of the topics they may want to address.

> *Use the following:*
>
> Salutation: Estimado Sr. (Estimada Sra.) _____,
> Closing: Cordialmente, [your name]

16 An exchange student who was staying with you has written you telling you about his/her trip back. He/she tells you that he/she lost his/her luggage and has not received it yet. Write a note in Spanish expressing your concern and hope that he/she will receive it soon.
    In your note, you may wish to give your friend some advice, tell him/her that you will call the airline, and ask him/her to let you know as soon as he/she receives it.

Use the following:

Salutation: Querido (Querida) _____,
Closing: Un abrazo [your name]

17 On your last trip to Tijuana, Mexico you bought some shoes for your aunt in a department store. Write a note in Spanish to the manager of the store requesting that he/she change the shoes you bought because they do not fit your aunt.

     In your note you may want to include when you bought the shoes, the size you need, and ask for a refund if is necessary.

Use the following:

Salutation: Estimados señores, _____,
Closing: Cordialmente, [your name]

18 As part of your assignment for your Spanish class you need to consult some books you cannot find in the United States. A friend gives you the e-mail address of a company in Madrid, Spain. Write an e-mail message to the bookstore in Madrid requesting information about the books you need for the report.

     In your note you may wish to mention the type of books you are looking for and how soon you need them, and to inquire about the cost for the books and the shipping.

Use the following:

Salutation: Muy estimado Sr. (Muy estimada Sra.)
              _____,

Closing: Atentamente, [your name]

19 On your way back from Barcelona, you intended to call and make plans during a stopover in Madrid to meet your friend Mari Carmen at the airport. At the last minute, the flight was changed to a direct flight and you didn't have time to call her. Write her a letter explaining what happened and excusing yourself for not being able to see her.

Use the following:

Salutation: Querida Mari Carmen _____,
Closing: Cariños, [your name]

20 You are going to a party tomorrow and have just realized that the suit you were going to wear needs to be cleaned and fixed. Write a note to your roommate asking her/him to take it to the dry cleaners and explain what needs to be done. You must remind him/her that it has to be ready for to-morrow.

Use the following:

Salutation: Queridísimo (Queridísima) _____,
Closing: Un fuerte abrazo, [your name]

Practice

Directions (1–10): In Spanish, write a **story** about the situation shown in the picture below. It must be a story relating to the picture, **not** a description of the picture. Do **not** write a dialogue.

APPENDIX 1
Idiomatic Expressions

Idiomatic Expressions with *dar*

dar a—to face, to look out upon

dar con—to run into

dar la mano—to shake hands

dar las gracias—to thank

dar recuerdos a—to give regards to

dar un paseo—to take a walk

dar un paseo en coche—to go for a ride

dar una vuelta—to take a walk

darse cuenta de—to realize

darse prisa—to hurry

Idiomatic Expressions with *echar*

echar a perder—to spoil

echar (una carta, etc.)—to mail (a letter, etc.)

echar de menos—to miss

echar la culpa—to blame

Idiomatic Expressions with *hacer*

hace poco—a little while ago

hacer caso—to pay attention

hacer daño—to hurt

hacerle falta—to need, to be lacking

hacer la cama—to make the bed

hacer la maleta—to pack one's suitcase

hacer un viaje—to take a trip

hacer una pregunta—to ask a question

WEATHER:

hacer (mucho) frío (calor)—to be (very) cold (hot)

hacer buen (mal) tiempo—to have good (bad) weather

hacer fresco—to be cool

hacer sol—to be sunny

hacer viento—to be windy

¿Qué tiempo hace?—How is the weather?

Idiomatic Expressions with *tener*

tener (algo, mucho) que hacer—to have (something, a lot) to do

tener (mucha) hambre—to be (very) hungry

tener (mucha) sed—to be (very) thirsty

tener (mucha) suerte—to be (very) lucky

tener (mucho) calor, frío—to be (very) hot (cold)

tener celos (de)—to be jealous (of)

tener cuidado—to be careful

tener deseos de—to feel like, to have an urge to

tener dolor de (cabeza, espalda, estómago etc.)—to have (a headache, a backache, a stomachache, etc.)

tener éxito—to be successful

tener ganas de—to feel like, to have an urge to

tener la culpa de—to be to blame for

tener lugar—to take place

tener miedo de—to be afraid of

tener prisa—to be in a hurry

tener razón—to be right; no tener razón—to be wrong

tener sueño—to be sleepy

tener suerte—to be lucky

tener vergüenza de—to be ashamed of

tener . . . años—to be . . . years old

Other Idiomatic Expressions with Verbs

aprender de memoria—to memorize

cumplir . . . años—to turn . . . years old

dejar caer—to drop

estar de acuerdo con—to agree with

estar de buen (mal) humor—to be in a good (bad) mood

estar de moda—to be in vogue

estar enamorado(a) de—to be in love with

importarle a uno—to matter to someone

ir de compras—to go shopping

llevarse bien (mal) con—to get (not get) along with

parecer mentira—to be hard to believe

pasarlo bien (mal)—to have a good (bad) time

pedir prestado—to borrow

perder tiempo—to waste time

ponerse de acuerdo—to come to an agreement

querer decir—to mean

tocarle a uno—to be one's turn

valer la pena—to be worthwhile

Other Idiomatic Expressions

a causa de—on account of, because of

a fines de—at the end of

a la derecha (izquierda)—to the right (left)

a mediados de—in or about the middle of

a menudo—often

a pie—on/by foot

a principios de—at the beginning of

a propósito—by the way

a tiempo—on time

a veces—sometimes

a ver—let's see

ahora mismo—right now

al aire libre—in the open air

al contrario—on the contrary

claro que sí (no)—of course (not)

con mucho gusto—gladly

con permiso—excuse me

de ningún modo, de ninguna manera—not at all

de nuevo—again

de pronto—suddenly

de repente—suddenly

de vez en cuando—from time to time

en cambio—on the other hand

en seguida—at once

en voz alta (baja)—aloud (in a low voice)

lo mismo—the same thing

otra vez—again

para siempre—forever

poco a poco—little by little

por aquí—this way, through here

por desgracia—unfortunately

por ejemplo—for example

por eso—therefore

por favor—please

por fin—finally

por lo menos—at least

por supuesto—of course

sin duda—without a doubt

sin embargo—however

todavía no—not yet

todo el mundo—everybody

ya no—no longer

APPENDIX 2
Problem Words

Spanish—English

actualmente—at present, at the present time

actual—present, current (not *actual*)

anciano(a)—old man (woman)

antiguo(a)—ancient

arena—sand

asco—disgust

asistir a—to attend

atender—attend to

avergonzado—embarrassed

ayudar—to assist

biblioteca—library

bien educado—well-mannered

campamento—camp

campo—field, countryside

collar—necklace

conferencia—lecture

confianza—confidence, trust

cuerdo—sane

darse cuenta de—to realize (become aware of)

diario—daily; el diario— newspaper

disgusto—unpleasantness

editor—publisher

embarazada—pregnant

en realidad—actually

éxito—success

fábrica—factory

grabar—to record

grande—large

idioma—language

ignorar—not to know

introducir—to introduce

jabón—soap

largo(a)—long

lectura—reading

librería—bookstore

mantel—tablecloth

mayor—older

modismo—idiom

no hacer caso—to ignore

padres—parents

pariente—relative

presentar—to introduce (a person)

realizar—to carry out, fulfill

realmente—actually

recordar—to remember

redactor—editor

salida—exit

sano—healthy

sopa—soup

suceso—event, happening

tela—fabric

vaso—glass

English—Spanish

actually—en realidad, realmente

ancient—antiguo(a)

assist—ayudar

attend to—atender

attend—asistir a

bookstore—librería

camp—campamento

carry out (fulfill)—realizar

collar—cuello

daily—diario; newspaper—el diario

disgust—asco

editor—redactor

embarrassed—avergonzado(a)

event, happening—suceso

exit—salida

fabric—tela

factory—fábrica

field, countryside—campo

glass—vaso

healthy—sano

idiom—modismo

ignore—no hacer caso

introduce (a person)—presentar

introduce—introducir

language—idioma

large—grande

lecture—conferencia

library—biblioteca

long—largo(a)

mayor—alcalde

necklace—collar

not to know—ignorar

old man (woman)—anciano(a)

older—mayor

parents—padres

pregnant—embarazada

present—actual

publisher—editor

reading—lectura

realize (become aware of)—darse cuenta de

record (to)—grabar

relative—pariente

remember—recordar

sand—arena

sane—cuerdo

soap—jabón

soup—sopa

success—éxito

tablecloth—mantel

unpleasantness—disgusto

vase—florero, jarrón

well-mannered—bien educado

More Problem Words

ask (a question)—preguntar, hacer una pregunta

ask for (request)—pedir

become (change in physical or emotional state)—ponerse + adjective

become (gradual change over time)—llegar a ser

become (suddenly)—volverse

become (through effort)—hacerse

but (rather)—sino

but—pero

know (a fact, or how to do something)—saber

know (a person or be acquainted with a person or place)—conocer

leave (behind)—dejar

leave (go out)—salir, irse, partir

play (a musical instrument)—tocar

play—jugar

return (give back)—devolver

return (to a place)—volver, regresar

take (transport from one place to another)—llevar

take (in one's hand)—tomar

APPENDIX 3
Transition Words

Writers often give cues to generalize, give examples, or make a transition from one point to another. These cues make it easier to follow a reading passage and, as a result, make it more comprehensible and interesting.

The following list of words is useful when you are trying to understand what someone else has written and also when you are writing in Spanish.

SOME WORDS THAT CAN BE USED WHEN STATING A GENERALIZATION:

(casi) nunca—(almost) never

(casi) siempre—(almost) always

a menudo—frequently, often

con frecuencia—frequently

de costumbre—usually

frecuentemente—frequently

generalmente   generally

por lo general—generally

probablemente—probably

rara vez—rarely

todo el mundo—all, everyone

todos—all, everyone

usualmente—usually

SOME WORDS THAT CAN BE USED WHEN STATING SPECIFIC EXAMPLES, IDEAS, OR ARGUMENTS THAT SUPPORT, EXPLAIN, JUSTIFY, OR PROVE A MAIN POINT:

además—furthermore, in addition

así es que—so

de manera que—so

de modo que—so

en cambio—on the other hand

en otras palabras—in other words

en primer lugar—in the first place

en realidad—actually, in reality

es decir—in other words, that is to say

o sea—in other words, that is to say

para empezar—to begin with

por consiguiente—consequently, therefore

por ejemplo—for example

por eso—consequently, therefore

por lo tanto—consequently, therefore

por otra parte—on the other hand

por otro lado—on the other hand

sin duda—without a doubt

sin embargo—nevertheless

sobre todo—above all

también—also

SOME COMMON WORDS THAT CAN BE USED TO MAKE TRANSITIONS SMOOTHLY FROM SENTENCE TO SENTENCE AND ESPECIALLY FROM PARAGRAPH TO PARAGRAPH (IN ADDITION TO THOSE LISTED ABOVE):

a causa de—because of

a pesar de eso—in spite of

al contrario—on the contrary

en vez de—instead of

pero—but

porque—because

Don't forget to use the most general connecting expressions, which are those that indicate order:

antes—before

ahora—now

hoy día—nowadays

primero—first

entonces—then

luego—later, next

después—later, next

más tarde—later, next

por fin—finally

finalmente—finally

en conclusión—in conclusion

APPENDIX 4
Thematic Vocabulary

The Thematic Vocabulary is a list to help you with the most common words you may need to complete some of the exercises in this book. It is not meant to be an exhaustive list of vocabulary. Please note that under some headings there are particular instructions as to how the vocabulary appears on that list.

In general, keep in mind that all nouns appear in the singular form and adjectives appear in the masculine form.

The following abbreviations are used:

m. = masculine

f. = feminine

sing. = singular

pl. = plural

If a stem-changing verb appears on the list, the change is noted in parentheses, i.e. almorzar (ue).

1. The Family

Unless otherwise noted, the feminine form of the following nouns is formed by changing the -o to an -a. For example: novio—boyfriend, novia—girlfriend. When the feminine form is a different word, there is an asterisk next to the word.

boyfriend—novio	great-grandson—bisnieto
brother—hermano	husband—esposo ✓
brother-in-law—cuñado	mother—madre*
cousin—primo	nephew—sobrino
daughter-in-law—nuera*	relative—pariente
father-in-law—suegro	son—hijo ✓
father—padre*	son-in-law—yerno*
godfather—padrino*	stepbrother—hermanastro
godmother—madrina*	stepfather—padrastro*
godson—ahijado	stepmother—madrastra*
grandfather—abuelo	stepson—hijastro
grandson—nieto	uncle—tío
great-grandfather—bisabuelo	

2. Adjectives to Describe a Person

The adjectives appear in the masculine form, unless otherwise noted. The feminine is formed by changing the -o to an -a. Adjectives that end in an -e or -l are invariable.

TO DESCRIBE SOMEONE'S PHYSICAL APPEARANCE

big—grande

blond—rubio

dark complected—moreno

elegant—elegante

fat—gordo, grueso

good-looking—guapo

poor—pobre

redheaded—pelirrojo

rich—rico

short—bajo

small—pequeño

strong—fuerte

tall—alto

thin—delgado, flaco

ugly—feo

weak—débil

TO DESCRIBE SOMEONE'S PERSONALITY OR INTELLIGENCE

boring—aburrido

careful—cuidadoso

courageous—valiente

coward—cobarde

crazy—loco

decisive—decisivo

diplomatic—diplomático

disobedient—desobediente

dumb—tonto

frank—franco

fun—divertido

generous—generoso

happy—alegre

hard-working—trabajador (m.), trabajadora

honest—honesto, honrado

independent—independiente

intelligent—inteligente, listo

interesting—interesante

ironic—irónico

just—justo

kind—amable

lazy—perezoso

nice—simpático

obedient—obediente

optimist—optimista (m. & f.)

organized—organizado

pessimist—pesimista (m. & f.)

quiet—quieto

respectful—respetuoso

romantic—romántico

sad—triste

sane—cuerdo

serious—serio

sincere—sincero

slow—lento

unpleasant—antipático

3. Adjectives to Express Physical State, Feelings, and Emotions

The adjectives appear in the masculine form, unless otherwise noted. The feminine is formed by changing the -o to an -a. Adjectives that end in an -e or -l are invariable.

angry—enojado

anxious—ansioso

ashamed—avergonzado

busy—ocupado

calm—tranquilo

clean—limpio

depressed—deprimido

dirty—sucio

dry—seco

exhausted—agotado

furious—furioso

grateful—agradecido

happy—alegre, contento

healthy—saludable, sano

nervous—nervioso

relaxed—relajado

restless—inquieto

sad—triste

sick—enfermo

surprised—sorprendido

tired—cansado

ungrateful—desagradecido

wet—mojado

worried—preocupado

4. Parts of the Body

ankle—tobillo (m.)

arm—brazo (m.)

back—espalda (f.)

beard—barba (f.)

blood—sangre (f.)

body—cuerpo (m.)

brain—cerebro (m.)

cheek—mejilla (f.)

chest—pecho (m.)

chin—barbilla (f.)

ear—oreja (f.)

elbow—codo (m.)

eye—ojo (m.)

eyebrow—ceja (f.)

face—cara (f.)

finger—dedo (m.)

foot—pie (m.)

forehead—frente (f.)

hair—pelo (m.), cabello (m.)

hand—mano (f.)

head—cabeza (f.)

heart—corazón (m.)

inner ear—oído (m.)

knee—rodilla (f.)

leg—pierna (f.)

lip—labio (m.)

moustache—bigote (m.)

mouth—boca (f.)

nail—uña (f.)

neck—cuello (m.)

nose—nariz (f.)

shoulder—hombro (m.)

skin—piel (f.)

stomach—estómago (m.)

throat—garganta (f.)

tongue—lengua (f.)

tooth—diente (m.)

wrist—muñeca (f.)

5. Professions and Occupations

All professions and occupations appear in the masculine form first and then the feminine form.

accountant—contador, contadora

actor—actor, actriz

announcer—locutor, locutora

architect—arquitecto, arquitecta

astronaut—astronauta (m. & f.)

author—autor, autora

baker—panadero, panadera

barber—barbero

businessman—hombre de negocios

businesswoman—mujer de negocios

butcher—carnicero, carnicera

carpenter—carpintero, carpintera

dentist—dentista (m. & f.)

doctor—médico, doctor; médica, doctora

driver—conductor, conductora

engineer—ingeniero, ingeniera

flight attendant—asistente de vuelo (m. & f.)

hairdresser—peluquero, peluquera

housewife—ama de casa

journalist—reportero, reportera

lawyer—abogado, abogada

mechanic—mecánico, mecánica

nurse—enfermero, enfermera

photographer—fotógrafo, fotógrafa

programmer—programador, programadora

salesperson—vendedor, vendedora

secretary—secretario, secretaria

shoemaker—zapatero, zapatera

singer—cantante (m. & f.)

surgeon—cirujano, cirujana

taxi driver—taxista (m. & f.)

teacher—maestro, profesor; maestra, profesora

waiter—camarero, camarera

writer—escritor, escritora

6. Countries and Nationalities

SPANISH-SPEAKING COUNTRIES

Argentina—argentino(a)

Bolivia—boliviano(a)

Chile—chileno(a)

Colombia—colombiano(a)

Costa Rica—costarricense

Cuba—cubano(a)

Ecuador—ecuatoriano(a)

El Salvador—salvadoreño(a)

España—español, española

Guatemala—guatemalteco(a)

Honduras—hondureño(a)

México—mexicano(a)

Nicaragua—nicaragüense

Panamá—panameño(a)

Paraguay—paraguayo(a)

Perú—peruano(a)

Puerto Rico—puertorriqueño

República Dominicana—
dominicano(a)

Uruguay—uruguayo(a)

Venezuela—venezolano(a)

OTHER COUNTRIES

Alemania—alemán, alemana

Canadá—canadiense

China—chino(a)

Corea—coreano(a)

Francia—francés, francesa

Haiti—haitiano(a)

India—indio(a)

Inglaterra—inglés, inglesa

Irlanda—irlandés, irlandesa

Italia—italiano(a)

Japón—japonés, japonesa

Filipinas—filipino(a)

Portugal—portugués, portuguesa

Rusia—ruso(a)

7. In the House

add—agregar, añadir

alarm clock—(reloj) (m.)
despertador (m.)

apron—delantal (m.)

armchair—sillón (m.), butaca (f.)

balcony—balcón (m.)

bathe—bañarse

bathtub—bañera (f.)

bed—cama (f.)

blanket—frazada (f.), manta (f.)

boil—hervir (ie)

bookshelf—estante (m.)

burn—quemar

chair—silla (f.)

closet—armario (m.)

coffee table—mesita (f.)

cook—cocer (ue), cocinar

cup—taza (f.)

desk—escritorio (m.)

dishwasher—lavaplatos (m.),

dresser—cómoda (f.)

faucet—grifo (m.)

food—comida (f.), alimento (m.)

fork—tenedor (m.)

glass—vaso (m.)

hair dryer—secadora para el pelo
(f.)

hanger—percha (f.)

iron—plancha (f.)

iron—planchar

kitchen range—estufa (f.), cocina
(f.)

knife—cuchillo (m.)

lamp—lámpara (f.)

light—luz (f.)

meal—comida (f.)

microwave—microonda (f.)

mirror—espejo (m.)

napkin—servilleta (f.)

night table—mesita de noche (f.)

oven—horno (m.)

pillow—almohada (f.)

pillowcase—funda (f.)

plate—plato (m.)

poster—cartel (m.)

put makeup on—maquillarse

refrigerator—refrigerador (m.),
nevera (f.)

rug—alfombra (f.)

set the table—poner la mesa (irr.)

shave—afeitarse

sheet—sábana (f.)

shower—ducha (f.)

shower—ducharse

soap—jabón (m.)

sofa—sofá (m.)

spoon—cuchara (f.)

stair—escalera (f.)

sweep—barrer

tablecloth—mantel (m.)

teaspoon—cucharita (f.)

television set—televisor (m.)

toilet—retrete (m.), inodoro (m.)

toilet paper—papel higiénico (m.)

towel—toalla (f.)

wash—lavar

wash—lavarse

wash dishes—fregar (ie)

washbasin—lavamanos (m. sing. &
pl.)

8. In School

attend—asistir a

backpack—mochila (f.)

ballpoint pen—bolígrafo (m.)

book—libro (m.)

chalkboard—pizarra (f.)

classroom—aula (f.), salón de
clases (m.)

desk—pupitre (m.)

elementary school—escuela
primaria (f.)

fail—salir mal, ser suspendido

get good (bad) grades—sacar
buenas (malas) notas

grade—nota (f.)

graduate—graduarse

graduation—graduación (f.)

high school—escuela secundaria
(f.)

homework—tarea (f.)

learn—aprender

lesson—lección (f.)

major (in), specialize (in)—
especializarse

notebook—cuaderno (m.)

pass—salir bien, aprobar

pencil—lápiz (m.)

principal—director (m.), directora
(f.)

register—matricularse

report—informe (m.)

schedule—horario (m.)

scholarship—beca (f.)

student—estudiante (m. & f.),
alumno (m.)

subject—asignatura (f.)

take notes—tomar apuntes

teach—enseñar
teacher—maestro

test—examen (m.)

9. In the Movie House/Theater

act—acto (m.)

actor—actor (m.)

actress—actriz (f.)

be about—tratarse de

box office—taquilla (f.)

character—personaje (m.)

comedy—comedia (f.)

drama—drama (m.)

stage, scenery—escenario (m.)

musical—obra musical (f.)

performance—función (f.)

play a role—hacer el papel de

plot—trama (f.)

row—fila (f.)

scene—escena (f.)

screen—pantalla (f.)

seat—asiento (m.)

ticket—entrada (f.)

tragedy—tragedia (f.)

work—obra (f.)

10. In the Bank

account—cuenta (f.)

bill—billete (m.)

borrow—pedir prestado

cash—cobrar

cash—dinero en efectivo (m.)

change (loose coins)—suelto (m.),
  cambio (m.)

check—cheque (m.)

checking account—cuenta de
  cheques (f.), cuenta corriente (f.)

coin—moneda (f.)

credit card—tarjeta de crédito (f.)

deposit—depositar, hacer un
  depósito

exchange—cambiar

loan—préstamo (m.)

money—dinero (m.)

save—ahorrar

savings account—cuenta de ahorros
  (f.)

traveler's check—cheque de viajero
  (m.)

withdraw—sacar

11. In the Post Office

address—dirección (f.)

air mail—correo aéreo (m.)

deliver—repartir

letter—carta (f.)

mail carrier—cartero

mailbox—buzón (m.)

money order—giro postal (m.)

package—paquete (m.)

post office box—apartado postal
  (m.)

postcard—tarjeta postal (f.)

send—enviar, mandar

sender—remitente (m.)

shipping charge—costo de envío (m.)

stamp—estampilla (f), sello (m.)

telegram—telegrama (m.)

window—ventanilla (f.)

zip code—zona postal (f.)

12. At the Hairdresser/Barber

beard—barba (f.)

cut—cortar

dye—teñir (i)

haircut—corte de pelo (m.)

hairdresser—barbero, peluquero

handkerchief—pañuelo (m.)

manicure—manicura (f.)

moustache—bigote (m.)

pedicure—pedicura (f.)

shampoo—champú (m.)

shave—afeitar (se)

sideburn—patilla (f.)

trim—recorte (m.)

13. At the Clothing Store

be in style—estar de moda

belt—cinturón (m.)

blouse—blusa (f.)

coat—abrigo (m.), sobretodo (m.)

cap—gorra, gorro

dress—vestido (m.)

fabric—tela (f.)

fit well—quedarle bien; not fit— quedarle mal

glove—guante (m.)

handkerchief—pañuelo (m.)

hat—sombrero (m.)

jacket—chaqueta (f.)

match—hacer juego con

measure—medir (i)

pants—pantalones (m.)

pay cash—pagar al contado/en efectivo

pocketbook—bolso (m.), bolsa (f.)

raincoat—impermeable (m.)

scarf—bufanda (f.)

shirt—camisa (f.)

size—talla (f.)

skirt—falda (f.)

sock—calcetín (m.)

stocking—media (f.)

suit—traje (m.)

sweater—suéter (m.)

swimsuit—traje de baño (m.)

t-shirt—camiseta (f.)

tie—corbata (f.)

14. In the Shoe Store

boot—bota (f.)

fit—quedarle bien; not fit—
  quedarle mal

heel—tacón (m.)

high heels—tacones altos

leather—cuero (m.)

measure—medir (i)

narrow—estrecho

pair—par (m.)

sandal—sandalia (f.)

shoe—zapato (m.)

shoelaces—cordones (m.)

size—número (m.)

sneakers—zapatos de tenis

sole—suela (f.)

vest—chaleco (m.)

wide—ancho

15. In the Doctor's Office

ache—dolor (m.)

bandage—vendaje (m.), venda (f.)

chill—escalofrío (m.)

cold—catarro (m.), resfriado (m.)

cough—tos (f.)

cough—toser

dizzy—mareado

ear—oído (m.)

earache—dolor de oído

fever—fiebre (f.)

flu—gripe (f.)

headache—dolor de cabeza (m.)

hurt—tener dolor de . . .

injection—inyección (f.)

break—romperse (+ part of the
  body)

sick—enfermo

sneeze—estornudar

sore throat—dolor de garganta (m.)

stomachache—dolor de estómago
  (m.)

symptom—síntoma (m.)

weigh—pesar

16. Food Stores

bakery—panadería (f.)

butcher shop—carnicería (f.)

fish store—pescadería (f.)

grocery store—bodega (f.)

market—mercado (m.)

supermarket—supermercado (m.)

17. In the Restaurant

appetizers—entremeses (m.)

check—cuenta (f.)

dessert—postre (m.)

fish—pescado (m.)

fried—frito

fruit—fruta (f.)

house specialty—especialidad (f.)
  de la casa

main course—plato principal (m.)

meat—carne (f.)

menu—menú (m.)

salad—ensalada (f.)

soup—sopa (f.)

tip—propina (f.)

vegetables—vegetales (m.),
  legumbres (f.)

waiter—camarero (m.)

waitress—camarera (f.)

18. At the Hotel

air conditioning—aire
  acondicionado (m.)

available—disponible

bath—baño (m.)

bed—cama (f.)

bellhop—botones (m.)

bill—cuenta (f.)

cashier—cajero (m.)

clerk—recepcionista (m. & f.)

elevator—ascensor (m)

full—lleno

guest—huésped (m., f.)

heat—calefacción (f.)

key—llave (f.)

registration—recepción (f.)

reservation—reservación (f.),
  reserva (f.)

room service—servicio de cuartos
  (habitaciones) (m.)

room—cuarto (m.), habitación (f.)

swimming pool—piscina (f.)

19. Using the Telephone

area code—código de área (m.)

busy—ocupado

call—llamada (f.)

collect call—llamada con cobro
  revertido (f.)

dial tone—tono (m.), señal (f.)

dial—marcar

hang up—colgar (ue)

local—local

long-distance—larga distancia (f.)

message—mensaje (m.)

number—número (m.)

operator—operador(a),
  telefonista (f.)

person-to-person—de persona a
  persona

pick up—descolgar (ue), responder

ring—sonar (ue)

telephone book—guía telefónica (f.)

telephone booth—cabina telefónica (f.)

wrong number—número equivocado (m.)

20. Sports

ball—balón (m.) (soccer)

ball—pelota (f.) (baseball, tennis, etc.)

baseball—béisbol (m.)

basket—canasta (f.), cesto (m.)

basketball—baloncesto (m.), básquetbol (m.)

court—cancha (f.)

football—fútbol americano (m.)

lose—perder (ie)

match—partido (m.)

net—red (f.)

play—jugar (ue)

player—jugador (m.), jugadora (f.)

racket—raqueta (f.)

referee—árbitro (m.)

soccer—fútbol (m.)

sprain—torcerse (ue)

team—equipo (m.)

tennis—tenis (m.)

throw—lanzar

tournament—torneo (m.)

train—entrenar (se)

volleyball—vólibol (m.)

win—ganar

21. Means of Transportation

arrival—llegada (f.)

brake—frenar

bus—autobús (m.)

delay—demora (f.)

departure—salida (f.)

destination—destino (m.)

early—adelantado

express—espreso

gas—gasolina (f.)

horn—bocina (f.)

late—con retraso, atrasado

license—permiso de conducir

luggage—equipaje (m.)

on time—a tiempo

one way—sencillo (m.)

platform—andén (m.)

rent—alquilar

reserved—reservado

ride a bike—montar en bicicleta

ride a horse—montar a caballo

round trip—viaje de ida y vuelta (m.)

schedule—horario (m.)

start (a motor)—arrancar

start the car—poner el coche en marcha

station—estación (f.)

stop—parar

suitcase—maleta (f.)

tank—tanque (m.)

ticket window—ventanilla (f.)

ticket—boleto (m.), billete (m.)

tire—neumático (m.)

train—tren (m.)

trunk—maletero (m.)

waiting room—sala de espera (f.)

22. At the Airport

agent—agente (m. & f.)

arrival—llegada (f.)

available—disponible

board, go aboard—embarcarse

boarding gate—puerta de embarque (f.)

boarding pass—tarjeta de embarque (f.)

change planes—cambiar de avión

check—facturar

counter—mostrador (m.)

customs agent—aduanero

customs declaration—declaración (f.) de aduana

declare—declarar

departure—salida (f.)

destination—destino (m.)

fare—tarifa (f.)

fasten the seat belt—abrocharse el cinturón de seguridad

first class—primera clase

flight attendant—asistente de vuelo (m. & f.)

flight—vuelo (m.)

fly—volar (ue)

full—lleno, completo

label, tag—etiqueta (f.)

land—aterrizar

luggage—equipaje (m.)

make a line—hacer cola

nonstop—sin escala

on the aisle—en el pasillo

passaport—pasaporte (m.)

passenger—pasajero

personal belongings—efectos personales

row—fila (f.)

seat—asiento (m.)

security check—control de seguridad (m.)

stop—escala (f.)

suitcase—maleta (f.)

take off—despegar

terminal—terminal (f.)

ticket—boleto (m.)

tourist card—tarjeta de turista (f.)

visa—visa (f.)

23. Animals, Insects, etc.

ant—hormiga (f.)

bear—oso

bee—abeja (f.)

bull—toro (m.)

butterfly—mariposa (f.)

camel—camello (m.)

cat—gato

chicken—pollo (m.)

cow—vaca (f.)

deer—venado

dog—perro

dolphin—delfín (m.)

donkey—burro

duck—pato

eagle—águila (f.)

elephant—elefante (m.)

fish—pez (live), pescado

fly—mosca (f.)

fox—zorro

frog—rana (f.)

giraffe—jirafa (f.)

goat—cabra (f.)

hen—gallina (f.)

horse—caballo (m.)

lamb—oveja (f.)

lion—león (m.)

mare—yegua (f.)

mosquito—mosquito

mouse—ratón (m.)

parakeet—perico

pig—cerdo (m.)

rabbit—conejo

rat—rata (f.)

roach—cucaracha (f.)

rooster—gallo (m.)

serpent—serpiente (f.)

spider—araña (f.)

squirrel—ardilla (f.)

tiger—tigre (m.)

turtle—tortuga (f.)

whale—ballena (f.)

wolf—lobo (m.)

zebra—cebra (f.)

24. Days of the Week

All days of the week are masculine in Spanish.

Monday—lunes

Tuesday—martes

Wednesday—miércoles

Thursday—jueves

Friday—viernes

Saturday—sábado

Sunday—domingo

25. Months of the Year

January—enero

February—febrero

March—marzo

April—abril

May—mayo

June—junio

July—julio

August—agosto

September—septiembre

October—octubre

November—noviembre

December—diciembre

26. The Seasons of the Year

spring—primavera (f.)

summer—verano (m.)

autumn—otoño (m.)

winter—invierno (m.)

APPENDIX 5
Numbers

Cardinal Numbers

All cardinal numbers are masculine in Spanish.

0 cero	28 veintiocho
1 un(o), una	29 veintinueve
2 dos	30 treinta
3 tres	40 cuarenta
4 cuatro	50 cincuenta
5 cinco	60 sesenta
6 seis	70 setenta
7 siete	80 ochenta
8 ocho	90 noventa
9 nueve	100 ciento (cien)
10 diez	101 ciento uno (una)
11 once	102 ciento dos (tres, cuatro, etc.)
12 doce	200 doscientos, as
13 trece	300 trescientos, as
14 catorce	400 cuatrocientos, as
15 quince	500 quinientos, as
16 dieciséis	600 seiscientos, as
17 diecisiete	700 setecientos, as
18 dieciocho	800 ochocientos, as
19 diecinueve	900 novecientos, as
20 veinte	1,000 mil
21 veintiuno	2,000 dos mil (tres mil, cuatro mil, etc.)
22 veintidós	100,000 cien mil
23 veintitrés	200,000 doscientos, (-as) mil
24 veinticuatro	1,000,000 un millón (de + noun)
25 veinticinco	2,000,000 dos millones (de + noun)
26 veintiséis	1,000,000,000 mil millones (de + noun)
27 veintisiete	

Keep in mind the following points when expressing numbers in Spanish:

- You may write the numbers 16 through 19 and 21 through 29 as three words *(diez y seis, diez y siete, diez y ocho, diez y nueve, veinte y uno, veinte y dos, veinte y tres, veinte y cuatro, veinte y cinco, veinte y seis, veinte y siete, veinte y ocho, veinte y nueve)*. Note that no accent is needed.
- *Un* is not used before *cien(to)* and *mil*.

  cien libros—a (one) hundred books
  mil árboles—a (one) thousand trees

- *Ciento* changes to *cien* when it is immediately in front of nouns, and in front of *mil* and *millones (de)*.

  cien discos compactos—a hundred compact disks
  cien mil dólares—one hundred thousand dollars
  cien millones de habitantes—one hundred million inhabitants

- In front of a feminine noun the ending *-cientos* changes to *-cientas*.

  doscientos escritorios—two hundred desks
  doscientas sillas—two hundred chairs

- Thousands are indicated with periods instead of commas in Spanish.

Ordinal Numbers

first—primero (primer), primera

second—segundo, segunda

third—tercero (tercer), tercera

fourth—cuarto, cuarta

fifth—quinto, quinta

sixth—sexto, sexta

seventh—séptimo, séptima

eighth—octavo, octava

ninth—noveno, novena

tenth—décimo, décima

Keep in mind the following when using ordinal numbers:

- Ordinal numbers agree in gender and number with the nouns they modify.

  Tenemos que terminar la primera lección
  We have to finish the first lesson.

- Ordinal numbers may be placed in front of or after the noun.

El segundo acto (El acto segundo) es mi favorito.
The second act is my favorite.

- In front of a masculine singular noun *primero* and *tercero* drop the final *-o*.

El ascensor no para en el primer (tercer) piso.
The elevator does not stop in the first (third) floor.

APPENDIX 6
Dates

- To find out the date in Spanish, you may use any of the following questions.

¿Cuál es la fecha?	Es el quince de junio.
¿A cómo estamos?	Estamos a dos de enero.
¿A cuántos estamos?	Estamos a primero de agosto.

- When writing a date you must remember that cardinal numbers are used, except for the first of the month. They are preceeded by the article *el.*

Hoy es el primero de octubre.
Today is the first of October.

El examen es el tres de mayo.
The exam is May third.

- The names of the months are never capitalized in Spanish.

- *De* is used between the month and the year.

Diego nació el doce de abril.
Diego was born April 12.

- When writing the date on a letter, the article *el* is omitted.

San Francisco, 14 de diciembre de 1990.
San Francisco, December 14, 1990.

APPENDIX 7
Telling Time

- To find out the time in Spanish, you ask:

  ¿Qué hora es?   What time is it?

  ¿Qué hora tiene(s)?   What time do you have?

- The verb *ser* and the feminine article *la* or *las* are used to express the hour.

  Es la una.   It's one o'clock.

  Son las tres.   It's three o'clock.

Note that the singular form of the verb as well as the singular form of the article are used to express one o'clock.

- *Menos* and *y* are used to express the time before or after the hour.

  Son las cuatro menos diez.
  It's ten minutes to four.

  Es la una y veinte.
  It's twenty minutes after one.

- To express the quarter and half hour you use:

  y cuarto—a quarter after (past)
  y media—half past (thirty minutes past)
  menos cuarto—a quarter to

- The preposition *a* is used to express *at.*

  ¿A qué hora empiezas las clases? A las ocho menos cuarto.
  At what time do you start classes? At a quarter to eight.

- Noon is *mediodía,* and midnight, *medianoche.*

- *En punto* is used to express *sharp/on the dot.*

  Tienes que llegar a las dos en punto.
  You have to arrive at two o'clock sharp/on the dot.

- *At about* is expressed by *a eso de.*

  Salgo a eso de las ocho.
  I leave at about eight o'clock.

- To make it clear whether it is morning, afternoon, or evening use *de la mañana, de la tarde, de la noche.*

  La reunión es a las tres de la tarde.
  The meeting is at three o'clock in the afternoon.

APPENDIX 8
Accentuation

All words in Spanish are stressed according to some specific rules. Any word that does not follow the specific rules must have a written accent to indicate the correct stress.

- Words that end in a vowel or *n* or *s* are usually stressed on the next to the last syllable.

camisa	ayudan	tenis
persona	reciben	grupos

- Words that end in a consonant, except *n* or *s,* are stressed on the last syllable.

recibir	verdad	hotel	actriz

- Any word that does not fall under the two categories above needs a written accent on the stressed syllable

conversación	sábado	francés	película
matemáticas	crímenes	siéntese	lápiz

APPENDIX 9
Capitalization

The only cases in which capital letters are used in Spanish are:

- At the beginning of a sentence or a title

  Hace buen tiempo.
  The weather is nice.

  La mejor película es *Como agua para chocolate.*
  The best movie is *Like Water for Chocolate.*

- In proper names of people and places

  Voy a España con María.
  I'm going to Spain with María.

- In abbreviations

  ¿Es Ud. el presidente de los EE.UU.?
  Are you the president of the United States?

APPENDIX 10
Answer Key for Grammar Exercises

In order for you to verify whether or not you have understood the material you are studying, we have provided the answer to every other question in each of the grammar exercises. A page number (in parentheses) indicates the first page of exercise A in each group of exercises. Other exercises in the group (B, C, etc.) will not be followed by a page number.

As you are doing each exercise, keep in mind that:

* In some instances there is only one possible response.

* When more than one response is possible, the heading "Answers will vary." is followed by several possible answers. These answers are not meant to be an exhaustive list of possible answers.

Unit 1—Socializing

LESSON 1
Part A
Exercises (p. 2)
A. Answers will vary.
  1.—¡Buenos días!
  3.—Bien, ¿y a ti?
  5.—Buenas tardes.
B. Answers will vary.
  1.—Muy bien, señorita López, ¿y Ud.?
  3.—Hola, Sra. García.
  5.—Buenos días, Sra. Iglesias.

Part B
Exercises (p. 3)
  Answers will vary.
  1.—¡Hasta el sábado!
  3.—Adiós.
  5.—Hasta la próxima.

Part C
Exercises (p. 4)
  Answers will vary.
  1.—(name) y (name), quisiera
    presentarles a mi amigo Ricardo.
    —Encantado (name), (name).
    —Mucho gusto, Ricardo.
  3.—Este es (name).
    —Encantado(a).
    —Mucho gusto.
More exercises (p. 5)
A. Answers will vary.
  1.—¡Hola!

  3.—¡Hasta luego!
  5.—Regular, ¿y tú?
  7.—El gusto es mío.
B. Answers will vary.
  —¡Hola!
  —Mucho gusto, Sebastián.
    Encantado.
  —Bien, ¿y a ti?
  —Hasta pronto.
C. Answers will vary.
  —Buenos días Sr./Sra./Srta. (name).
  —Buenos días.
  —Le presento a mi amigo(a) (name).
  —Mucho gusto.
  —Mucho gusto.
  —Hasta luego.
  —Adiós.

Parts D & E
Exercises (p. 7)
  Answers will vary.
  1.—Mucho gusto./Encantado(a).
    /El gusto es mío.
  3.—Lo siento (mucho)./Perdón.
  5.—Adiós./Hasta la próxima./Hasta
    luego.
  7.—Con permiso.

Part F
Exercises (p. 9)
  Answers will vary.
  1.—Aló./Bueno./Diga./Dígame.
  3.—Aló./Bueno./Diga./Dígame.
  5.—¿De parte de quién?/¿Quién
    habla?/Un momento, por favor.

Part G
Exercises (p. 11)
Answers will vary.
1. —Estimado(a).../Muy señor
   mío./Muy señor(a) nuestro(a), etc.
   Atentamente, /Suyo(a) afectísimo(a),
   etc.
3. —Muy estimado(a) Sr. (Sra.)
   (name),/Muy
   señor(a) nuestro(a), etc.
5. —Te/Le agradezco tu/su carta
   de.../He recibido tu/su carta..., etc.
7. —Besos y abrazos,/Un abrazo
   de,/Con todo el cariño de, etc.

Unit 2—Providing and Obtaining Information

LESSON 2
Part A
Exercises (p.14)
Answers will vary.
A. 1.—Vamos al parque, ¿verdad?
   3.—¿Tienes dinero?
   5.—¿Vamos juntos(as)?
   7.—Llevamos el postre, ¿no?
B. 1.—Sí, (yo) vivo en el campo./No,
      (yo) no vivo en el campo./No,
      (yo) vivo en la ciudad.
   3.—Sí, el barrio es muy bueno./No, el
      barrio no es muy bueno./No, el
      barrio es malo.
   5.—Sí, salgo de compras en el
      barrio./No, no salgo de compras
      en el barrio./No, voy al centro.
   7.—Sí, (nosotros) vamos en coche./No,
      (nosotros) no vamos en coche./No,
      (nosotros) vamos en autobús.
Exercises (p. 18)
A. 1. Quién
   3. Por qué
   5. Cuándo
   7. Cuánto
B. 3. ¿Adónde quieren ir (ellos)?
   5. ¿Dónde vive (ella)?
   7. ¿Cuándo viene (ella)?
   9. ¿Cuándo va de compras (Graciela)?
   11. ¿Por qué va (Graciela) al
       supermercado?
   13. ¿Quién limpia la casa?
   15. ¿A dónde van a cenar?
   17. ¿Qué tiene (Carlos)?
   19. ¿Cómo es?
   21. ¿Para quién es la otra bicicleta?
   23. ¿Cuántos años tienen sus hermanas?
C. 1. ¿Cuánto cuesta (la blusa)?
   3. ¿De quién es (la mochila)?
   5. ¿A qué hora es la cita?

7. ¿Cuándo regresan/vuelven?
9. ¿Cuánto cuestan las hamburguesas?

Part B
Exercises (p. 24)
1. el, El, el.
3. la, La.
5. el, El.
7. El, el.
9. la, La, el.
Exercises (p. 26)
1. X, al, las, la, el, el, El, el, X, El, el,
   X, el.
Exercises (p. 28)
A. X, X, un, X, un, X, X, X, X.
B. 1. la, el, un, una, la, los/unos, unos.
Exercises (p. 30)
A. 1. las manzanas
   3. los melones
   5. las lechugas
   7. los tomates
   9. las fresas
   11. los mangos
B. 1. una manzana
   3. unas lechugas
C. Cierto, media, mil, cien, otro.
D. 1. Es juez/abogado.
   3. Es escritora/autora.
   5. Son periodistas/reporteros.
   7. Es cartero.
E. 1. Ricardo es un carnicero muy bueno.
   3. El Sr. Rodríguez y la Sra. Ruíz son
      unos dentistas excelentes.
   5. Inés es una traductora fenomenal.
F. Answers will vary.
   En mi cuarto hay una cama, dos
   estantes, un televisor, una ventana, etc.
G. Answers will vary.
   1. —¿Hay muchos estantes (en tu
      cuarto)?
   3. —¿Tienes una alfombra?
   5. —¿Hay un radio?

Part C
Exercises (p. 34)
A. Answers will vary.
   1. Mi mejor amigo es simpático. Es
      inteligente. También es optimista.
   3. Mi profesora de español es
      interesante. Es divertida. También
      es cubana.
   5. Mis clases son emocionantes. Son
      grandes. También son difíciles.
B. 1. Louise es canadiense.
   3. Christophe es francés.
   5. Sofía es nicaragüense.
C. Answers will vary.
   1. Mi actriz favorita tiene el pelo
      negro, los ojos pardos, la cara
      ovalada, la boca ancha y la nariz
      grande.

Part D
Exercises (p. 34)
A. Answers will vary.
  1. Antes de un examen, Alicia está
    preocupada.
  3. Si nosotros no tenemos nada que
    hacer, nosotros estamos aburridos.
  5. Cristóbal y Julia corren diez millas,
    ellos están cansados.
  7. El novio de Inés está en El Salvador
    desde el año pasado, ella está triste.
B. Answers will vary.
  1. No puedo entrar en el cuarto porque
    la puerta está cerrada.
  3. Orlando trabaja mucho. No hagas
    ruido, él está dormido.
  5. Aquí está la invitación para la fiesta,
    todos nosotros estamos invitados.

Part E
Exercises (p. 39)
A. 1. No, no están encima de la mesa,
    están debajo de la mesa.
  3. No, no está aquí, está allí.
  5. No, no están lejos de la caja, están
    cerca de la caja.
B. 1. cerca de
  3. detrás de
  5. dentro del

Part F
Exorcicos (p. 10)
A. 1. Los lápices son de Juanita. *Or,* Son
    los lápices de Juanita.
  3. La mochila es de Luis. *Or,* Es la
    mochila de Luis.
  5. Los cuadernos son de Antonio. *Or,*
    Son los cuadernos de Antonio.
B. 1. Las tizas son de los maestros. *Or,*
    Son las tizas de los maestros.
  3. La bolsa es de Diego. *Or,* Es la
    bolsa de Diego.
  5. Las plumas son de Juan y Tito. *Or,*
    Son las plumas de Juan y Tito.
Exercises (p. 42)
A. 1. mi
  3. su
  5. tus
  7. sus
B. Answers will vary.
  1. Tengo la pluma de mi papá.
  3. Es mi almuerzo.
  5. Son mis lápices.
Exercises (p. 44)
A. 1. mías
  3. mío
  5. tuya/suya
  7. suyo
Exercises (p. 45)
A. 1. Sí, son míos.
  3. Sí, son nuestras.
  5. Sí, son suyos.

Exercises (p. 46)
Answers will vary.
  Tengo una manzana, dos camisetas,
  cuatro libros y tres pares de medias
  en mi gaveta.

Part G
Exercises (p. 48)
A. 1. Guillermo es más simpático que
    Adela.
  3. Tomás es menos trabajador que
    Georgina.
  5. Teresa y Domingo son menos
    curiosos que Isabel.
  7. Juan José es más alto que Leticia
    y Sandra.
B. 1. En la clase de español hay
    más (menos) de veinte estudiantes.
  3. En la clase de matemáticas hay
    más (menos) de diez estudiantes.
  5. En la clase de educación física hay
    más (menos) de veinte y cinco
    estudiantes.
C. Answers will vary.
  1. El profesor de español es el más
    exigente de todos los profesores.
  3. El entrenador de natación es el menos
    pesimista de los entrenadores.
  5. Mi amiga es la más perezosa de la
    clase.
D. 1. Carl Lewis corre más rápido que yo.
  3. Yo aprendo más fácilmente que tú.
  5. Tú hablas español menos claramente
    que esos chicos.
Exercises (p. 52)
A. 1. El socialismo es peor que la demo-
    cracia.
  3. La situación política de los países
    en vía de desarrollo es menos
    grave que la situación política de
    los países desarrollados.
  5. La economía del Perú está peor.
B. Answers will vary.
  1. Yo tengo menos discos compactos
    que mis amigos.
  3. Mis amigos tienen más vídeos que yo.
  5. Yo tengo más suerte que mis amigos.
  7. Yo como en menos restaurantes
    caros que mis amigos.
C. 1. El clima es malo en Alaska, pero es
    mejor en la Florida.
  3. Mi hermano mayor lleva su abrigo
    más viejo cuando esquía.
  5. Agosto es el mes más caliente del año.
  7. La primavera es la mejor estación
    en Washington.

Part H
Exercises (p. 55)
A. Answers will vary.
  1. Oprah Winfrey tiene tanto dinero
    como Bill Gates.

3. Los Rockefeller tienen tantos edificios como Donald Trump.
5. Esta tienda vendió tantos discos de Janet Jackson como esas tiendas.
7. Elton John está tan dedicado a las causas de los pobres como el Presidente Carter.
B. Answers will vary.
 1. Las clases son tan buenas este año como el año pasado.
 3. Este año las diversiones son mejores que el año pasado.
 5. El tiempo en California es peor este año que el año pasado.
 7. Este año los partidos de fútbol son más interesantes que el año pasado.
C. Answers will vary.
 1. Mi amigo Pedro tiene más energía que Michael Jordan.
 3. Mis amigos José y Julio tienen tanta fuerza como mi padre.
 5. Mi amiga Elena tiene tanta intuición como mi madre.
D. Answers will vary.
 1. No, el río es larguísimo.
 3. No, la avenida es muy ancha.
 5. No, el periódico es liberalísimo.

Part I
Exercises (p. 59)
 1. Nosotros/Nosotras compramos un televisor.
 3. El/Ella/Ud. quiere pantalones nuevos.
 5. Yo leo novelas de misterio.
 7. El/Ella/Ud. arregla el coche de su padre.
 9. Tú tocas el piano.
Exercises (p. 61)
A. Answers will vary.
 1. Las hago por la tarde.
 3. La prefiero porque es muy divertida.
 5. Sí, las usan siempre.
 7. Sí, la discutimos todos los días.
B. 1. (El) me conoce bien.
 3. El y su esposa nos visitan.
 5. (El) tiene dos hijas, Andrea y Celia. (Yo) no las veo a menudo.
 7. (El) me llama si me necesita cuando (ellas) necesitan practicar el vocabulario.
Exercises (p. 64)
A. 1. Yo les leo los cuentos a mis hermanos.
 3. Nosotros les pedimos dinero a mis padres.
 5. Tú nos das las recetas a nosotros.
 7. Yo les hago la cama a ustedes.
B. 1. Me gustan las frutas.
 3. Te gustan los dulces.
 5. (A Uds.) les gusta el arroz con pollo.
 7. (A Ud.) le gusta la comida italiana.

Exercises (p. 66)
A. 1. Yolanda me las regala.
 3. Ellos se los compran.
 5. El se los recomienda.
 7. Yo se lo pregunto.
B. 1. Se lo das al aduanero.
 3. Se la muestras al policía.
 5. Me la das a mí.

Part J
Exercises (p. 68)
A. Answers will vary.
 1. No, me gustan estos zapatos rojos.
 3. No, me gusta esta camiseta blanca.
 5. No, compro ese sombrero negro.
B. 1. estos, aquella
 3. aquellos, esos
 5. ese, esta
Exercises (p. 70)
A. 1. esa, ésta
 3. esta, ésa
 5. Este, ése
 7. Eso
B. Answers will vary.
 1. No, ésta es más grande que ésa.
 3. No, me gustan aquéllos más que éstos.
 5. No, aquélla es más barata que ésta.

Part K
Exercises (p. 73)
A. 1. No tienes nada en el bolsillo.
 3. No hablan con ningún estudiante.
 5. No ayudamos a nadie.
 7. ¿Los experimentos? ¿No preparaste ninguno?
B. Answers will vary.
 1. No, nunca aprendo nada interesante.
 3. No, ellos no están ocupados nunca.
 5. No, no conozco a nadie antipático.
 7. No, nunca soy amable con ninguno de mis amigos.

LESSON 3
Part A
Exercises (p. 76)
A. 1. prometen, promete, prometemos, prometes
 3. sufro, sufre, sufrimos, sufres
 5. sacas, sacamos, saca, sacan
B. 1. asisten
 3. escribe
 5. cenamos
 7. baila
 9. corre
C. Answers will vary.
 1. Durante la semana yo desayuno a las siete y media.
 3. Durante la semana mis padres y yo escuchamos las noticias.
 5. Durante los fines de semana mis amigos corren en el parque.

Exercises (p. 80)
A. 1. doy, da, dan, das
   3. conoces, conozco, conocen, conoce
   5. conduce, conduces, conducen, conduzco
   7. ve, veo, ve, vemos
   9. salimos, sales, salgo, sale
B. Answers will vary.
   1. (Yo) hago la tarea temprano.
   3. Sí, (yo) sé hacer apuntes en las clases.
   5. Sí, (yo) salgo con ellos los fines de semana.
   7. Sí, (yo) les doy apoyo.
Exercises (p. 82)
A. 1. Dicen, Decimos, Dicen, Dice
   3. vienen, viene, venimos, vienen
   5. vas, vamos, va, va
   7. soy, es, eres, es
B. vienen, vamos, están, digo, son, oigo, vamos, tengo, viene, dicen, soy, están, Eres, estoy, tienes
Exercises (p. 83)
   Answers will vary.
   1. Hay treinta estudiantes en mi clase.
   3. Hay carteles en las paredes.
   5. Hay siete profesores de español.
Exercises (p. 85)
A. 1. convenzo, convencemos, convence, convences
   3. cogemos, cojo, coge, cogen
B. Answers will vary.
   1. Sí, escojo a mis amigos bien.
   3. No, nunca finjo estar enfermo para no ir a la escuela.
   5. Sí, dirijo un grupo muy bueno.
Exercises (p. 89)
A. 1. quiero, queremos, quieren, quieres
   3. prefiere, prefieres, prefiere, preferimos
   5. cuestan, cuesta, cuesta, cuestan
B. Answers will vary.
   1. Ellos miden cinco pies dos pulgadas.
   3. Nosotras almorzamos en casa de mi tía.
   5. Ud. puede ir de viaje durante la primavera.
C. Answers will vary.
   1. Pienso que son muy trabajadores.
   3. No, no mentimos nunca.
   5. Sí, confieso mis errores a mis padres.
   7. Los ciudadanos consiguen cambiar las leyes a veces.
D. Answers will vary.
   1. Mis amigos no entienden por qué los padres son estrictos.
   3. Siempre pido ayuda a la policía.
   5. Mi amiga Elena tiembla delante de un artista famoso.
Exercises (p. 92)
A. 1. confían, confiamos, confían, confío
   3. actúa, actúa, actúo, actuamos

B. Answers will vary.
   1. Sí, confío en mis amigos.
   3. No, a veces no actúo con madurez.
   5. Los celos destruyen muchas relaciones personales.

Part B
Exercises (p. 94)
A. Answers will vary.
   1. Hace tres años que aprendo español.
   3. No salgo con mis amigos hace una semana.
   5. Hace cinco años que leo el periódico regularmente.
   7. No nado en la piscina pública hace dos años.
   9. Hace tres meses que no duermo en casa de un amigo.
B. Answers will vary.
   1. Estudio español hace tres años.
   3. Hace dos meses que no salgo a cenar a un restaurante.
   5. No visito a mis parientes hace dos semanas.
   7. Hace un año que sirvo la cena en casa.
   9. Distribuyo los libros en clase hace cuatro meses.
C. Answers will vary.
   1. ¿Cuánto (tiempo) hace que montas en bicicleta?
   3. ¿Cuánto (tiempo) hace que lees novelas de aventuras?
   5. ¿Cuánto (tiempo) hace que juegas videojuegos?

Part C
Exercises (p. 97)
A. Answers will vary.
   1. Sí, voy a las tiendas a menudo.
   3. No, nunca practico ningún deporte.
   5. Voy a esquiar de vez en cuando.
   7. A veces hago un viaje durante las vacaciones.
   9. Rara vez pongo la mesa para la cena.
   11. Siempre oigo música rock.
B. Answers will vary.
   1. Construyo modelos de puentes muy mal.
   3. Cuento chistes bien.
   5. Escojo novelas interesantes muy bien.
   7. Pinto mal.

Part D
Exercises (p. 100)
A. 1. me canso, nos cansamos, se cansan, se cansa
   3. nos acordamos, se acuerda, me acuerdo, se acuerda
   5. se aburren, me aburro, se aburre, te aburres
B. Answers will vary.
   1. Me encuentro con mis amigos en la calle.

3. Se entristecen cuando saco malas notas.
5. Nos enfadamos cuando alguien llega tarde.
7. Sí, se quejan a menudo.
C. Answers will vary.
Por la mañana me despierto y me levanto a las seis y media.
Luego me baño, me visto. Antes de salir me despido de mis padres.
Por la noche me lavo y me acuesto.
Entonces, leo las noticias en el periódico. Generalmente, me duermo a las once.
D. Answers will vary.
Mis padres se levantan a las seis de la mañana. Se bañan y se visten. Mi madre no se maquilla pero mi padre se afeita.
E. Answers will vary.
1. Nunca me olvido de un examen.
3. Rara vez me enojo con mi mejor amigo.
5. Nunca me niego a ayudar a un amigo.
F. Answers will vary.
1. Me asusto.
3. Me desmayo.
5. Me enojo.
7. Me apresuro.
9. Me río.

Exercises (p. 105)
A. 1. Se vende un coche del año.
3. Se buscan secretarias bilingües.
5. Se necesitan traductores e intérpretes.
B. 1. Se practican muchos deportes. *Or,* No se practican muchos deportes.
3. Se conoce a mucha gente. *Or,* No se conoce a mucha gente.
5. Se come muy mal en la cafetería. *Or,* No se come muy mal en la cafetería.

Part E
Exercises (p. 107)
A. 1. Nosotros (no) estamos prestándole atención al profesor (a la profesora).
3. Mi amigo (no) está durmiéndose.
5. Tú (no) estás repitiendo las frases.
B. 1. ...estoy estudiando todo lo posible.
3. ...estoy aprendiendo a usar una computadora.
5. ...estoy aprendiendo un idioma extranjero.
Answers will vary.
1. ...estoy leyendo mucho.
3. ...estoy pidiendo información acerca de varias universidades.

Part F
Exercises (p. 109)
A. 1. Nosotros vamos a practicar un deporte. *Or,* Nosotros no vamos a practicar ningún deporte.

3. Mis amigos van a dormir. *Or,* Mis amigos no van a dormir.
5. Mi amigo y yo vamos a estudiar. *Or,* Mi amigo y yo no vamos a estudiar.
7. Tú vas a escribir un ensayo. *Or,* Tú no vas a escribir un ensayo.
B. Answers will vary.
1. Voy a hacer ejercicio este fin de semana.
3. Voy a comprar unas revistas esta tarde.
5. Voy a graduarme el año próximo.
7. Voy a prepararme para un examen esta noche.
9. Voy a hacer la cama mañana.

LESSON 4
Part A
Exercises (p. 111)
1. No, acabo de almorzar.
3. No, acabo de saludarlo.
5. No, acaban de ir al cine.
7. No, acabo de ir al centro.

Part B
Exercises (p. 113)
A. 1. recibí, recibió, recibimos, recibieron
3. terminaron, terminamos, terminó, terminé
B. 1. Gilda terminó los estudios universitarios.
3. Nosotros viajamos por cuatro países latinoamericanos.
5. Yo prometí casarme con Susana.
7. Uds. descubrieron unos programas de computadora interesantísimos.
C. Answers will vary.
1. No, no cené en la cafetería de la escuela, cené en casa.
3. Sí, las miré con mis padres.
5. Sí, ayudé a mis padres con los quehaceres de la casa./Sí, los ayudé./Sí, lavé los platos y barrí la cocina./etc.
D. me desperté, Me levanté, me lavé, me cepillé, Me miré, me peiné, me desayuné, Salí, tomé, Bajé, corrí, Tomé, salí.
Exercises (p. 116)
A. 1. trajiste, trajeron, trajo, trajeron
3. dije, dijimos, dijiste, dijo
5. condujeron, condujiste, condujo, condujeron
7. Vinieron, Vino, Viniste, Vino
9. estuviste, estuvo, estuve, estuvimos
B. estuvo, condujimos, anduvimos, traduje, se puso, dije, trajo, vinimos, llamó, dijo, hicimos
C. Answers will vary.
1. Sí, nos pusimos botas.
3. No, no conduje el coche, mi padre lo condujo.

5. No, mis hermanos no vinieron. Ellos se quedaron en casa.
7. Ricardo jugó en la nieve.

Exercises (p. 119)
A. 1. Tuvo, tuvo
3. conociste, conocí
5. Pudiste, no pude
B. 1. Did Ricardo receive any news about Tina? Yes, he received news about her. She had an accident.
3. Did you meet her here or in Argentina? I met her here.
5. Did you succeed in convincing him? No, I did not succeed in convincing him.
C. Answers will vary.
1. Supimos su nombre cuando lo presentaron.
3. Sí, tuvimos que hacer cola por dos horas.
5. Vimos al artista pero no lo conocimos.

Exercises (p. 121)
A. 1. fuimos, fui, fueron, fue
3. Viste, Vio, Vio, Vieron
B. fuimos, vimos, fue, fui, fue, vi, dio, di, fui

Exercises (p. 123)
A. cayó, leí, leyó, oyó, cayeron, creyó, distribuyeron, huyeron, incluyeron, contribuyeron
B. 1. Los sindicatos contribuyeron a la campaña del Sr. Mederos.
3. Leyó datos políticos.
5. Oímos comentarios positivos.
7. Sí, (él) creyó lo que dijo el Sr. Mederos.

Exercises (p. 127)
A. 1. busqué, buscamos, buscaron, buscó
3. entregué, entregó, entregaste, entregó
5. empecé, empezaron, empezamos, empezaste
B. Answers will vary.
1. Almorcé en el parque.
3. ¡Claro que sí! Abracé a mis padres cuando llegué.
5. Comencé a estudiar a las siete.
C. toqué, practiqué, llegué, habló, me tranquilicé, Rogué, me equivoqué, terminé, abracé, di

Exercises (p. 130)
A. 1. nos divertimos, me divertí, se divirtieron, te divertiste
3. dormiste, durmieron, durmió, durmió
5. vistió, vestí, vistieron, vestimos
B. decidió, hizo, se despidió, se fue, llegó, se sintió, encontró, conocieron, se sintieron, se divirtieron, fueron, durmieron, consiguieron

Part C
Exercises (p. 131)
A. Answers will vary.
1. Hace tres semanas que yo viajé por avión.
3. Mis amigos y yo hicimos una fogata en el campo hace seis meses.
5. Hace dos años que mis padres fueron a un baile de fin de año.
B. Answers will vary.
1. ¿Cuánto (tiempo) hace que tú montaste a caballo?
3. ¿Cuánto (tiempo) hace que tú hiciste alguna locura?
5. ¿Cuánto (tiempo) hace que tú fuiste al cine?

Exercises (p. 133)
Answers will vary.
1. El fin de semana pasado yo fui al cine y vi *Titanic.*
3. La semana pasada mi mejor amigo celebró su cumpleaños y recibió muchos regalos.
5. Anoche nosotros visitamos a mis abuelos y cenamos con ellos.

Part D
Exercises (p. 135)
A. 1. estaba, hacía, estábamos, hacíamos, estaban, hacían, estabas, hacías
3. venían, venía, venías, venían
B. era, iba, íbamos, tenía, tenía, tenía, jugábamos, gustaba, íbamos, llevaba, comíamos, bebíamos, compraba, venía, comía, eran, pasábamos
C. Answers will vary.
1. Yo jugaba al ajedrez siempre también.
3. A menudo yo pedía ayuda cuando no entendía la tarea.
5. Por lo general yo no hacía buenos regalos.
D. Answers will vary.
1. Yo salía por la noche rara vez.
3. Tú te aburrías en las clases a veces.
5. El limpiaba el cuarto todos los días.
7. Ella dormía hasta muy tarde de vez en cuando.
E. 1. jugaba, me caí
3. Llovía, aterrizó
5. Hacía, saliste
7. regaba, empezó
9. hablaba, abrió

Part E
Exercises (p. 139)
A. 1. Cuando regresó a la escuela hacía diez días que Juan estaba ausente.
3. Cuando terminó las puertas hacía una semana que el carpintero las arreglaba.

5. Cuando vendieron su casa hacía treinta años que mis abuelos vivían allí.
B. 1. ¿Cuánto hacía que Diego leía el periódico? *Or,* ¿Desde cuándo leía el periódico Diego?
3. ¿Cuánto hacía que hablabas con Genaro? *Or,* ¿Desde cuándo hablabas con Genaro?
5. ¿Cuánto hacía que dormías? *Or,* ¿Desde cuándo dormías?

Part F
Exercises (p. 142)
A. fui, compré, Había, tuve, me encontré, estaba, mostró, Era, invitaron, fuimos, comimos, me despedí, tomé, llegué, estaba, quería, estaba, decidí, regresamos
B. fuimos, invitamos, era, Era, fui, compré, hice, trajo, contribuyó, hacía, podíamos (pudimos), llegamos, conseguimos, estaba, comíamos, escuchamos (escuchábamos), vimos, se emocionó, vi, sonreía, tenía

Part G
Exercises (p. 144)
A. 1. me he bañado, me he vestido, he desayunado
3. hemos limpiado nuestro cuarto, hemos oído el pronóstico del tiempo, hemos ido a comprar leche
B. 1. has puesto
3. hemos salido
5. han corrido

Part H
Exercises (p. 146)
A. 1. había estado en mi casa, había traído los programas para mi computadora, había arreglado el impresor
3. no habías hecho nada, no habías escogido el tema para tu informe, no habías pensado en las consecuencias
B. 1. Ignacio y Roberto habían limpiado la casa.
3. Graciela había preparado la cena.
5. Ignacio y yo habíamos escrito nuestros informes para la clase.

LESSON 5
Part A
Exercises (p. 149)
A. Answers will vary.
1. Yo deseo conseguir un buen trabajo.
3. Mi mejor amigo y yo pensamos viajar alrededor del mundo.
5. Mi mejor amiga quisiera trabajar en el extranjero.

7. Tú esperas ser arquitecto.
B. Answers will vary.
1. Sí, debo continuar mis estudios porque quiero ser abogada.
3. Sí, mis padres necesitan trabajar mucho porque tienen muchos gastos.
5. No, no quisiera vivir en un país extranjero.
C. Answers will vary.
1. No quisiera asistir a una universidad lejos de mi casa.
3. Me gustaría ser famoso.
5. Quisiera viajar al espacio.
7. No me gustaría jugar en un equipo profesional.

Part B
Exercises (p. 152)
A. Answers will vary.
1. Es aconsejable dormir mucho antes de salir.
3. Es importante llamar a nuestros padres frecuentemente.
5. Hay que llevar mucha comida.
7. Es mejor no conducir muy rápido.
B. 1. Es importante no tener secretos.
3. Es necesario decir la verdad.
5. Hay que tener paciencia.

Part C
Excercises (p. 154)
A. Answers will vary.
1. tienen mucha suerte.
3. tengo mucho frío.
5. tenemos mucho sueño.
7. tiene mucho miedo.
B. 1. Tenemos mucha sed.
3. Necesito comprar un abrigo. Mi hermana tiene mucho frío.
5. Mis amigos tienen sueño.

LESSON 6
Part A
Exercises (p. 158)
A. 1. A mí me gustan los vegetales, a mi amigo le gusta la carne.
3. A mí me gusta la camisa roja, a mi amigo le gusta la camisa azul.
5. A mí me gusta salir por las noches, a mi amigo le gusta salir por las mañanas.
B. Answers will vary.
1. A mí no me gusta correr en la lluvia.
3. A mí me encanta viajar en tren.
5. A mí me gusta nadar en el río.
C. 1. A mí me duele la cabeza.
3. A Ignacio le duele el brazo.
5. A ti te duelen los pies.
D. 1. Me preocupa la contaminación.
3. Les interesan las ideas nuevas.
5. ¿Cuánto dinero les falta para el proyecto?

Part B
Exercises (p. 162)
A. Answers will vary.
   1. ¡Qué pena!
   3. ¡Qué sorpresa!
   5. ¡Qué desastre!
   7. ¡Qué malo!
B. Answers will vary.
   1. Es malo fumar.
   3. No es bueno tener mucho tiempo libre.
   5. Es maravilloso vivir en un país tropical.
C. Answers will vary.
   1. ...juega muy bien.
   3. ...estudiamos mucho.
   5. ...es muy simpático(a).
D. Answers will vary.
   1. Tengo miedo de no asistir a una buena universidad.
   3. Me enojo de tener que esperar a un amigo mucho tiempo.
   5. Me alegro de recibir un regalo de un amigo.
   7. Siento llegar tarde a una cita.
E. Answers will vary.
   1. Me enorgullezco de ayudar a mi hermanito.
   3. Mis padres se enojan de tener que pagar muchos impuestos.
   5. Sí, mi profesor siente no tener vacaciones más largas.
F. Answers will vary.
   1. ...participar en una fiesta tan exclusiva.
   3. ...ayudar a alumnos que tienen poco dinero.
   5. ...no poder asistir.

Unit 3—Expressing Personal Feelings

LESSON 7

Part A
Exercises (p. 169)
   1. escriba, escriba, escribamos, escriban
   3. diseñemos, diseñes, diseñe, diseñen
   5. nos aburramos, te aburras, me aburra, se aburran
Exercises (p. 171)
   1. crucemos, cruces, cruce, cruce
   3. paguen, paguen, pagues, pague
Exercises (p. 173)
   1. empiece, empiecen, empecemos, empieces
   3. prefieras, prefiramos, prefieran, prefiera
Exercises (p. 174)
   1. te acuerdes, nos acordemos, se acuerde, se acuerden

   3. se duerman, me duerma, nos durmamos, te duermas
Exercises (p. 175)
   1. se ría, nos riamos, se rían, te rías
   3. sirvan, sirva, sirvan, sirvas
Exercises (p. 176)
   1. des, den, demos, dé
   3. vaya, vaya, vayas, vayan
   5. sepan, sepas, sepa, sepa

Part B
Exercises (p. 177)
A. 1. hayan visitado
   3. haya ido
   5. hayamos traído
B. Answers will vary.
   1. Yo estoy encantado de que ella haya tenido una oportunidad tan especial.
   3. Nosotros nos alegramos de que sus parientes hayan venido a despedirse de ella.
   5. Su novio teme que ella no le haya echado de menos.
Exercises (p. 179)
A. puedan, es, puede, conozcan, viva, venga, pueda, tengamos, encontremos, vaya, van, se sientan
B. 1. ¡Qué lástima que haya nevado tanto!
   3. Temo (Tengo miedo de) que no haya electricidad esta noche.
   5. ¡Qué maravilloso que nadie haya muerto en la tormenta!
   7. La señora Fontana está triste de que su casa esté destruida.

Part C
Exercises (p. 182)
A. 1. se case
   3. vaya
   5. empiecen
   7. te gradúes
B. 1. Dudo que él sepa cantar.
   3. No creo que él gane mucho dinero.
   5. Es probable que él conozca todas las canciones.
C. 1. ...mejore pronto.
   3. ...no sea problemática.
   5. ...tengan mucho dinero para ayudar a los necesitados.
Exercises (p. 185)
   Answers will vary.
   1. Quizás él le pida ayuda a sus profesores.
   3. No dudo que vamos a merendar en el parque.
   5. Puede ser que yo vaya con Uds.
   7. Es seguro que mis padres van a ir a verlo.
   9. Es imposible que podamos salir esta noche.

Part D
Exercises (p. 187)
A. 1. anduvieron   anduviera
    3. dijeron   dijera
    5. estuvieron   estuviera
    7. hicieron   hiciera
    9. leyeron   leyera
   11. pudieron   pudiera
   13. quisieron   quisiera
   15. supieron   supiera
   17. sirvieron   sirviera
   19. vinieron   viniera
B. 1. llegaran, llegáramos, llegaras,
     llegaran
    3. perdieran, perdiéramos, perdiera,
     perdiera
    5. se despertara, se despertara, te
     despertaras, se despertaran

Exercises (p. 189)
A. 1. reaccionara
    3. pudieran
    5. aplaudiera
    7. vinieran
B. Answers will vary.
    1. No pensé que hubiera tanta gente
     en la playa.
    3. Fue imposible que no nos
     divirtiéramos.
    5. Nos alegramos de que hiciera buen
     tiempo.
    7. Fue maravilloso que el dinero fuera
     suficiente.

Exercises (p. 191)
A. 1. hubieran terminado, hubiéramos
     terminado, hubiera terminado,
     hubieran terminado
    2. hubieran hecho, hubiera hecho,
     hubieran hecho, hubiera hecho
B. 1. hubiera hecho
    3. hubiéramos ayudado
    5. hubiera defendido

Unit 4—Getting Others to Adopt a Course of Action

LESSON 8

Part A
Exercises (p. 194)
A. 1. ¡No cruce la calle en esa esquina!
    3. ¡Póngase el abrigo antes de salir!
    5. ¡Compre las medicinas allí!
    7. ¡Venga a cenar en mi casa!
B. 1. Sepan todos los nombres.
    3. Estén en el auditorio temprano.
    5. Preparen algunas preguntas para ellos.

Part B
Exercises (p. 197)
    1. ¡No vayas a la escuela en metro!

    3. ¡Compra boletos para una obra de
     teatro!
    5. ¡Asiste a todas las clases!
    7. ¡Ten paciencia si no entiendes el
     inglés!
    9. ¡No salgas de la escuela demasiado
     tarde!

Exercises (p. 199)
A. 1. ¡Despiértate!
    3. ¡Aféitate primero!
    5. ¡Vístete rápidamente!
    7. ¡No te lo pongas!
    9. ¡No la pongas en la cama!
B. 1. ¡Devuélvelo a la biblioteca!
    3. ¡Échala en el cesto!
    5. ¡Dáselo a tu padre!
    7. ¡No la dejes en la cama!

LESSON 9
Exercises (p. 202)
A. Answers will vary.
    1. Ellos desean que nosotros salgamos
     bien en los exámenes.
    3. Ellos exigen que yo no llegue muy
     tarde a casa.
    5. Ellos aconsejan que mis hermanos
     no mientan nunca.
    7. Ellos permiten que nosotros
     almorcemos siempre en la
     cafetería.
B. 1. El profesor espera que yo limpie
     los instrumentos.
    3. El profesor sugiere que tú hagas
     el experimento cuidadosamente.
    5. El profesor prefiere que Uds.
     terminen antes del fin de la clase.
    7. El profesor pide que ellas lean toda
     la información antes de empezar.
C. Answers will vary.
    1. Mis padres prohiben que yo vaya al
     cine durante la semana.
    3. Sí, permiten que yo asista a un
     campamento durante el verano y
     que juegue al vólibol con el equipo
     de la escuela.
    5. Sí, prefieren que yo salga durante
     los fines de semana porque durante
     la semana quieren que me quede en
     casa y haga la tarea.

Exercises (p. 205)
A. Answers will vary.
    1. Es importante que tú no te pongas
     nervioso.
    3. Es mejor que tú te acuestes temprano.
    5. Es necesario que tú hagas apuntes
     de la información.
B. Answers will vary.
    1. ...llame al teatro.
    3. ...les pidamos dinero a nuestros
     padres.
    5. ...te levantes temprano para terminarlo.

Exercises (p. 206)
A. 1. lleves
 3. dé
 5. declares
 7. pierdan
 9. consigan
B. 1. hayas limpiado
 3. hayan dado
 5. haya enviado
Exercises (p. 208)
A. 1. nos levantáramos
 3. vinieran
 5. recogiera
 7. hiciéramos
B. 1. hubiéramos dormido
 3. hubieras hecho
 5. hubiéramos comprado
 7. hubiéramos quedado

LESSON 10
Exercises (p. 211)
A. 1. ¡Ojalá que haga buen tiempo!
 3. ¡Ojalá que ellos traigan las pelotas para jugar al fútbol!
 5. ¡Ojalá que no haya muchos insectos!
 7. ¡Ojalá que tú convenzas a tus padres para poder venir!
 9. ¡Ojalá que el sol salga temprano!
B. Answers will vary.
 1. ¡Ojalá que sea feliz!
 3. ¡Ojalá que consiga un trabajo!
 5. ¡Ojalá que pueda viajar a Europa!
Exercises (p. 212)
A. 1. ¡Ojalá que mis amigos me visitaran!
 3. ¡Ojalá que el museo estuviera abierto!
 5. ¡Ojalá que yo tuviera ganas de leer!
 7. ¡Ojalá que mis amigos y yo pudiéramos jugar al fútbol!
B. 1. ¡Ojalá que hubiera pasado más tiempo en el Yunque!
 3. ¡Ojalá hubiera podido quedarme más tiempo en San Juan!
 5. ¡Ojalá que hubiera hecho más amigos en Mayagüez!
 7. ¡Ojalá que hubiera leído la guía antes de salir de Nueva York!

Unit 5—Hypothesizing

LESSON 11
Part A
Exercises (p. 217)
A. 1. valdrán, valdrán, valdrá
 3. pondremos, pondrá, pondrán, pondré
 5. podremos, podrá, podré, podrán
 7. querrán, querrá, querrán, querrás
 9. haré, harán, harás, hará
 11. decorarán, decoraremos, decorará, decoraré

B. Answers will vary.
 1. Ignacio no lo sabrá.
 3. Habrá muchas personas allí.
 5. ¿Caminará a la fiesta?
 7. Valdrá mucho.
C. Answers will vary.
 1. Sí, iré porque me encantan los conciertos en el parque.
 3. Si conocen a la familia, me permitirán quedarme en casa de un amigo.
 5. Me pondré una camiseta y unos vaqueros.
 7. Tocarán música rock.
 9. No sé. Tendré que invitarlo.

Part B
Exercises (p. 221)
A. Answers will vary.
 1. Si tengo tiempo, iré a casa de mi amiga Elena.
 3. Si tengo mucho trabajo, no podré practicar un deporte.
 5. Si hace mal tiempo durante las vacaciones, me enojaré mucho.
 7. Si mis maestros no son muy estrictos, les pediré permiso para comer durante la clase.
B. Answers will vary.
 1. Si mi profesor de inglés tiene hambre, va a un restaurante chino.
 3. Si mi mejor amigo no puede salir de su casa hoy, juega con la computadora.
 5. Si mis padres no quieren cocinar hoy, vamos a comer pizza.
 7. Si sirven comida hispana en la cafetería, mis compañeros van a almorzar allí.

LESSON 12
Part A
Exercises (p. 224)
A. 1. llegamos
 3. anunciaron
 5. entramos
 7. volvió
B. Answers will vary.
 1. ...mi tío Antonio nos visita.
 3. ...nos relajamos.
 5. ...llego a casa.
 7. ...abren las salas de clases.
Exercises (p. 226)
A. 1. estés
 3. se mueran
 5. reciba
 7. sepas
B. 1. reciba
 3. empiece
 5. aprenda
 7. conduzca

Part B
Exercises (p. 228)
A. 1. pierda
   3. tengamos
   5. se pongan
B. 1. ...nos dé una extensión.
   3. ...planeemos.
C. Answers will vary.
   1. ...pagues las entradas.
   3. ...sea muy popular.

Part C
Exercises (p. 230)
A. Answers will vary.
   1. Nosotros debemos tener más fiestas a fin de que todos los alumnos se diviertan juntos.
   3. Yo le voy a pedir a los profesores que apoyen nuestro club para que vengan más personas.
   5. La entrada a los bailes tiene que ser más barata a fin de que los alumnos se entusiasmen a venir.
B. Answers will vary.
   1. ...salga temprano de mi casa.
   3. ...esté preparado para la lluvia.
   5. ...tener el fin de semana libre.

Part D
Exercises (p. 231)
A. 1. me regalen
   3. venden
   5. es
B. Answers will vary.
   1. ...no tenga mucho dinero.
   3. ...le expliquemos lo que pasó.
   5. ...fue esta mañana.

LESSON 13
Part A
Exercises (p. 235)
A. 1. dir-   dirían
   3. podr-   podrías
   5. querr-   querría
   7. saldr-   saldríamos
   9. valdr-   valdrían
   11. cabr-   cabrías
B. 1. haríamos, haría, harían, haría
   3. podríamos, podría, podría, podrías
   5. dirías, dirían, diría, diría
C. 1. escribiríamos
   3. visitarías
   5. daría
D. Answers will vary.
   1. Antonio quisiera ir a la heladería.
   3. Nos gustaría dar un paseo.
   5. A Uds. les gustaría patinar en el hielo.

Part B
Exercises (p. 237)
A. 1. Si ella fuera el presidente, destruiría las armas nucleares.

3. Si mi amigo pudiera comprar un disco compacto, compraría el de Janet Jackson.
5. Si ellos fueran profesores, nunca darían tarea.
7. Si nosotros no miráramos tanto la televisión, saldríamos mejor en las clases.
9. Si Ud. condujera en las calles de Nueva York, se pondría muy nervioso.
B. Answers will vary.
   1. Si yo fuera profesor, daría una prueba cada día.
   3. Si yo supiera hablar ruso, podría trabajar en la ONU.
   5. Si yo viviera en Alaska, necesitaría más abrigos.
   7. Si yo fuera un actor famoso, ganaría mucho dinero por cada película.
C. Answers will vary.
   1. Si mi mejor amigo(a) fuera profesor(a), nunca daría pruebas.
   3. Si mi mejor amigo(a) supiera hablar ruso, iría a Rusia.
   5. Si mi mejor amigo(a) viviera en Alaska, yo le echaría de menos.
   7. Si mi mejor amigo(a) fuera un actor famoso (una actriz famosa), él (ella) construiría una cancha de tenis en el patio de su casa.

Part C
Exercises (p. 240)
A. 1. Eduardo ayuda a los pobres como si fuera rico.
   3. Yolanda y Benito caminan por la calle como si conocieran a todo el mundo.
   5. Adelaida corre como si huyera de alguien.
   7. Nosotros actuamos como si llegáramos a la clase a tiempo siempre.
B. 1. Carlos come como si no hubiera comido en meses.
   3. Los niños gritan como si hubieran visto un fantasma.
   5. Uds. recomiendan remedios como si hubieran estudiado medicina.
   7. Tú caminas como si te hubieras roto una pierna.

LESSON 14
Exercises (p. 243)
A. 1. esté, tenga
   3. sea
   5. se sienta
   7. sepa
B. 1. Necesito un puesto que pague bien.
   3. Necesitamos trabajar en una oficina que tenga muchas ventanas.
   5. Buscamos un jefe que no sea demasiado exigente.

Answer Key for Unit 7—Preparing for the New York State Regents Examination

Part 1—Speaking
Answers will vary.

Part 2—Listening Comprehension

(1)	1	(8)	3	(15)	2	(22)	4
(2)	4	(9)	1	(16)	3	(23)	2
(3)	2	(10)	2	(17)	3	(24)	3
(4)	3	(11)	4	(18)	4	(25)	1
(5)	4	(12)	2	(19)	1	(26)	4
(6)	1	(13)	4	(20)	2		
(7)	4	(14)	3	(21)	3		

Part 3—Reading Comprehension

(1)	1. 2	2. 4	3. 3	4. 1	5. 3
(2)	1. 2	2. 1	3. 2	4. 1	5. 4
(3)	1. 2	2. 1	3. 4	4. 4	5. 3
(4)	1. 2	2. 3	3. 4	4. 1	5. 2
(5)	1. 3	2. 1	3. 4	4. 4	5. 2

(6) 3, 1	(11) 4, 3	(16) 3	(21) 2
(7) 1, 2	(12) 4	(17) 4	(22) 1
(8) 2, 4	(13) 2	(18) 3	(23) 3
(9) 2, 3	(14) 2	(19) 2	(24) 1
(10) 1, 4	(15) 1	(20) 1	(25) 4

(26)	1. 2	2. 3	3. 1	4. 4	5. 1
(27)	1. 3	2. 1	3. 2	4. 4	5. 3
(28)	1. 2	2. 4	3. 1	4. 4	5. 1
(29)	1. 2	2. 3	3. 1	4. 2	5. 3
(30)	1. 1	2. 4	3. 3	4. 2	5. 1

Part 4—Writing
Answers will vary.

Examination June 2000

Comprehensive Examination in Spanish

PART 1

Your performance on Part 1, Speaking (24 credits), has been evaluated prior to the date of this written examination.

PART 2

Answer all questions in Part 2 according to the directions for *a* and *b*. [30]

a Directions (1-9): For each question, you will hear some background information in English *once*. Then you will hear a passage in Spanish *twice* and a question in English *once*. After you have heard the question, the teacher will pause while you read the question and the four suggested answers. Choose the best suggested answer and write its *number* in the space provided. Base your answer *on the content of the passage, only*. The passages that the teacher will read aloud to you are found in the ANSWERS section, Part 2, at the end of this examination. [18]

1 What does the airline offer?
  1 better in-flight service
  2 a free flight to Japan
  3 more flights to Japan
  4 more modern airplanes   1 _____

2 What is the purpose of this announcement?

    1 to promote a new children's game
    2 to warn parents of the danger of a toy
    3 to advertise a new health clinic
    4 to introduce faster mail service   2 _____

3 What did the message say?

    1 The item you ordered is no longer made.
    2 Your rebate is in the mail.
    3 The company has changed its address.
    4 The product you wanted is now on sale.   3 _____

4 What is being advertised?

    1 health foods
    2 a set of cookware
    3 kitchen cabinets
    4 a new heating system   4 _____

5 What kind of television program begins soon?

    1 musical show   3 historical drama
    2 game show   4 soap opera   5 _____

6 What is being offered to the public?

    1 a new Latin dance club
    2 a new chain of music stores
    3 an easier way to purchase music
    4 a chance to meet a Latin star   6 _____

7 Who would be most interested in this announcement?

    1 those planning to take adult education courses
    2 those wishing to visit their child's school
    3 those seeking information about college
    4 those hoping to work with schoolchildren   7 _____

8 What service has been initiated?

    1 a safe way of sending credit information

    2 a special new charge card for Spanish-speaking countries

    3 a computer program for managing clients' financial records

    4 a guarantee of the lowest interest rates available   8 _____

9 Who would be most interested in this announcement?

    1 someone wanting a driver's license

    2 someone with a medical problem

    3 someone going on a field trip

    4 someone looking for employment   9 _____

b Directions (10-15): For each question you will hear some background information in English *once*. Then you will hear a passage in Spanish *twice* and a question in Spanish *once*. After you have heard the question, the teacher will pause while you read the question and the four suggested answers. Choose the best suggested answer and write its *number* in the space provided. Base your answer *on the content of the passage, only*. The passages that the teacher will read aloud to you are found in the ANSWERS section, Part 2, at the end of this examination. [12]

10 ¿De quién se habla en este pasaje?

    1 una autora   3 una cantante

    2 una deportista   4 una ilustradora   10 _____

11 Según este anuncio, ¿qué hará el cantante Carlos Vives?

    1 Va a cambiar su estilo.
    2 Va a cantar en otras lenguas.
    3 Va a dar más dinero a su comunidad.
    4 Va a actuar en una película.   11 _____

12 ¿Qué discute el médico?

    1 dónde hacer ejercicios
    2 cómo seleccionar zapatos
    3 la práctica del atletismo
    4 el cuidado de los pies   12 _____

13 Según el agente, ¿qué puedes hacer si vas de vacaciones a Veracruz?

    1 viajar a las ruinas prehistóricas
    2 visitar muchos museos y monumentos
    3 competir en un consurso de geografía
    4 gozar de mucha acción en la naturaleza   13 _____

14 ¿Qué ventaja tiene este hotel?

    1 Está en un buen sitio para negocios.
    2 Está cerca del supermercado.
    3 Está en un lugar tranquilo.
    4 Está cerca de la estación de trenes.   14 _____

15 ¿Para quiénes es este anuncio?

    1 para estudiantes interesados en ir a un concierto
    2 para estudiantes que quieren visitar museos
    3 para estudiantes interesados en participar en una obra teatral
    4 para estudiantes que quieren aprender a dibujar   15 _____

PART 3

Answer all questions in Part 3 according to the directions for *a*, *b*, and *c*. [30]

a Directions (16-20): After the following passage, there are five questions or incomplete statements. For *each,* choose the word or expression that best answers the question or completes the statement *according to the meaning of the passage,* and write its *number* in the space provided. [10]

La carrera artística de Miriam Colón se puede describir en tres palabras: Teatro Rodante Puertorriqueño. Este teatro fundado por ella hace más de treinta años, es motivo de orgullo y es su destino, aunque algunas veces es un dolor de cabeza. El Teatro Rodante Puertorriqueño es para Miriam Colón, el drama de su vida.

A principios de los años 50, ella era una adolescente que estudiaba en la escuela Baldorioty del Viejo San Juan, en Puerto Rico. "La noche de la última función de la producción escolar donde debuté como actriz, me di cuenta de que me había enamorado del teatro", recuerda ella. Hoy, casi cincuenta años después, su entusiasmo es el mismo. Se le ilumina la cara cuando habla de sus grandes pasiones: la producción de teatro latino y el descubrir y estimular el talento joven.

Comenzó sus estudios en la Universidad de Puerto Rico. Poco después, el profesorado de esta universidad se dio cuenta de su gran talento y le dio una beca para que Miriam continuara sus estudios en Nueva York. Entonces Miriam tenía solamente 17 años. Más tarde estudió en el famoso Actors Studio. "Fui la primera puertorriqueña que estudió allí", dice con un brillo en sus ojos oscuros.

A principios de los años 60, Colón comenzó su carrera cinematográfica en Hollywood. "Imagínate cómo sería para mí, una jibarita de Ponce, el poder actuar junto con Marlon Brando: ¡Lo máximo!", dice. Luego se desilusionó con los papeles pequeños que le ofrecían a las actrices hispanas y decidió buscar otras maneras de satisfacer su ambición.

En 1967, organizó en Nueva York un teatro rodante similar al de la Universidad de Puerto Rico, que daba representaciones gratis a los pueblos de la isla. Ahora, todos los veranos el Teatro Rodante Puertorriqueño lleva funciones al aire libre y gratuitas a los vecindarios de Nueva York. Además de las presentaciones en inglés y español aquí se ofrecen también talleres para actores y Miriam Colón participa en todo.

Pero a pesar de los títulos honorarios, de los premios recibidos como actriz y como líder en la comunidad, Miriam Colón piensa que no ha tenido un éxito completo. "Producimos producciones de primera clase en el Teatro Rodante, la crítica es excelente, pero nos faltan miles de dólares para llevar al público una obra. Ojalá que en el futuro haya latinos que quieran producir teatro, en vez de esperar sombrero en mano, que ocurra un milagro", dice la célebre puertorriqueña.

El Teatro Rodante acaba de celebrar sus 30 años. Colón se siente satisfecha, y en cuanto al futuro dice, "Me gustaría encontrar una persona a quien le apasione el teatro y que tenga la voluntad necesaria para dirigir una organización artística hispana. Cuando la encuentre, me haré a un lado y le diré, 'Aquí está, mi hijo. Qué Dios te bendiga'."

16 ¿Cuándo descubrió Miriam su gran pasión?

   1 cuando era muy joven
   2 cuando tenía 50 años
   3 cuando viajó a Nueva York
   4 cuando terminó la universidad   16 _____

17 ¿Qué le entusiasma a ella todavía?

   1 trabajar como profesora de lengua española
   2 dar becas a los jóvenes con talento excepcional
   3 actuar con el grupo de la escuela Baldorioty
   4 crear teatro latino y animar a jóvenes actores   17 _____

18 ¿Qué empezó Miriam en el año 1967?

   1 un teatro para los estudiantes de la Universidad de Puerto Rico
   2 un teatro rodante que no cobra dinero por sus presentaciones
   3 una escuela de música para niños
   4 una compañía para construir nuevos teatros   18 _____

19 ¿Cuál es uno de los problemas que tiene que enfrentar Miriam Colón?

   1 la falta de dinero
   2 la crítica negativa
   3 la falta de buenos actores
   4 la gente que no habla español   19 _____

20 ¿Qué espera Miriam Colón en el futuro?

   1 encontrar un edificio nuevo para su teatro
   2 encontrar un nuevo líder para la organización
   3 producir otro tipo de teatro en Nueva York
   4 obtener más títulos honorarios de la comunidad   20 _____

b *Directions* (21-25): Below each of the following selections, there is either a question or an incomplete statement. For *each*, choose the word or expression that best answers the question or completes the statement *according to the meaning of the selection,* and write its *number* in the space provided. [10]

21

LA HIGIENE EN LA COCINA

■ Conviene tener dos termómetros: uno en el congelador (la temperatura debe ser inferior a los 32 grados Fahrenheit y otro en la nevera donde debe haber 40 grados para que los alimentos se mantengan frescos.

■ Utiliza las sobras refrigeradas al cabo de uno o dos días. Al congelar las carnes, no las coloques encima de las cubeteras de hielo porque los líquidos en el paquete podrían escurrirse y contaminar los cubitos.

■ Guarda los restos de comida que no contengan carne y los de las salsas durante menos de una semana.

■ Guíate con la fecha sellada en los paquetes que dice "úsese antes del día..." para los productos que se echan a perder como la leche. Estas fechas están determinadas por la agencia que regula la sanidad de los alimentos— para asegurar que el público los consuma frescos y sanos.

What is this article about?

1 the importance of balanced, nutritious meals
2 the need to wash frequently
3 the importance of handling and storing food safely
4 the need to keep an activities calendar in the kitchen

21 _____

22

¿Sabía usted...?

A esta fecha ya se han invertido más de $12 millones en restaurar la preciosa joya verde de Nueva York, el Parque Central, incluyendo un nuevo lago para pescar, el Discovery Center, donde usted puede alquilar la caña de pescar y comprar carnada, para pescar en el lago. Igualmente, finalizaron las obras de renovación del New York Botanical Garden, en el Bronx, a un costo de $165 millones. Este Jardín Botánico tiene una extensión de 250 acres.

Tompkin Square Park, que incluye canchas de "handball" y baloncesto, así como una elegante fuente, se ha reabierto, a un costo de $5.5 millones. En la zona de Queens, el área de Flushing Meadows - Corona State Park, ya está en pleno disfrute de una restauración que costó $5 millones. Ahí se encuentra el Unisphere.

Después de dos años de reparación, ya abrió el Aquarium Wildlife Conservation, donde se pueden ver delfines y leones marinos. Lo que antes fue el Brooklyn's Floyd Bennet Field, se ha convertido en un complejo municipal para educación y recreo. Este fue el primer aeropuerto municipal de Nueva York.

Desde este año, Brooklyn disfruta ya de una arena deportiva y un estadio, construidos a un costo de $70 millones, donde acaban de celebrarse los Juegos de Buena Voluntad. ❀

What is this article about?

1 information for tourists on how to travel to important places
2 the lack of money for renovations in recreational sites
3 improvements made to recreational sites in New York City
4 the closing of various places of interest in New York City

22 _____

23

LIBROS
Por Elizabeth Subercaseaux
"HUMO DE TRENES"

Poli Délano. Editorial Andrés Bello.
Cada día se escuchan más y más voces
de padres preocupados por la escasa
literatura para sus hijos adolescentes
que se está escribiendo hoy día. Los
chiquillos de 12, 13, y 14 años no leen
y muchas veces no lo hacen no porque
no les guste leer, sino porque no
tienen qué leer. Pasan medio día
pegados a la televisión y de libros,
poco o nada.

Pero ahora tenemos una buena
noticia. "Humo de trenes", novela para
adolescentes, escrita por el reconocido
escritor chileno Poli Délano, autor de
novelas y libros de cuentos ("En este
Lugar Sagrado", "Dos lagartos en una
botella", "Sin morir del todo", "La
misma esquina del mundo" y "Cuentos
mexicanos", entre otros). Premio Casa
de las Américas en 1973. Premio
Nacional de Cuento en México en
1975. Ha publicado esta deliciosa
novela para sacar a los adolescentes
del hipnotismo de la televisión e
invitarlos, en cambio, a la literatura.

Why did Poli Délano write this novel?

1 to show how a television series is produced
2 to encourage adolescents to read novels written
  for them
3 to inform teenagers about the pleasures of travel-
  ing by train
4 to provide parents with advice on raising
  adolescents.

23 _____

24

> ### Señora Directora:
>
> Nosotros los ciudadanos de Medellín, Colombia, nos sentimos muy halagados por el excelente artículo que su revista "Geomundo" de septiembre ha publicado sobre nuestra bella ciudad. Créanos que ha sido un honor el sentirnos incluidos en una de las revistas más importantes del mundo de habla hispana.
>
> Por su intermedio deseo agradecerle a la periodista Olga Lucía Jaramillo y al fotógrafo Jorge Ernesto Bautista por su magnífico artículo y bellas fotografías.
>
> Medellín siempre será su casa, cuente con nuestra permanente colaboración; no podemos olvidar a los amigos que entienden bien esta ciudad y realzan sus bondades.
>
> Reciba un cordial y afectuoso saludo.
>
> **Atentamente,**
> **Luis Bernardo Duque Osorio**
> **Director de Fomento y Turismo**
> **de Medellín.**

Why did Luis Bernardo write to the magazine?

1 to compliment them for an article they printed
2 to find out how to contact the photographer
3 to renew his subscription for another year
4 to complain about inaccurate statements   24 _____

25

PARA OBTENER INFORMACIÓN CON FACILIDAD...llame directamente a las oficinas siguientes marcando el número 808 seguido de los números que aparecen al lado de los nombres a continuación:

Plan de estudios de música y arte..2333
Director atlético, y salud 2420
Presupuesto...2016
Programas comunitarios..2071
Plan de estudios para estudiantes de comercio...2236
Curso de estudios de inglés..2060
Curso de estudios de lenguas extranjeras..2073
Servicios de consejería..2035
Programa sobre estrategias de aprendizaje..2232
Servicios alimenticios..2040
Curso de estudios de matemáticas..2180
Servicios médicos..2050
Programa para estudiantes superdotados...2230
Centro de información para padres..2174
Programa de Pre-escolar..2039
Servicios estudiantiles, trabajo social, servicios
    psicológicos, habla, asistencia...2425
Departamento de investigaciones, pruebas y
    evaluación...2248
Curso de estudios de ciencias...2172
Curso de estudios sociales..2037
Oficina de información estudiantil..2438
Transporte, autobuses escolares...2057
Voluntarios..2013

These telephone listings are all related to

1 a hotel   3 a hospital
2 an employment agency   4 a school   25 _____

c *Directions* (26-30): In the following passage, there are five blank spaces numbered 26 through 30. Each blank space represents a missing word or expression. For each blank space, four possible completions are provided. Only one of them makes sense *in the context of the passage.*

First, read the passage in its entirety to determine its general meaning. Then read it a second time. For each blank space, choose the completion that makes the best sense and write its *number* in the space provided.   [10]

La fiesta:
herencia cultural española

España está siempre de fiesta, más de 25.000 al año. Cada veinte minutos se celebra una fiesta en cualquier parte del país. Algunas fiestas se originaron hace muchos siglos; otras empezaron en los recientes   (26)   . Para los españoles cualquier razón es buena para tener una fiesta.

Ningún país del mundo tiene tantas fiestas, celebraciones, carnavales, corridas, desfiles, procesiones, y alegría en general para gritar, bailar, comer,   (27)   y disfrutar de la vida. Los historiadores y autores clásicos son muy aficionados a estudiar este carácter de alegría nacional. "Descansemos hoy, necesitamos la energía para celebrar mañana. ¡Qué buena vida es ésta!" dicen los españoles.

Hay fiestas de origen histórico, pero la mayoría son religiosas, como las procesiones, y las ofrendas navideñas. Al mismo tiempo existen fiestas como la Tomatina, donde los participantes se tiran tomates como manera de divertirse. De hecho, España es una fiesta constante que empezó hace ya muchos siglos, y que no va a   (28)   muy pronto.

Hay más fiestas que ciudades. Hay fiestas donde el motivo es expresar   (29)   con música, risas, gritos, y ruidos tan altos que podrían dañar los oídos.

El antropólogo Enrique Gil Calvo escribió en su libro *Estado de Fiesta* que los pueblos mediterráneos presentan unas de las manifestaciones más coloridas del continente europeo. Para Gil Calvo, la fiesta es una expresión más de la capacidad humana de demostrar sus sentimientos.

Esplendor, alegría e imaginación popular son características básicas de las fiestas españolas. Las grandes celebraciones festivas que tienen lugar cada año tienen al pueblo como protagonista y como espectador. Las fiestas son parte de la herencia cultural, fenómeno propio de la vitalidad española. Hay celebraciones en diferentes lugares y en todas las estaciones del año sin ninguna interrupción. El viajero encontrará siempre el momento apropiado para asistir a algunos de estos eventos mágicos y espectaculares que alteran el ritmo cotidiano de la ___(30)___ .

(26) 1 clubes   3 tiempos
     2 puertos   4 pensamientos   26 _____

(27) 1 callar   3 seguir
     2 criticar   4 jugar   27 _____

(28) 1 terminar   3 animar
     2 interesar   4 nacer   28 _____

(29) 1 la alegría   3 la ayuda
     2 la información   4 el miedo   29 _____

(30) 1 edad   3 sociedad
     2 enfermedad   4 verdad   30 _____

PART 4

Write your answers to Part 4 according to the directions for *a* and *b*. [16]

a Directions: Write **one** well-organized note in Spanish as directed below. [6]

> Choose **either** question 31 **or** 32. Write a well-organized note, following the specific instructions given in the question you have chosen. Your note must consist of **at least six clauses.** To qualify for credit, a clause must contain a verb, a stated or implied subject, and additional words necessary to convey meaning. The six clauses may be contained in fewer than six sentences if some of the sentences have more than one clause.

31 A Spanish-speaking classmate is recovering from an illness and will not be at school for several days. Write a note in Spanish to your classmate offering your help to him or her.

In your note, you may wish to include an expression of sympathy and/or hope for a quick recovery. You may wish to make a general offer to help or you may wish to suggest something specific, such as taking notes in class, providing homework assignments, or performing some errands that he or she needs to have done. **Be sure to accomplish the purpose of the note, which is *to offer to help your classmate.***

> *Use the following:*
>
> Salutation: Querido/Querida [classmate's name],
> Closing: [your name]

The salutation and closing will *not* be counted as part of the six required clauses.

32 Your pen pal is visiting from Spain. You would like to bring him or her to your Spanish class. Write a note in Spanish to your Spanish teacher about bringing your pen pal to class.

In your note, you may wish to include where your pen pal is from, when he or she is coming, and what he or she can contribute to the class. You may also wish to tell your teacher other details about your pen pal. **Be sure to accomplish the purpose of the note, which is *to write about bringing your Spanish pen pal to Spanish class.***

Use the following:

Salutation: Estimado Profesor/Estimada Profesora,
Closing: [your name]

The salutation and closing will *not* be counted as part of the six required clauses.

b *Directions:* Write **one** well-organized composition in Spanish as directed below. [10]

Choose **either** question 33 **or** 34. Write a well-organized composition, following the specific instructions given in the question you have chosen. Your composition must consist of **at least 10 clauses.** To qualify for credit, a clause must contain a verb, a stated or implied subject, and additional words necessary to convey meaning. The 10 clauses may be contained in fewer than 10 sentences if some of the sentences have more than one clause.

33 In Spanish, write a story about the situation shown in the picture below. It must be a story relating to the picture, **not** a description of the picture. Do **not** write a dialogue.

34 Schools are sometimes the subject of criticism. Your Spanish teacher would like to know your ideas about what is positive and/or good about your school. In Spanish, write a letter to your Spanish teacher discussing what is positive and/or good about your school.

You <u>must</u> accomplish the purpose of the letter, which is *to discuss what is positive and/or good about your school.*

In your letter, you may wish to mention and give some examples of how certain teachers, friends, classes, sports, art, music, drama, clubs, and/or afterschool activities make attending your school a good and positive experience.

You may use any or all of the ideas suggested above *or* you may use your own ideas. **Either way, you must discuss what is positive and/or good about your school.**

Use the following:

Dateline:	el 20 de junio de 2000
Salutation:	Sr./Sra. [your teacher's name],
Closing:	[your name]

The dateline, salutation, and closing will *not* be counted as part of the 10 required clauses.

Answers
June 2000

Comprehensive Examination in Spanish

PART 1

This part of the examination was evaluated prior to the date of this written examination. [24 credits]

PART 2

The following passages are to be read aloud to the students according to the directions given for this part at the beginning of this examination. The correct answers are given after number 15. [30 credits]

1 You hear a representative of an airline make this announcement:

Los gobiernos de los Estados Unidos y el Japón firmaron un tratado de aviación que nos permite ofrecer más vuelos competitivos y accesibles entre los dos países. Me complace anunciar que con este nuevo servicio extendido al Japón, ahora tendrá la oportunidad de llegar a su destino más fácil—y más rápidamente que antes. Este es el resultado de muchos años de negociaciones con el gobierno japonés para un servicio más rápido y más frecuente.

What does the airline offer?

2 While watching television in Spain, you hear this announcement:

Ayúdenos a retirar este producto del mercado. El juguete se llama "Osito Meloso". Hemos detectado que si un bebé se lo pone en la boca, podría obstruirle la respiración. Por esto, hemos decidido quitarlo del mercado inmediatamente. Si su hijo tiene este juguete, por favor, envíelo por correo certificado. Incluya una carta donde nos indique su nombre y apellidos, dirección completa con código postal y teléfono. Para nosotros la seguridad de su bebé es lo primero.

What is the purpose of this announcement?

3   You hear this message on your answering machine:

Lo sentimos mucho, pero la bicicleta que usted pidió la semana pasada ya no se fabrica. La compañía interrumpió la fabricación de ese modelo hace seis meses. Si quiere le podemos enviar una de otro modelo más moderno, pero tiene un costo adicional. O si prefiere le devolveremos su dinero sin ningún problema. En todo caso, por favor llame nuestra oficina para indicarnos su decisión.

What did the message say?

4   While watching a Spanish television station, you hear this commercial announcement:

Por más de 50 años, nuestra compañía ha traído a la cocina una línea completa de sartenes, ollas, y cacerolas de alta calidad, diseñada para un estilo de vida saludable. Nuestro exclusivo equipo de cocina se distingue por su bella construcción y por su rápida distribución de calor. Es fácil de limpiar. Cocina con un mínimo de energía. Es tan durable, que nosotros ofrecemos una garantía de por vida.

What is being advertised?

5   You are in Mexico watching television. You hear an announcer say:

El actor brasileño Guy Ecker será el protagonista central de "La mentira", la telenovela que se empieza a transmitir el próximo lunes.

"La mentira" es muy diferente. Tiene características interesantes, distintas a la telenovela tradicional; el tema es el drama de la vida moderna y los personajes tienen actitudes muy dramáticas.

What kind of television program begins soon?

6   While you are listening to some music on the radio, you hear the announcer say:

Apreciado aficionado a la música latina: ¿Recuerda cuando la pasión por la música latina crecía en todas partes ... pero la selección disponible era escasa y difícil de conseguir?

Nosotros mismos hemos sentido esa falta. En 1991 nosotros, los aficionados a la música latina decidimos formar el Club Música Latina, un club con una misión: ofrecer el mejor servicio a nuestra comunidad con la facilidad de comprar desde su casa la mejor selección de música latina.

What is being offered to the public?

7 The principal of a school is being interviewed on a local television channel in Spain. The principal says:

Se les invita a todos los padres a visitar la escuela de sus hijos. Todos los visitantes deben ir primero a la oficina. Todos los que deseen reunirse con un maestro o con el director de la escuela, deben llamar primero para hacer una cita. Si desea entrar en el salón de clase de su hijo, debe hablar con el director para que le indique la fecha y la hora en que lo puede hacer.

Who would be most interested in this announcement?

8 You are listening to the radio and hear this commercial:

El Banco de Santander ha iniciado en Colombia un programa de comercio electrónico seguro que permitirá a los consumidores comprar con seguridad en la red mundial. Esta nueva tecnología garantiza la integridad de la información de crédito que se envía por la Internet. Este servicio fue creado para la división de América Latina y el Caribe del Banco de Santander.

What service has been initiated?

9 While you are visiting a school in Puerto Rico, you hear this announcement:

Todos los jóvenes entre las edades de 14 y 18 años necesitan un permiso para trabajar. Los estudiantes de la escuela pueden obtener los formularios en la oficina de la enfermera o en la oficina del sub-director. El solicitante necesita que uno de sus padres o su tutor firme la solicitud. También necesita un documento que pruebe su edad y un certificado de salud de su médico o del médico de la escuela. Los permisos para trabajar serán procesados y otorgados en las oficinas indicadas.

Who would be most interested in this announcement?

10 You are listening to a program and hear this information:

Es joven, hermosa y bilingüe. María del Carmen Romero es una poetisa chilena que acaba de publicar su tercera antología de poemas, *Recuerdos,* en la que resaltan su simplicidad, su preocupación social y sus sentimientos románticos. Según lo confiesa al iniciar su colección de poemas, cada palabra que escribe es un escape. Se mueve entre el pasado y el presente, e intenta tocar la esencia de la vida. El libro está ilustrado con dibujos en negro y rojo. El negro simboliza lo concreto en su vida y el rojo sus sentimientos o los sentimientos del arte en relación a lo que escribe.

¿De quién se habla en este pasaje?

11 You are listening to the radio and hear this report:

"Tengo fe", el nuevo álbum del artista Carlos Vives que hizo popular por todo el mundo el vallenato, una música típica colombiana, ha batido records de venta en su país. El disco tiene temas escritos por él, con una mezcla de ritmos que mantienen la esencia de la música vallenata. Aunque todo el álbum es en español, el primer día vendió 300.000 copias en su país, lo que le valió seis discos de platino. Carlos Vives piensa grabar en otros idiomas para dar a conocer mejor su música por el mundo entero.

Según este anuncio, ¿qué hará el cantante Carlos Vives?

12 You are listening to the radio and hear this commentary from a doctor:

Probablemente, todos tenemos o hemos tenido algún problema con los pies, pero casi siempre limitamos su cuidado a cortar las uñas. El primer paso en el cuidado de los pies es la prevención, y realmente, es muy simple. Lavar y secar escrupulosamente los pies sólo requiere unos instantes. ¿Cuántos de nosotros tenemos esta rutina?

¿Qué discute el médico?

13 While you are at a travel agency in Mexico, the agent tells you about Veracruz:

Caer de una cascada de agua de 30 metros de altura, arrojarse desde un globo en pleno vuelo, navegar contra la fuerza del agua mar abierto o de los ríos, escalar montañas, andar en bicicleta, ¡todo es adrenalina pura! Gracias a su favorable geografía, Veracruz es reconocido por la Secretaría de Turismo como el estado de mayor actividad ecoturística.

Según el agente, ¿qué puedes hacer si vas de vacaciones a Veracruz?

14 A travel agent in Mexico City tells you about a hotel. The travel agent says:

Por encontrarse en un lugar céntrico, el hotel Bristol satisface las necesidades de los ejecutivos más exigentes. Situado a sólo dos calles del Paseo de la Reforma, detrás de la embajada de Estados Unidos y a un paso de la Zona Rosa—con sus tiendas, restaurantes y boutiques—usted encontrará los bancos y comercios más importantes para resolver todos sus asuntos.

¿Qué ventaja tiene este hotel?

15 You are an exchange student in Valencia, Spain. While visiting your host's school, you hear this announcement:

¿Tienes talentos artísticos? ¿Te gustaría actuar? Si respondiste que sí a estas dos preguntas, ven a nuestra reunión esta tarde. Este año vamos a presentar una obra del escritor español Alejandro Casona. Necesitamos todo tipo de ayuda ... y si no quieres actuar, puedes ayudar con el diseño del escenario o del programa, la venta de boletos y muchas otras actividades.

¿Para quiénes es este anuncio?

PART 2

(1) 3	(4) 2	(7) 2	(10) 1	(13) 4
(2) 2	(5) 4	(8) 1	(11) 2	(14) 1
(3) 1	(6) 3	(9) 4	(12) 4	(15) 3

PART 3

(a) (16) 1	(b) (21) 3	(c) (26) 3
(17) 4	(22) 3	(27) 4
(18) 2	(23) 2	(28) 1
(19) 1	(24) 1	(29) 1
(20) 2	(25) 4	(30) 3

PART 4

(a) Notes in writing

For each note, an example of a response worth six credits follows. The slash marks indicate how each sample note has been divided into clauses.

31 Querido Carlos,

Oí/$_1$ que estás enfermo./$_2$ ¡Lo siento!/$_3$ ¿Te puedo ayudar con algo?/$_4$ Si quieres,/$_5$ te traigo la tarea y los apuntes./$_6$ Dime cuando puedo ir a tu casa.

José

32 Estimada Profesora,

Mi amiga Carolina acaba de llegar de Aravaca./₁ Quiere visitar nuestra clase./₂ Ella puede hablar de su país y de las costumbres españolas./₃ ¿Cuándo le parece mejor/₄ que venga a la clase?/₅ Estará acá por dos semanas./₆ Le hablaré a Ud. más tarde.

Teresa

(b) Narrative based on picture/letter

For each narrative/letter, an example of a response worth 10 credits follows. The slash marks indicate how each sample narrative/letter has been divided into clauses.

33. (Picture)

Fernando e Isabel están muy preocupados./₁ Acaban de tomar un examen muy difícil en la clase de ciencias./₂ Fernando se queja/₃ porque no tuvo bastante tiempo/₄ para terminar el examen./₅ Pero Isabel estudió mucho/₆ y no le pareció tan difícil./₇ El siempre ha tenido más problemas con las ciencias./₈ Ellos saben/₉ que van a recibir sus notas mañana./₁₀ Isabel dormirá muy tranquila.

34. (Letter)

el 20 de junio de 2000

Sra. Soto,

Aunque existen muchos problemas en nuestro colegio,/₁ en mi opinión hay muchas cosas buenas también./₂ Por ejemplo, aunque hay mucha construcción,/₃ vamos a tener muchas clases nuevas y una nueva biblioteca./₄ Además, nuestra escuela hoy día ofrece muchas actividades,/₅ y con las renovaciones podríamos tener más conciertos, partidos y bailes./₆ Hay muchos estudiantes aquí/₇ que pueden tomar cursos para crédito universitario./₈ Tenemos también un buen equipo de baloncesto/₉ que es conocido en todo el estado./₁₀ Me gusta asistir a este colegio.

Sinceramente,

Miguel

Examination January 2001

Comprehensive Examination in Spanish

PART 1

Your performance on Part 1, Speaking (24 credits), has been evaluated prior to the date of this written examination.

PART 2

Answer all questions in Part 2 according to the directions for *a* and *b*.   [30]

a Directions (1–9): For each question, you will hear some background information in English *once*. Then you will hear a passage in Spanish *twice* and a question in English *once*. After you have heard the question, the teacher will pause while you read the question and the four suggested answers. Choose the best suggested answer and write its *number* in the space provided. Base your answer *on the content of the passage, only*. The passages that the teacher will read aloud to you are found in the ANSWERS section, Part 2, at the end of this examination.   [18]

1 What is this person's complaint?
   1 The interview was not long enough.
   2 The interview did not include songs.
   3 The interview was not previously advertised.
   4 The interview was not interesting.   1 _____

2 What is the main idea of this announcement?

   1 Children should get regular exercise to promote good health.

   2 Parents should encourage their children to develop new hobbies.

   3 Watching television may be helpful for some children.

   4 It is important to stimulate an interest in reading in children.   2 _____

3 What does the Spanish Radio-Television Network plan to do?

   1 offer the cable at discount prices

   2 offer more programs in English

   3 increase its listening and viewing audience

   4 move its main network offices to Mexico   3 _____

4 What was just announced?

   1 A popular Spanish singer appeared in a video with an Irish group.

   2 Boyzone performed in concert in Latin America.

   3 Boyzone invited English fans to appear in a new video.

   4 Enrique Iglesias toured Europe with the Irish group.   4 _____

5 What does this advertisement promote?

   1 an exercise program

   2 helpful medicines

   3 new cooking utensils

   4 a healthier way of cooking   5 _____

6 What does the flight attendant advise you to do?

   1 remember to take all personal belongings
   2 stay seated during takeoff
   3 store your carry-on luggage carefully
   4 keep your seat belt fastened   6 _____

7 What is this announcement about?

   1 certain telephone numbers that can be called for
      free
   2 the chance to receive a free telephone
   3 the opportunity to make telephone calls in taxis
   4 procedures to follow to comment on taxi service   7 _____

8 What is a distinguishing feature of Costa Rica?

   1 There has been widespread rebellion for many
      years.
   2 It has a long history of freedom and democracy.
   3 Its economy has changed little since it became a
      republic.
   4 Swiss investments have significantly affected the
      economy of Costa Rica.   8 _____

9 What new service does this company now offer?

   1 laptops for business-class passengers
   2 additional frequent-flier miles
   3 more comfortable accommodations
   4 ticket purchases online   9 _____

b Directions (10–15): For each question, you will hear some background information in English *once*. Then you will hear a passage in Spanish *twice* and a question in Spanish *once*. After you have heard the question, the teacher will pause while you read the question and the four suggested answers. Choose the best suggested answer and write its *number* in the space provided. Base your answer *on the content of the passage, only*. The passages that the teacher will read aloud to you are found in the ANSWERS section, Part 2, at the end of this examination. [12]

10 ¿Cuál es el propósito de este anuncio?

   1 ofrecer excursiones a Disneylandia en Europa
   2 hablar de una película nueva
   3 anunciar vacaciones por el nuevo barco de Disney
   4 inaugurar un nuevo hotel en las Bahamas   10 _____

11 ¿Qué hacía Antonio cuando era un chico de 13 años?

   1 Distribuía los periódicos.
   2 Sacaba fotos.
   3 Arreglaba bicicletas.
   4 Escribía libros.   11 _____

12 ¿Qué producto se anuncia?

   1 gafas de último estilo
   2 loción para la piel
   3 nuevos maquillajes para la cara
   4 un nuevo método de aprender matemáticas   12 _____

13 ¿Por qué llamó tu amiga?

   1 Quiere informarte de una noticia.
   2 Quiere agradecerte el regalo.
   3 Quiere verte pronto.
   4 Quiere invitarte a su casa.   13 _____

14 ¿Qué vende la compañía?

   1 instrumentos musicales
   2 viajes turísticos
   3 videocintas educacionales
   4 novelas históricas   14 _____

15 ¿Cuál es el tema de esta noticia?

   1 un nuevo programa de computadoras para el año
      2000
   2 clases ofrecidas en una universidad
   3 la inauguración de un centro comercial
   4 la conservación de la naturaleza   15 _____

PART 3

Answer all questions in Part 3 according to the directions for *a*, *b*, and *c*. [30]

a Directions (16–20): After the following passage, there are five questions or incomplete statements. For *each,* choose the word or expression that best answers the question or completes the statement *according to the meaning of the passage,* and write its *number* in the space provided. [10]

Una Entrevista con Luis Miguel

Vestido completamente de negro y bronceado por el sol de Los Angeles, Luis Miguel luce la mejor de sus sonrisas. Confiesa estar satisfecho de volver a España para dar unos conciertos después de seis meses de ausencia, seguramente porque no esperaba el éxito que aquí está cosechando. El cantante mexicano empezó su carrera artística a los 12 años en 1982 con su producción titulada "Luis Miguel, un sol". Ahora con 28 años, una carrera consolidada con esfuerzo y recompensada por gran cantidad de premios—cuatro Grammys entre ellos—viene dispuesto a ofrecer lo mejor de sí mismo en los cinco conciertos programados en Madrid, Barcelona, Valencia, Murcia, y Málaga. "Quiero agradecer a todo el público por su cariño incondicional y por haberme seguido siempre. Su amor interminable me inspiró y me dio energías en aquellos momentos cuando llegué a pensar que nunca descubriría el éxito actual. A ellos les dedico mi esfuerzo, ya que por ellos he logrado la fama mundial que tengo", comentó el cantante.

Luis Miguel fue nombrado el artista del Año 2000 y también fue reconocido como el cantante con más conciertos ofrecidos en el Auditorio Nacional. Estos reconocimientos se unen a los 346 discos de platino que ha obtenido en los 18 años de exitosa carrera, durante la cual ha vendido más de 37 millones de discos a nivel mundial.

El periodista: ¿Esperabas tan buena aceptación en España?

Luis Miguel: Desde luego que me ha sorprendido porque no esperaba una hospitalidad tan cálida y agradable. Me siento como en casa. Ahora vengo por poco tiempo, pero me gusta tanto estar aquí que a lo mejor me quede a vivir en España.

El periodista: ¿Cuáles son las claves de tu éxito?

Luis Miguel: No conozco el secreto del éxito. Creo que he tenido éxito porque elijo las canciones con las que me identifico y trabajo mucho.

El periodista: ¿Disfrutas cantando boleros?

Luis Miguel: Soy un enamorado del bolero y otras canciones de emoción de ternura. Cuando canto un bolero, puedo expresarme con todo mi corazón y mis sentimientos. No sabría elegir uno en especial de todos los que canto.

El periodista: Tú mantienes tu residencia principal en Los Angeles. ¿No has pensado cantar en inglés para entrar más directamente en el mercado americano?

Luis Miguel: No. El español es una lengua muy importante en el mundo y creo que hay que defenderla por encima de todo. No he considerado cantar en otro idioma.

El periodista: ¿Qué le pides a la vida?

Luis Miguel: Más música, más público y seguir evolucionando como intérprete musical.

El periodista: ¿Qué valor y significado tiene en tu vida el amor?

Luis Miguel: El amor lo es todo. Llevo toda mi vida cantando a ese grandioso sentimiento que rejuvenece y llena el corazón de las personas.

El periodista: Finalmente, ¿es cierto que te has casado?

Luis Miguel: Por el momento, no; pero estoy muy enamorado y aún tengo la esperanza de casarme en un futuro cercano y formar una gran familia.

16 ¿Por qué ha regresado Luis Miguel a España?

1 para conocer este país mejor
2 para casarse con su primer amor
3 para descansar después de mucho trabajo
4 para cantar sus últimas canciones   16 _____

17 ¿Cómo le ha recibido el público español a este cantante?

1 con mucho entusiasmo
2 con mucha melancolía
3 con mucha tristeza
4 con mucho disgusto   17 _____

18 Según Luis Miguel, ¿a qué atribuye su triunfo musical?

1 a su vida estable en Los Angeles
2 a su lugar del nacimiento
3 a su esfuerzo y relación personal con su música
4 a su apariencia juvenil   18 _____

19 ¿Por qué le gusta cantar boleros?

1 porque son canciones sentimentales
2 porque expresan sus ideas políticas
3 porque describen su país natal
4 porque contienen temas folklóricos   19 _____

20 ¿Qué planes incluye su futuro?

1 Quiere tener una familia algún día.
2 Quiere regresar a México para vivir.
3 Quiere grabar canciones en inglés.
4 Quiere dejar de trabajar pronto.   20 _____

b Directions (21–25): Below each of the following selections, there is either a question or an incomplete statement. For *each*, choose the word or expression that best answers the question or completes the statement *according to the meaning of the selection*, and write its *number* in the space provided.   [10]

21

Para visitar Perú

Con el lema de "Destino Perú", la cadena hotelera Utell extiende una invitación a los turistas para visitar Perú, desde ahora hasta el 21 de diciembre de este año, en once de sus hoteles, con un ahorro de hasta el 65 por ciento. La oferta incluye desayunos y alojamiento gratis para los niños. Los hoteles que participan en esta oferta son: Picoga Hotel y Golden Tulip, en Cuzco; Miraflores Park Plaza y Las Américas Hotel en Lima; Libertador, en Arequipa. Los visitantes a Perú podrán tener la experiencia de ver algunas de las ruinas arqueológicas entre las 84 zonas de este tipo que hay en el país. Entre las ruinas que están incluidas en el programa está Moche y Chimu, restos del imperio inca, y recorridos por las junglas del Amazonas y las montañas andinas.

Utell International es una empresa que representa 7,700 hoteles en 180 países, para todos los presupuestos. Para mayor información consulte a su agente de viajes.

Who is advertising a trip to Peru?

1 the government of Peru
2 an airline
3 a university
4 a group of hotels   21 _____

22

> ## *Ojo con la TV*
>
> Si los pequeños se aburren en sus ratos libres, no es lo más recomendable animarlos a ver televisión como rutina. Mucho mejor es propiciar que realicen actividades al aire libre, que—de paso— los ayudan a ejercitarse. Es casi imposible evitar que vean televisión, pero su uso debe ser vigilado por los adultos. Aunque puede resultar un medio muy educativo, los padres deben asumir una posición crítica y activa ante los programas favoritos de los niños, así como tener varios vídeos que puedan entretenerlos de manera sana si la programación no resulta la más conveniente. Nunca se les debe dejar la TV encendida todo el tiempo. También los niños necesitan desarrollar su imaginación.

To whom is this article directed?

1 television producers
2 teenagers
3 advertisers
4 parents of small children   22 _____

23

MarcaV☉z℠

La manera más fácil y rápida de hacer sus llamadas más frecuentes.

Ahora con el nuevo *Servicio MarcaVoz℠** de NYNEX, usted puede llamar a cualquier persona o lugar con sólo decir el nombre de la persona o del sitio al que desea llamar, y su llamada será marcada automáticamente.

Con el *Servicio MarcaVoz,* usted no tendrá que marcar los números a los que llama con más frecuencia, y no importa si su llamada es a la vuelta de la esquina, a otra ciudad, estado o alrededor del mundo, el *Servicio MarcaVoz* marcará sus llamadas con el sonido de su voz.

El *Servicio MarcaVoz* no necesita equipo especial y funciona con cualquier teléfono de teclas (touch-tone) o de discado giratorio, en su hogar.

La programación es fácil, y todas las instrucciones son en español. ¡Usted puede programar hasta 50 nombres (en español o inglés) en su teléfono! Luego, usted sólo tiene que decir el nombre de la persona o del lugar al que desea llamar, y el *Servicio MarcaVoz* marcará por usted.

Piénselo: no tendrá que buscar más el "papelito" donde anotó un número telefónico importante; no tendrá que marcar esos largos números para hacer sus llamadas internacionales; y no volverá a marcar números equivocados.

Compruebe porqué con el *Servicio MarcaVoz* es más fácil y rápido hacer sus llamadas más frecuentes.

This announcement provides information about

1. low international telephone rates
2. bilingual telephone operators
3. voice-activated telephone dialing
4. additional free telephone lines

23 _____

24

Estimados señores:

La presente es para manifestarles mi asombro que, como ferviente seguidor de su revista, me causó el imperdonable error cometido en la edición No. 10 del presente año en el artículo "Conquistadores", al imputarle en la página 366 la fundación de Bogotá a Sebastián de Belalcázar, cuando el fundador de Santa Fe de Bogotá fue el conquistador Gonzalo Jiménez de Quesada el 6 de agosto de 1538.

Sebastián de Belalcázar fundó Santiago de Cali y Popayán.

Sin otro particular, y seguro de haber logrado claridad, me despido de ustedes.

Cordialmente:
Arq. Ricardo Alfonso, Pedraza Trujillo
Santa Fe de Bogotá, Colombia.

Why did this reader write the letter?

1 to thank the magazine staff for an article on conquerors
2 to ask for a previous edition of the magazine
3 to inform the magazine staff of a mistake they printed
4 to find out about subscription prices

24 _____

25

Si Ud. siempre quiso aprender a tocar guitarra, ésta es su gran oportunidad.

El método más sencillo, agradable y en VIDEO. En su propio hogar, sin tener que ir a una escuela y con canciones hermosas y de moda. Las canciones que aprenderá son muy conocidas, por ejemplo: El Reloj, Tu Cárcel, Amor Eterno, La Montaña, La Puerta Negra y muchas más.

Le enseñamos a tocar guitarra igual que sus padres le enseñaron a hablar. Sin ejercicios aburridos ni reglas complicadas.

Ud. aprendió a hablar, . . . hablando. Nosotros le enseñamos a tocar guitarra tocando, con canciones hermosas donde todo es alegría y casi sin darse cuenta, estará tocando en forma FA-CI-LI-SIMA.

Ud. aprende con canciones de artistas famosos como Roberto Carlos, Juan Gabriel, Los Bukis y muchos más. Además en vídeo donde el maestro no se cansa de repetir hasta que Ud. aprende. Su costo es sumamente módico . . . sólo $24.95. Incluye un libro con instrucciones, un vídeo de larga duración y se está regalando un juego de cuerdas de nilón para su guitarra con valor de $12.00, completamente GRATIS.

Han sido varios años de estudio e investigación para desarrollar el método que hace que tocar guitarra sea fácil . . . facilísimo. Además, super económico, ya que no tienen que pagar grandes cantidades por clases particulares. Algunos maestros cobran $30.00 por 1/2 hora; el vídeo es equivalente a muchísimas horas de estudio, por lo que el costo es mínimo.

Ordene su método hoy mismo o pídalo en su librería o tienda de discos favorita.

Y la SUPER GARANTIA, si en 60 días no aprende, puede devolver su método para un reembolso de su dinero y por supuesto, se puede quedar con las cuerdas. Pregunte a sus amigos, estamos seguros que ya han oído hablar de GUITARRA FACILISIMA. Tanta gente satisfecha no se puede equivocar. Ordene su curso hoy mismo y empiece a ser feliz.

1-800-244-1153

| Enviar cheque o money order por $24.95 más $6.00 para gastos de envío a nombre de IMPERIAL MUSIC 1110 W. OLYMPIC BLVD., SUITE "D", LOS ANGELES, CA 90015 | Nombre_____ Dirección_____ Ciudad___ Estado___ Código Postal___ Teléfono _____ SE ACEPTAN VISA, MASTER CARD Y DISCOVER |

According to this advertisement, where can you learn to play the guitar?

1 in the offices of Imperial Music in Los Angeles
2 in your own home
3 in your favorite music store
4 in the Juan Gabriel music studio

25 _____

c *Directions* (26–30): In the following passage, there are five blank spaces numbered 26 through 30. Each blank space represents a missing word or expression. For each blank space, four possible completions are provided. Only one of them makes sense *in the context of the passage*.

First, read the passage in its entirety to determine its general meaning. Then read it a second time. For each blank space, choose the completion that makes the best sense and write its *number* in the space provided. [10]

La Danza

La danza es una forma de expresión tan antigua como el hombre. Desde la más remota antigüedad, el bailar ha sido una actividad inherente a la expresividad humana. La danza, o baile, está considerada en algunas culturas como la madre de todas las artes. El bailar es una actividad exclusiva del hombre. Forma parte de las actividades más naturales e instintivas de la especie humana.

El baile es una actividad ___(26)___, relajante, y beneficiosa para la salud. Nos ayuda a mejorar nuestro estado físico y psíquico, nos permite mejorar nuestras relaciones sociales y ayuda a proyectar nuestra personalidad. Es una de las actividades más completas y exigentes de todas las disciplinas gimnásticas que mantienen en forma nuestro ___(27)___. Nos proporciona fuerza, flexibilidad, resistencia y ritmo.

Los ejercicios físicos necesarios para aprender determinadas técnicas se coordinan con la música, y al mismo tiempo que vamos entrenando nuestro cuerpo mejoramos nuestra figura y adquirimos un sentido del ritmo y del equilibrio. Las personas que practican el baile ___(28)___ con equilibrio, elegancia y ritmo.

Al principio, la danza se practicaba como un rito

religioso. Después de muchos siglos el baile ha
evolucionado hasta convertirse en un agradable
___(29)___. Existen múltiples tipos de bailes, unos
orientados a favorecer nuestra forma física y otros a
potenciar nuestra expresividad corporal. Se puede
decir que las formas de practicar el baile son el
ballet clásico, el gim jazz, la danza regional y
los bailes sociales. Y cada una de estas formas da
beneficios a sus practicantes.

La danza también favorece las relaciones sociales.
Tanto el baile en grupos como el baile de salón en
pareja ayudan a crear nuevas amistades. Es decir
que el baile nos ayuda a conocer a nuevos amigos en
poco tiempo. La proximidad, el movimiento del
cuerpo y el contacto físico hacen que se rompa el
hielo, estimulando la relación interpersonal y
provocando que el conocimiento sea más rápido y
relajado.

También a través del baile podemos transmitir
sensaciones y sentimientos. Podemos eliminar
tensiones y conseguir una relajación física y mental
similar a la que se obtiene en la práctica de cualquier
otro ejercicio aeróbico. Como disciplina y práctica
deportiva es una actividad ideal para producir
efectos calmantes en nuestro sistema nervioso.
Además, está comprobado que danzar ejerce un
efecto ___(30)___ sobre nuestra mente produciendo
efectos similares a los que dan la psicoterapia y el
yoga.

(26) 1 física   3 pasiva
      2 inadecuada   4 obscura   26 _____

(27) 1 empleo   3 cuerpo
      2 hogar   4 espanto   27 _____

(28) 1 se oyen   3 se visten
      2 se comprenden   4 se mueven   28 _____

(29) 1 viaje   3 castigo
      2 pasatiempo   4 monumento   29 _____

(30) 1 molestoso   3 temeroso
      2 celoso   4 beneficioso   30 _____

PART 4

Write your answers to Part 4 according to the directions for *a* and *b*.   [16]

a Directions: Write **one** well-organized note in Spanish as directed below.   [6]

> Choose **either** question 31 **or** 32. Write a well-organized note, following the specific instructions given in the question you have chosen. Your note must consist of **at least six clauses.** To qualify for credit, a clause must contain a verb, a stated or implied subject, and additional words necessary to convey meaning. The six clauses may be contained in fewer than six sentences if some of the sentences have more than one clause.

31 You are in a restaurant in San Juan. At the end of your meal, you are asked to evaluate the restaurant. You are given some notepaper so you may immediately express your thoughts. Write a note in Spanish to the manager expressing your opinion of the restaurant.

In your note, you may wish to include your opinion about the service, price, cleanliness, selection, quality of food, and/or friendliness of the staff. **Be sure to accomplish the purpose of the note, which is *to express your opinion of the restaurant.***

Use the following:

Salutation: Señor/Señora,
Closing: Sinceramente, [your name]

The salutation and closing will *not* be counted as part of the six required clauses.

32 You are an exchange student at a school in Mexico. You would like to change one of the classes you are taking. Write a note in Spanish to your guidance counselor about changing one of your classes.

In your note, you may wish to mention which classes you have, which class you would like to change, which other class you prefer, why you are requesting the change, when your classes meet, and/or where each class is held. **Be sure to accomplish the purpose of the note, which is to *ask about changing one of your classes.***

Use the following:

Salutation: Querido Señor/Querida Señora
        [your counselor's name],
Closing: [your name]

The salutation and closing will *not* be counted as part of the six required clauses.

b Directions: Write **one** well-organized composition in Spanish as directed below. [10]

Choose **either** question 33 **or** 34. Write a well-organized composition, following the specific instructions given in the question you have chosen. Your composition must consist of **at least 10 clauses.** To qualify for credit, a clause must contain a verb, a stated or implied subject, and additional words necessary to convey meaning. The 10 clauses may be contained in fewer than 10 sentences if some of the sentences have more than one clause.

33 In Spanish, write a story about the situation shown in the picture below. It must be a story relating to the picture, **not** a description of the picture. Do **not** write a dialogue.

34 The Spanish Club's newspaper is sponsoring an essay contest in your school. Each student has been asked to write about a person he or she admires. In Spanish, write a letter to the newspaper to tell about a person you admire.

You <u>must</u> accomplish the purpose of the letter, which is *to tell about a person you admire.*

In your letter, you may wish to identify the person and mention the person's physical characteristics and/or character traits, the person's occupation, what the person did that was noteworthy, why you chose the person, how you got to know the person, and what effect the person has had on you or others. You may use any or all of the ideas suggested above *or* you may use your own ideas. **Either way, you must tell about a person you admire.**

Use the following:

Dateline:	el 25 de enero de 2001
Salutation:	La tribuna española:
Closing:	Atentamente, [your name]

The dateline, salutation, and closing will *not* be counted as part of the 10 required clauses.

Answers January 2001

Comprehensive Examination in Spanish

PART I

This part of the examination was evaluated prior to the date of this written examination. [24 credits]

PART 2

The following passages are to be read aloud to the students according to the directions given for this part at the beginning of this examination. The correct answers are given after number 15. [30 credits]

1. You are listening to the radio and the announcer reads this letter from a listener:

   El propósito de mi carta es darles las gracias por la entrevista en el mes de febrero con la cantante Ana Gabriel. Ella es mi cantante favorita y preferida. Me agradó mucho su entrevista, pero al mismo tiempo lamento que no haya sido más extensa. ¿Les sería posible entrevistar a Ana Gabriel por mucho más tiempo, la próxima vez?

   What is this person's complaint?

2. You are watching television in Mexico City and hear this announcement:

   Establecer el amor a la lectura es menester hoy día para la juventud. Hay que enseñar a temprana edad el amor a la lectura. Es un hábito para toda la vida que vale la pena. Aquí tiene usted unas reglitas importantes para tener éxito en este campo.
   Es importante que el niño seleccione lo que él desea leer. Visite la biblioteca frecuentemente para ver los libros recién llegados. Otra exce-

lente idea es darle al niño varios libros para leer antes de acostarse. Si es posible, pase tiempo leyendo al niño.

What is the main idea of this announcement?

3. While listening to the radio in Spain, you hear this announcement:

La Radiotelevisión Española planea extender su señal por el sur de los Estados Unidos. La Compañía de Radiotelevisión Española piensa llevar programas de cable a los estados de California, Nuevo México y Texas. También espera alcanzar otro acuerdo que permitirá distribuir su programación por las redes de cable de Florida. Esta señal internacional llegará a 800.000 hogares adicionales.

What does the Spanish Radio-Television Network plan to do?

4. You are watching the Spanish television channel on cable and hear:

¿Irlandeses cantando en español? Dada la presente popularidad de la música latina, todo es posible. O por lo menos es lo que piensa el grupo de muchachitos que integran Boyzone, un quinteto irlandés que está causando sensación entre las jovencitas de Europa y América. ¿El secreto? Boyzone canta en inglés y español e incluye temas de cantantes latinos. El éxito de este grupo empezó en Europa, con su primer álbum "Said and Done". Para satisfacer la alta demanda de música latina, los chicos de Boyzone no dudaron en invitar a alguien muy especial, el talentísimo Enrique Iglesias, para participar en su nuevo video.

What was just announced?

5. While listening to the radio, you hear this advertisement:

En Miami, Florida, Thais Carreño ha creado un sistema revolucionario de comidas a domicilio o "cantinas". La razón es que Carreño ha diseñado la manera de cocinar la rica comida cubana, manteniendo al mínimo el uso de grasa y usando elementos de la comida criolla cubana que son muy saludables. Esta preparación es completamente conforme con las sugerencias dietéticas de la Asociación Norteamericana del Corazón; logrando una comida baja en grasa y calorías y al mismo tiempo riquísima.

What does this advertisement promote?

6. You are on a flight to Spain. You hear the flight attendant make this announcement:

Como pasajero, usted hace un papel muy importante en su seguridad personal. Lo más importante y sencillo que Úd. puede hacer es asegurarse de siempre mantener su cinturón de seguridad abrochado. A pesar de los mejores esfuerzos de nuestros pilotos, ocasionalmente nos encontramos con turbulencias inesperadas. Comenzando este verano, Delta requerirá que todos sus pasajeros se queden sentados y que mantengan sus cinturones de seguridad abrochados mientras estén en sus asientos.

What does the flight attendant advise you to do?

7. While listening to a Spanish-language radio station, you hear this news broadcast:

La Administración municipal de Nueva York piensa autorizar a los taxis de la ciudad a equiparse con teléfonos portátiles para el uso de los clientes. Los primeros vehículos con teléfono, que permitirán hacer llamadas pero no recibirlas, funcionarán este verano. Las empresas de taxi y las compañías telefónicas discuten las condiciones del mantenimiento de los aparatos y las tarifas.

What is this announcement about?

8. You are listening to an exchange student from Costa Rica talk about her country. She says:

Costa Rica tiene una de las democracias más antiguas de América. Es una república libre e independiente. A diferencia de muchos otros países en América Latina, los habitantes de Costa Rica han disfrutado de plena estabilidad política. En Costa Rica no se oye de revoluciones ni guerras civiles como en otras naciones centroamericanas. Por ser una nación libre y democrática se le llama "La Suiza Centroamericana".

What is a distinguishing feature of Costa Rica?

9. You are listening to the radio and hear this advertisement:

La aerolínea española Iberia ahora ofrece un nuevo servicio a sus clientes, la venta de boletos electrónicos por la red mundial. Con este nuevo servicio, el cliente podrá hacer la reserva y pagar por su billete utilizando el ordenador. Usted puede pedir que le manden el boleto a su domicilio, o si prefiere, lo puede reclamar en el aeropuerto el día de su vuelo. Como siempre, Iberia está dispuesta a mejorar sus servicios para complacer a sus clientes.

What new service does this company now offer?

10. You are in Puerto Rico watching a television program. You hear the announcer say:

La compañía Disney comenzó a operar recientemente un nuevo crucero. El crucero sale desde Miami y viaja hasta las Bahamas, parándose en la isla privada de Disney, Castaway.

Los costos por persona para los turistas son de $2,000 y hasta $4,000. Estos precios diseñados para paquetes de siete noches, incluyen tarifa aérea, entrada a todos los parques y gastos del hotel en el Reino Mágico y las comidas dentro del crucero en nave.

¿Cuál es el propósito de este anuncio?

11. Your teacher is telling you a story about a famous photographer. The teacher says:

Antonio Pérez tenía 13 años cuando tuvo su primera experiencia con el periodismo. Todos los días, al salir de clases, recorría en bicicleta las calles de su barrio en el sur de Chicago distribuyendo el Diario, un pequeño periódico local. Cinco años más tarde, Pérez se convirtió en fotoperiodista y por coincidencia, su primera foto apareció publicada en el Diario.

¿Qué hacía Antonio cuando era un chico de 13 años?

12. While listening to a Spanish radio station, you hear this commercial:

La geometría de las caras humanas es muy variada. Así que tenemos caras cuadradas, caras redondas, triangulares, y hasta ovaladas. Esto importa a la hora de seleccionar las gafas. Existe una nueva línea de gafas tan individuales como cada consumidor. Para la cara cuadrada, tienes marco de curva, la cara redonda necesita monturas de línea recta o angular de color negro. Cada estilo nos hace ver mejor. Esta nueva línea también nos protege contra los rayos ultravioletas.

¿Qué producto se anuncia?

13. You received a telephone call from a friend. This is the message on the answering machine:

¡Hola! Soy María Mercedes. Llamo porque hoy mismo recibí los dulces que me mandaste. ¡Gracias por este regalo tan rico! Me acuerdo de haberlos comido cuando era niña. Son mis favoritos.

¿Por qué llamó tu amiga?

14. A representative of a production company is speaking to a club at your school. The representative says:

Narrada en inglés por la actriz Phylicia Rashad, esta videocinta les explica a los niños, en 25 minutos, la historia, la geografía y el folklore de Puerto Rico y la situación de los puertorriqueños que viven en los Estados Unidos. Compuesta de varios segmentos, la grabación abarca desde los carnavales en Ponce, hasta la presentación de un coro escolar acompañado de instrumentos típicos de la isla. Los segmentos son bastante cortos como para mantener la atención y el interés de los niños.

¿Qué vende la compañía?

15. While listening to the Spanish news on television, you hear this information:

"Haciendo Ambiente 2000" es un programa para enseñar a la comunidad en general sobre la importancia de conservar las especies en peligro de extinción. El miércoles 15 se llevará a cabo el Primer Eco Tour Ambiental. Ese día se regalarán 1,000 árboles, habrá talleres de siembra y del reciclaje de papel, y se dará información de cómo conservar el medio ambiente. Se presentará también un programa de reciclaje en los comercios participantes para mantener la ciudad de Ponce limpia.

¿Cuál es el tema de esta noticia?

PART 2

(1) 1	**(4)** 1	**(7)** 3	**(10)** 3	**(13)** 2
(2) 4	**(5)** 4	**(8)** 2	**(11)** 1	**(14)** 3
(3) 3	**(6)** 4	**(9)** 4	**(12)** 1	**(15)** 4

PART 3

(a) **(16)** 4	**(b)** **(21)** 4	**(c)** **(26)** 1
(17) 1	**(22)** 4	**(27)** 3
(18) 3	**(23)** 3	**(28)** 4
(19) 1	**(24)** 3	**(29)** 2
(20) 1	**(25)** 2	**(30)** 4

PART 4

(a) Notes in writing

For each note, an example of a response worth six credits follows. The slash marks indicate how each sample note has been divided into clauses.

31. Señor,

Anoche, fui a cenar con mis amigos al Parador Azul/₁ y nos gustó mucho./₂ La comida era deliciosa/₃ y el servicio era excelente./₄ El lugar es muy bonito/₅ y está muy limpio./₆ Además los camareros eran muy simpáticos.

Sinceramente,
Marcelo

32. Querido Señor,

Necesito su ayuda./$_1$ La clase de matemáticas que tengo/$_2$ es demasiado fácil para mí./$_3$ ¿Hay otra clase más avanzada?/$_4$ Prefiero quedarme con el mismo profesor./$_5$ También, si es posible/$_6$ deseo tener la clase más temprano. Me gustaría tomar la clase a las diez. Muchas gracias por su ayuda.

Su estudiante,
Ricardo

(b) Narrative based on picture/letter

For each narrative/letter, an example of a response worth 10 credits follows. The slash marks indicate how each sample narrative/letter has been divided into clauses.

33. (Picture)

La semana pasada Juan y su padre fueron a un partido de béisbol./$_1$ Antes de volver a casa,/$_2$ ellos decidieron ir al café/$_3$ para comer algo./$_4$ Juan estaba muy contento/$_5$ porque su equipo ganó./$_6$ Ahora tiene mucha hambre./$_7$ Va a comer tres hamburguesas y un perro caliente./$_8$ También quiere un helado./$_9$ Su padre está cansado/$_{10}$ y le gustaría ir a casa inmediatamente porque mañana tiene que trabajar temprano.

34. (Letter)

el 25 de enero de 2001

La tribuna española:

Hay muchas personas/$_1$, que yo admiro/$_2$ pero mi abuelo es la persona más especial para mí./$_3$ Me encanta mi abuelo/$_4$ porque él es un hombre muy generoso./$_5$ Siempre tiene tiempo/$_6$ para ayudarme con la tarea/$_7$ o para pasar horas conmigo hablando./$_8$ Me gusta contarle mis problemas/$_9$ porque él me da consejos prácticos/$_{10}$ y no me critica. Mi abuelo me enseñó a tener paciencia con mis hermanitos y a apreciar más a mis padres. Es una lección que podré usar el resto de mi vida.

Atentamente,
Margarita

INDEX

Notes

Notes

Notes

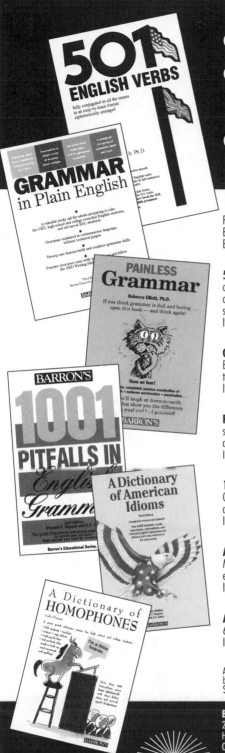